T0382596

An Introduction to Metaphilosophy

What is philosophy? How should we do it? Why should we bother to? These are the kinds of questions addressed by metaphilosophy – the philosophical study of the nature of philosophy itself. Students of philosophy today face a confusing and daunting array of philosophical methods, approaches and styles, and also deep divisions such as the notorious rift between analytic and continental philosophy. This book takes readers through a full range of approaches – analytic versus continental, scientistic versus humanistic, 'pure' versus applied – enabling them to locate and understand these different ways of doing philosophy. Clearly and accessibly written, it will stimulate reflection on philosophical practice and will be invaluable for students of philosophy and other philosophically inclined readers.

SØREN OVERGAARD is Associate Professor of Philosophy at the University of Copenhagen. He is the author of *Husserl and Heidegger on Being in the World* (2004) and *Wittgenstein and Other Minds* (2007), and co-editor (with Sebastian Luft) of *The Routledge Companion to Phenomenology* (2011).

PAUL GILBERT is Emeritus Professor of Philosophy at the University of Hull. He is the author of *New Terror, New Wars* (2003), *The World, the Flesh and the Subject* (with Kathleen Lennon, 2005), and *Cultural Identity and Political Ethics* (2010).

STEPHEN BURWOOD is Head of the Department of Humanities at the University of Hull. He is the author of *Philosophy of Mind* (with Kathleen Lennon and Paul Gilbert, 1998).

An Introduction to Metaphilosophy

SØREN OVERGAARD
PAUL GILBERT
STEPHEN BURWOOD

CAMBRIDGE
UNIVERSITY PRESS

CAMBRIDGE
UNIVERSITY PRESS

University Printing House, Cambridge CB2 8BS, United Kingdom

Cambridge University Press is part of the University of Cambridge.

It furthers the University's mission by disseminating knowledge in the pursuit of education, learning and research at the highest international levels of excellence.

www.cambridge.org
Information on this title: www.cambridge.org/9780521175982

© Søren Overgaard, Paul Gilbert and Stephen Burwood 2013

This publication is in copyright. Subject to statutory exception and to the provisions of relevant collective licensing agreements, no reproduction of any part may take place without the written permission of Cambridge University Press.

First published 2013

A catalogue record for this publication is available from the British Library

Library of Congress Cataloguing in Publication data
Overgaard, Søren, author.
  An introduction to metaphilosophy / Søren Overgaard, Paul Gilbert, and Stephen Burwood.
    pages   cm. – (Cambridge introductions to philosophy)
  Includes bibliographical references.
  ISBN 978-0-521-19341-2 (hardback) – ISBN 978-0-521-17598-2 (paperback)
  1. Philosophy.   I. Gilbert, Paul, author.   II. Burwood, Stephen, 1959– author.
  III. Title.
  B53.O94   2013
  101–dc23   2012036676

ISBN 978-0-521-19341-2 Hardback
ISBN 978-0-521-17598-2 Paperback

Cambridge University Press has no responsibility for the persistence or accuracy of URLs for external or third-party internet websites referred to in this publication, and does not guarantee that any content on such websites is, or will remain, accurate or appropriate.

Contents

Preface

This book is an introduction to metaphilosophy – the branch of philosophy that asks what philosophy is, how it should be done and why we should do it. As far as we know, it is the first such introduction in English; at least we are fairly certain it is the only one currently in print. As a consequence, we wrote this book feeling that we had entered completely uncharted territory, and while the idea of writing the first introduction to the field of metaphilosophy was an exciting one, the task was also daunting and extremely difficult. But if this book can generate more interest in metaphilosophy, and perhaps induce others to write rival introductions, pointing out the mistakes and limitations in our approach, we will consider our mission accomplished.

We have tried to make each chapter as accessible and student-friendly as possible, though no doubt in many cases we have failed in this endeavour. But then, as P. F. Strawson remarked: 'There is no shallow end to the philosophical pool' (1992: vii). This goes for metaphilosophy as much as for the rest of philosophy.

Several people have helped us at various stages of this project. We would like to thank David Cerbone, Antony Hatzistavrou, Bob Plant, Suzanne Uniacke and the readers for Cambridge University Press for providing input of various kinds. We are especially grateful to our clearance reader for making a number of useful suggestions. Some of the material included in Chapter 4 was presented at the Ph.D. seminar 'Intuitions in Philosophy', organised by Mikkel Gerken at the University of Copenhagen in December 2011. We are grateful to the participants for helpful questions and comments. Special thanks are due to Hilary Gaskin and Anna Lowe of Cambridge University Press for their patience and assistance.

1 Introduction: what good is metaphilosophy?

'What do you do?'; people sometimes ask me. 'I am a philosopher.' If I am lucky, the conversation ends there, but often it continues: 'Well, I suppose we are all of us philosophers in our different ways; I mean we all have our own ideas about the purpose of life. Now what I think ...' Or else: 'A philosopher: I envy you in these difficult times. To be able to take things calmly, to rise above the petty vexations that trouble us ordinary men.' Or again: 'That must be fascinating: really to understand people, to be able to reach their souls. I am sure you could give me some good advice.' Or, worst of all: 'What *is* philosophy?'[1]

Most students and practitioners of philosophy, we suspect, have felt something of the unease Ayer expresses in this quote. Sometimes we would prefer no one asks what we do. And if we cannot avoid that, then at least we would like the topic dropped after the confession, 'I am a philosopher'. But often, to our discomfort, it continues in one of the ways mentioned by Ayer.

Of the possible continuations of the conversation Ayer imagines, one is, perhaps, less frequent nowadays, whereas the other three are very common. It isn't clear that many people today associate philosophy with the ability to remain calm in the face of adversity. Indeed, this conception of philosophers and philosophy has long been lampooned, from Shakespeare's 'For there was never yet philosopher. That could endure the toothache patiently' to Oscar Wilde's 'Philosophy teaches us to bear with equanimity the misfortunes of others'. Nevertheless, the broader idea that philosophy can help us to deal with life's problems is still current. A book published a few years ago whose title echoed that of medieval philosopher Boethius's *The Consolation of Philosophy* received enthusiastic reviews

---

[1] Ayer 1969: 1.

from non-philosophers.[2] Even philosophers, reviewing the book much less favourably, did not question its presumption that philosophy can and should affect our lives.[3] Instead, they cast doubt on whether it should do so by way of consolation rather than by revealing possibly painful truths we must learn to live with. Much more common than this conception, however, is the popular assumption that the activity of philosophising consists mainly in expressing one's opinion on matters related to life and death or right and wrong. Or people associate it vaguely with the 'Mind, Body and Spirit' section in airport bookshops. Or indeed, perhaps most commonly of all, they have no clear idea of what philosophy is.

That people have misconceptions about what philosophy is and what philosophers do is not peculiar to philosophy. Some people don't know what a dermatologist is, and many have wrong ideas about the astronomer's profession. What may be peculiar to philosophy, however, is its practitioners' feeling that the request for clarification is, as Ayer puts it, the 'worst of all' – worse than the common misunderstandings. If a dermatologist is asked what she does, she is unlikely to feel particularly embarrassed. Nor will she feel uncomfortable if her interlocutor follows up with the question 'What is dermatology?' The astronomer might well become irritated by requests for horoscopes, but, again, he will hardly experience the embarrassment so well known to the philosopher, and is in fact likely to feel relieved if someone asks him to clarify what he does so that he can dispel any misconceptions. Why is the situation so different for the philosopher?

In part, this may have to do with the nature of philosophy. It is no easy matter to explain what we do, and this has to do, inter alia, with the fact that it isn't obviously the case that there is a particular region of objects (like stars and planets or diseases of the skin) that philosophers make it their special business to study. Even if we say we study the nature of right and wrong, the relation between mind and body and so forth, it is not clear what, if anything, draws such topics together into a single subject matter. Furthermore, while it may be evident that what philosophers do in studying them is not comparable to the kind of observational activity that dermatologists and astronomers engage in, what philosophers actually do seems hard to communicate except by getting people to do some

[2] de Botton 2000.   [3] Skidelsky 2000.

philosophising themselves. But this is only addressing the question of what philosophy is by demonstrating it in practice, not by giving an answer the recipient could use to pick out examples for himself or herself.

Partly, however, our embarrassment at the question of what we do may also reflect the fact that, to put this a bit provocatively, *we do not know.* We may know, to take some notions employed in philosophy, what a quale is, what disjunctivism is and what the doctrine of double effect states, but are we equally certain that we know what philosophy is? Perhaps not. For the question 'What is philosophy?' is very different from the question 'What is disjunctivism?' and much more like the question 'What is the structure of perceptual experience?' The former asks a question about a notion in philosophy to which there is a (more or less) definite answer; the latter is a difficult question philosophers ask themselves. So is 'What is philosophy?'

'What is philosophy?' is itself one of the fundamental questions of philosophy. It is a question in philosophy partly because philosophy asks a range of analogous questions about subjects of study that aim to provide us with knowledge or understanding of the world and of ourselves. It asks 'What is science?' or 'What is history?' not just to get the sort of answer a scientist or historian might give, but because we philosophers want to know what kind of knowledge or understanding such subjects might provide. We want to know as philosophers what knowledge and understanding are and how to attain them. Thus we ask the same sort of question about philosophy itself. That this is itself a philosophical question means, among other things, that there is controversy surrounding the correct answer to it.

On the other hand, one would imagine that even controversial answers can be given without too much embarrassment. Asked about the nature of perceptual experience, a committed disjunctivist can simply reply, '*I* believe such-and-such, but of course there are those who disagree'. There are two reasons, we think, why an answer of this sort isn't a very attractive option in the case of 'What is philosophy?' First, when you come to think of it, it is really rather odd to admit that you can only offer a controversial view of what people in your profession do. Astronomers and dermatologists – or for that matter plumbers and economists – rarely find themselves in disagreement with other members of their respective professions about what they do. And if historians or sociologists, say, disagree about what they do, on whether, for example, they are or should be putting forward theories that can be tested in the same way as theories in the physical sciences, then perhaps they are really airing a philosophical disagreement about the nature of their subject, for the reason just mentioned. They can disagree on this and still offer an uncontroversial answer about their subject matter and basic methods. Shouldn't such an answer about philosophy also be possible? Surely we need the ability to identify uncontroversially what it is that there is a disagreement about. Yet matters are not so simple. Even if they agree on what represents clear examples of philosophy, philosophers often disagree on what it is that makes them so. But the controversial nature of philosophy can hardly provide the source of the sort of embarrassment Ayer describes. Philosophers generally can cope with controversy, and those who cannot are probably in the wrong line of business.

The second reason that 'I believe philosophy is such-and-such, but of course there are others who disagree' isn't likely to prove an adequate reply is that, while philosophers work intensively on questions such as 'What is the structure of perceptual experience?', 'What is a just society?' or 'What is science?' in their ongoing research, they tend to all but ignore 'What is philosophy?' Metaphilosophy – the inquiry into the nature of philosophical questions and the methods (to be) adopted in answering them – is, as Colin McGinn puts it, 'perhaps the most undeveloped part of philosophy'.[4] In the words of another recent writer on metaphilosophy, it is a 'rather neglected' philosophical discipline.[5] If this simply reflected the obviousness of the right answer to the question 'What is philosophy?', then there would be little cause for worry: a quick look in a philosophical dictionary would settle the matter. However, as already pointed out (and as McGinn and Rescher both emphasise), metaphilosophy is no less fraught with controversy than other branches of the subject. So the second reason philosophers may find it awkward or difficult to offer even a controversial view of the nature of philosophy is that this isn't a topic to which they likely have devoted much serious thought. They may have thought a lot about how they should go about doing philosophy. But they may have thought very little about what it is they are doing when they are doing it, which is odd, because usually we need to know what it is we are trying to

[4] McGinn 2002: 199.   [5] Rescher 2001: 1.

do before wondering how we should get it done. One consequence of this neglect is the fact that this book is, as far as we know, the only available introduction to metaphilosophy.

Does the question matter?

Our occasional discomfort during a dinner party conversation aside, however, is there any reason we *should* know what philosophy is? Perhaps it is for a good reason that metaphilosophy remains undeveloped. Is 'What is philosophy?' an important question? Not everyone thinks so.

> I believe that the function of a scientist or of a philosopher is to solve scientific or philosophical problems, rather than to talk about what he or other philosophers are doing or might do. Any unsuccessful attempt to solve a scientific or philosophical problem, if it is an honest and devoted attempt, appears to me more significant than a discussion of such a question as 'What is science?' or 'What is philosophy?' And even if we put this latter question, as we should, in the slightly better form, 'What is the character of philosophical problems?', I for one should not bother much about it; I should feel that it had little weight, even compared with such a minor problem of philosophy as the question whether every discussion or every criticism must always proceed from 'assumptions' or 'suppositions' which themselves are beyond argument.[6]

The question we should ask here, of course, is how we are going to measure the importance of the question 'What is philosophy?' Compared with the search for a cure for cancer, surely our question will seem of little importance, but so will most other questions of philosophy. What we must ask is to what extent the question is *philosophically* important. Interestingly, Popper thinks the questions 'What is science?' and 'What is philosophy?' are alike in this respect. According to him, neither question is of any particular importance. But 'What is science?' is certainly a question that has traditionally been considered philosophically (if not scientifically) important. Presumably, Popper thinks otherwise since he makes no essential distinction between empirical science and philosophy. Both are in the business of solving problems. And the problems of philosophy owe whatever importance they have to matters vital to science and human life

[6] Popper 1968: 66.

in general. 'Genuine philosophical problems', writes Popper, 'are always rooted in urgent problems outside philosophy, and they die if these roots decay'.[7] When we ask what truth is, whether the mind can be regarded as just a part of nature or why we ought not to commit murder, our questions presumably have relevance to human life beyond the philosophical arm-chair. That link, it seems, is severed when we engage in metaphilosophical inquiry. Here philosophy turns its back on the world in idle navel gazing. To pause to think about what we are doing or might be doing, therefore, is merely a waste of precious time. In Popper's words, 'a philosopher should philosophise: he should try to solve philosophical problems, rather than talk about philosophy'.[8] Many philosophers have expressed somewhat similar sentiments. Bernard Williams writes that 'philosophy is not at its most interesting when it is talking about itself',[9] and Rorty sounds a note of scepticism regarding the utility of metaphilosophy: 'questions about "the method of philosophy" or about "the nature of philosophical problems"', he suggests, 'are likely to prove unprofitable'.[10] Ryle, finally, delivers the verdict that 'preoccupation with questions about methods tends to distract us from prosecuting the methods themselves. We run, as a rule, worse, not better, if we think a lot about our feet'.[11]

Popper's rejection of metaphilosophical inquiry as unimportant clearly presupposes a particular metaphilosophical view: a particular view of what genuine philosophical problems are and of what the activity of the philosopher consists in, or ought to consist in. In other words, Popper takes a particular metaphilosophy *for granted*. He does not produce arguments for one. But is this necessarily a problem? We all take certain things for granted without ever subjecting them to careful philosophical scrutiny. Perhaps some metaphysicians or philosophers of mind even take for granted particular political philosophies without ever having subjected these to the scrutiny to which they subject positions in their field of research. Perhaps some moral philosophers hold naïve realist views of perceptual experience without ever having seriously considered the problems associated with the view. We cannot all do serious research on *everything*, and can thus be excused for focussing on the problems that strike us as the most important ones. If this invariably means taking certain views or

[7] Popper 1968: 72.   [8] Ibid.: 68.   [9] Williams 2006: 169.
[10] Rorty 1992c: 374.   [11] Ryle 2009b: 331.

positions – philosophical or otherwise – for granted, then so be it. If this is right, then Popper's taking for granted a particular metaphilosophical view is only a problem if it can be shown that metaphilosophical questions are questions he should have recognised as important.

We might, however, wonder whether Popper can seriously think the question 'What is science?' has little or no philosophical importance. After all, he states elsewhere that 'the critical inquiry into the sciences, their findings, and their methods … remains a characteristic of philosophical inquiry'.[12] How is this different from a critical exploration of the question 'What is science?' – an inquiry into what scientists 'are doing or might do'? Yet if 'What is science?' is allowed back in among the respectable philosophical questions, and it is hard to see how anyone could seriously refuse this, then surely, 'What is philosophy?' is rehabilitated as well. This ought to be particularly obvious for anyone who, like Popper, views philosophy as something that never ought to be, and indeed 'never can be, divorced from science'.[13] But the point should really strike anyone as valid: if 'What is science?' and 'What is art?' are genuine philosophical questions, then 'What is philosophy?' must be as well. Nor will this then be mere navel gazing for reasons mentioned earlier. It will be part of a general philosophical investigation of the nature and possibility of knowledge and understanding.

Let us agree with Stanley Cavell, then, that 'philosophy is one of its own normal topics'.[14] Yet it still does not follow that lack of metaphilosophical reflection, beyond being the cause of occasional social awkwardness, is itself a philosophical shortcoming. For we still haven't given sceptics such as Popper a reason to consider such questions philosophically *important*. Thus, the core of Popper's objection remains intact: why not just get on with the business of solving philosophical problems and stop worrying about philosophy itself? A reply, however, is to hand. Traditionally it has been thought that we can tackle philosophical problems just by ruminating about them. In an episode of the popular British TV series *Inspector Morse*, virtually the only thing a potential suspect has been doing for several hours while sinister events have unfolded is 'thinking'. When Sergeant Lewis relates this to Morse, the latter reacts with an incredulous

[12] Popper 1975: 53.   [13] Ibid.

[14] Cavell 2002: xxxii. Timothy Williamson also insists that 'the philosophy of philosophy is automatically part of philosophy' (2007: ix).

stare. 'Well', Lewis explains, 'he *is* doing a doctorate in philosophy'. But if critics of the traditional methods of philosophising, such as the 'intuition sceptics' we discuss in Chapter 4, are right, then the way most of us go about solving philosophical problems is in fact radically inadequate to the task. In other words, if the critics of the standard methods of philosophising are right, then this *affects philosophy across the board*: epistemology, metaphysics, philosophy of science, moral and political philosophy and so on and so forth are all affected insofar as philosophers working in those areas employ the methods under criticism. Surely, any criticism that affects philosophy across the board in such a way is philosophically important, indeed crucial. However, to attempt to answer this question – to reflect on the methods of philosophising – is to do metaphilosophy. And once you have opened the discussion of philosophy's proper method(s), questions about what philosophy is or should be arise as well, since, as we said, to judge the appropriateness of a method we need to know what it is a method for.

But it is not only because metaphilosophical problems affect all of philosophy that metaphilosophy constitutes an important part of philosophy. Philosophy, however it is to be characterised more generally, has always been thought to include the critical examination of the forms and methods of human knowledge and understanding. Since philosophy is itself, at least on the vast majority of metaphilosophical views, a contribution of some sort to human knowledge or understanding, the philosophical project remains radically incomplete unless the critical light is directed at philosophy itself. Indeed, Sellars goes as far as to state: 'It is this reflection on the place of philosophy itself, in the scheme of things which is the distinctive trait of the philosopher,' so that 'in the absence of this critical reflection on the philosophical enterprise, one is at best but a potential philosopher'.[15] Whether or not that is an overstatement, it seems to us that Timothy Williamson is right – *pace* Ryle – to maintain that 'Philosophizing is not like riding a bicycle, best done without thinking about it – or rather: the best cyclists surely *do* think about what they are doing.'[16] Metaphilosophy is not just a part of philosophy, but an *important* part.

This still leaves the worries – articulated in the quotes from Rorty and Bernard Williams – that perhaps metaphilosophy is less interesting or

---

[15] Sellars 1991: 3.   [16] Williamson 2007: 8.

profitable than other areas of philosophical research. Yet whether some areas of philosophy are more or less interesting than others surely depends on who you ask. And the charge that metaphilosophical discussion is likely to prove 'unprofitable' is hard to evaluate. The question to ask here is, 'Profitable in terms of what?' In terms of effecting social or political change, say? In terms of clarifying important philosophical questions? Or are metaphilosophical discussions unprofitable because it is unlikely that they will lead to agreement and progress? But how much progress has been made in *other*, more developed parts of philosophy?

In his 2009 book on metaphilosophy, Gary Gutting suggests that two features have been responsible for making metaphilosophy particularly unprofitable and uninteresting:

> a dogmatic attitude that derives the nature of philosophy from controversial philosophical doctrines (e.g., idealist metaphysics or empiricist epistemology) and an abstract, overly generalized approach that pays no attention to the details of philosophical practice.[17]

Insofar as Gutting is right that metaphilosophy has been disproportionately characterised by these shortcomings, it is indeed hard to avoid the conclusion that it has been less satisfying and interesting than other parts of the subject. But unless there is reason to think it inevitable that metaphilosophy is marred by dogmatism and overgeneralisation, then the conclusion to draw from this is not that we shouldn't do metaphilosophy, but that we should strive to do it *better*.[18] Perhaps when good metaphilosophy replaces bad metaphilosophy, this part of philosophy will become as interesting and profitable as other parts of the subject.[19]

The aims of the book

This book is an introduction to metaphilosophy or 'the philosophy of philosophy', as it is also sometimes called. In it, we provide an overview of the central questions philosophers have asked about philosophy, we discuss the answers they have given to them and we suggest some of our own.

---

[17] Gutting 2009: 2.
[18] This, of course, is Gutting's conclusion as well.
[19] The criteria for profitability of any philosophy constitute a central metaphilosophical topic, which we discuss in Chapter 8.

Some philosophers, including Cavell and Williamson, have expressed dissatisfaction with the term 'metaphilosophy' because they think it suggests that the latter isn't itself a part of philosophy, as metaphysics is not, or at least not obviously, a part of physics.[20] When we have chosen to stick with the word 'metaphilosophy', it is not because we welcome the connotations of, in Williamson's words, looking down on philosophy 'from above, or beyond'. We agree that metaphilosophy is straightforwardly part of philosophy in the same way metaphysics or normative ethics is. 'Metaphilosophy', it seems to us, is simply the term most widely used for this particular part of philosophy.[21]

Introductions to (parts of) philosophy are always, explicitly or implicitly, opinionated – they are never entirely neutral. Our book is no exception. In fact, since it is an introduction to *meta*philosophy, it presents an interesting complication. Suppose one could write, say, an introduction to the philosophy of mind which presented all the major positions and their strengths and weaknesses in a balanced and fair manner. Such a book would not be opinionated with respect to any particular discussion within the area (philosophy of mind) covered. Yet it *would* express a particular *meta*philosophical view. By either excluding or including neuroscientific or other experimental research, for example, the book would express a particular view of the relation between philosophy and the empirical sciences. The same would go for books on epistemology, ethics and all other parts of philosophy.

The interesting thing about a book on metaphilosophy is thus that the very topic covered is the one on which it seems impossible not to take some sort of stand, however tacitly or implicitly. So our approach to the topics of metaphilosophy reflects a particular conception of the nature of philosophy – that is, a particular metaphilosophy. As will become obvious, we have not approached our topic in a 'naturalised' manner. That is, with one or two exceptions, we have not conducted or consulted empirical studies of the behaviour of philosophers, relations of influence among them, how philosophical theories get accepted, citation patterns in journals and so on and so forth.[22] If someone were to point out that this shows our sympathies

---

[20] Cavell 2002: xxxii; Williamson 2007: ix. See also Glock 2008: 6.

[21] There is even a respected journal called *Metaphilosophy*. In the first volume of *Metaphilosophy*, Morris Lazerowitz – a student of Wittgenstein – claims that he coined the term 'metaphilosophy' (or 'meta-philosophy') in 1940 (1970: 91).

[22] To get an idea of what such 'naturalised metaphilosophy' would be like, see Morrow and Sula 2011.

with a traditional understanding of philosophy as somehow set apart from the empirical sciences, we would have to plead guilty. But, first, as just pointed out, it does not seem possible to avoid taking a metaphilosophical stand of some sort, and so we are simply compelled to beg some of the very questions that we wish to discuss in a balanced, objective manner. Second, we do consider some of the rival naturalistic views, in a hopefully balanced way, in Chapter 4 and elsewhere. And finally, by adopting an 'armchair' approach to the questions of metaphilosophy, we are in line with the majority of the literature. Perhaps naturalised metaphilosophy is on the rise, and if so, one would probably have to write a very different introduction to metaphilosophy ten years from now. But at least for the time being, the majority of philosophers seems to share our bias (which is of course not to say that it is right).

We should note one more caveat. As just indicated, any piece of philosophising has metaphilosophical implications. By choosing to discuss *this* topic in the pages of a philosophy journal, a philosopher intimates something about the sorts of topics he or she deems worthy of philosophical attention; by employing a certain style and method, one implies that these are at least acceptable, and so on. Metaphilosophy is implicit in all of philosophy. But our main purpose in this book is not to discuss the implicit metaphilosophical views we can extract from contributions to other parts of philosophy, though we also do this from time to time – in Chapter 5 and elsewhere. The main purpose of this book is to serve as an introduction to metaphilosophy as a subdiscipline of philosophy, on a par with, say, epistemology or metaethics. For this reason, we mainly focus on what has been termed 'explicit metaphilosophy' – that is, explicit philosophical discussions on the nature of philosophy, the proper methods of philosophising and so on.[23]

It is helpful, we think, to divide the central metaphilosophical questions into three large groups: *What* is philosophy? *How* should we do it? and *Why* should we do it? It is important not to misunderstand this suggestion. We do not mean to deny the obvious fact that the three questions are closely related in many ways. Someone who thinks of philosophy as literally part of natural science will typically commit to certain methodological views

---

[23] For the distinction between implicit and explicit metaphilosophy, and a good example of a study that mainly focusses on implicit metaphilosophy, see Joll 2010.

as well – views about how philosophy is to be done – as well as views about the value that accrues to the activity or result of doing it. Indeed, for this reason most of the chapters in this book do not focus exclusively on one of the three questions. Nevertheless, to provide some order to the metaphilosophical topics, the distinctions among the 'What', 'How' and 'Why' questions are useful, and chapters in this book are exclusively dedicated to each of these: Chapter 2 asks what philosophy is, Chapter 4 examines how it is to be done and Chapter 8 reflects on why one might want to do it.

All three questions are more interesting if they are interpreted as inviting *prescriptive* rather than descriptive replies. A descriptive reply to the 'What' question would give a characterisation of what past and present philosophers have understood their discipline to be, or what it has been in their hands. Careful historical and sociological research should, it seems, settle this question conclusively. But this is not the only sort of 'What' question we are interested in. For philosophers think of their subject as continuous with that of their predecessors. Thus they seek features common to both past and present practice. The dictum that all philosophy consists of footnotes to Plato is an exaggeration, but it contains an element of truth. Whatever Plato understood himself to be doing or can be regarded as actually having done within the context of his time, subsequent generations of philosophers have continued to find in his work a valuable resource of problems and arguments. They have read him, and continue to read him, as if he conducted his work in philosophy in the same way as they themselves. So, since similar considerations apply to the whole canon of great philosophers, an account of philosophy is needed which covers what they can be thought of as doing as well as what philosophers do today. Philosophy would not be what it is without the history it tells about itself. But it tells this history by assuming that the great philosophers were doing what philosophers should be doing. Whatever else they did is discounted.

The philosophically more interesting question, then, is what philosophy *should* be: should it be part of the natural sciences, or transcendental reflection, or conceptual analysis or what? This is the prescriptive 'What' question. Similarly, the more interesting 'How' question is not how philosophers proceed (and have proceeded) or what methods they (have) use(d), but how they *ought* to proceed, what the *right* methods are. What we ought to do depends, in part, on what we can do. So one connection between the 'What' question and the 'How' question concerns the results philosophy could deliver. Could it, for example, produce the same sort of results, albeit at a higher level of generality, as the natural sciences? Philosophers of the past have often thought so and some philosophers still do. And here it is worth reminding ourselves that what we think of as the same subject has been pursued by different methods, though some methods are just too different from any of our own for their practitioners to count as philosophers. Among the factors accounting for methodological change, however, have been changes in philosophical conceptions of what is possible for the subject.

Finally, more philosophically interesting than the question of why people philosophise – which might be a psychological or sociological research topic[24] – is the question of whether there is any good reason to do philosophy, whether there is reason to think philosophy has any real value. And, like many other questions about values and the strength of reasons, this is a philosophical question. All of these questions, especially the last, should be of some interest to non-philosophers. But it will be principally practitioners and students of philosophy who should be concerned with these prescriptive questions. For they ought, we claim, to reflect on what they should be doing, how best to do it and why. We cannot claim to be able to remove their embarrassment when they are asked these questions by non-philosophers, but we hope to provide them with at least something to say.

Outline of the rest of the book

In the next chapter, we address the 'What' question in both its manifestations. First, we briefly examine possible replies to the descriptive question of what philosophy is. We distinguish between two opposing extremes – 'essentialist' and 'deflationary' replies – and suggest that both are problematic. We then inquire whether the truth might lie somewhere in the middle, and we tentatively suggest the possibility that an account in terms of family resemblances might single out a set of central issues and characteristic ways of dealing with them. The bulk of the chapter, however, is dedicated to the prescriptive question. This has been answered in

[24] As you will have noticed, here we just begged a major metaphilosophical question.

many different ways, ranging from the view that philosophy is literally a part of science to the argument that it is not a cognitive enterprise at all. Between these two extremes stand various other views, including the view that philosophy is immature science, the residue of science, a Platonic 'super-science', a quest for understanding, transcendental inquiry into the conditions of possibility of experience and cognition, among others. Along the way, we indicate some of the problems the various views face, though most of them are discussed in greater detail in later chapters.

In Chapter 3, we confront the dramatic claim that philosophy is dead because modern science has taken over its work, philosophy's apparent lack of progress having been due to its lack of scientific method. We concede that most contemporary philosophers hold naturalistic views, in the sense that they think the natural world is all that exists. But we raise doubts about whether this implies that the natural sciences have a monopoly on describing that world. In particular, the world of everyday objects in which we live is describable differently, and most of us find it difficult or impossible to recognise ourselves in many of the descriptions science provides of our behaviour. This leads us to consider the suggestion that, rather than having to be continuous with science if it is to have any validity, philosophy should properly be viewed as part of the humanities.

Chapter 4 approaches the question of how philosophy is to be done by focussing on two – arguably central – methods of traditional philosophising: phenomenological description and conceptual analysis. Both of these ways of philosophising assume, in one way or another, that it is possible to collect philosophical data from the proverbial 'armchair', and they have both been criticised on this account by methodological naturalists who argue that philosophers should instead employ the standard methods of empirical science. We discuss Daniel Dennett's critique of traditional phenomenology, and his plea for what he terms 'heterophenomenology', before turning to recent critical discussions of conceptual analysis put forth by 'experimental philosophers' and what we term 'intuition sceptics'. Although we offer no conclusive verdict on any of these issues, we do suggest that they illustrate the fruitfulness of appealing to more than one sort of data when philosophising.

In Chapter 5, we turn to the notorious distinction between so-called continental and analytic approaches to philosophy. We examine various attempts to show that these labels reflect real, insurmountable differences between two incommensurable visions of philosophy and suggest that there are plausible candidates for counterexamples to all proposed definitions of 'continental' or 'analytic'. Hence the labels, if they capture anything, probably pinpoint two different trails of influence, each of which may be associated with a loose set of family resemblances. While this might be enough to make it reasonable to continue to talk of 'continental' and 'analytical' traditions of philosophy, it conceives the borders of these traditions as fluid and porous rather than hard and impermeable. It thus lends no support to the idea of a gulf so wide as to exclude meaningful engagement. We end the chapter by briefly suggesting that such engagement might already be happening.

In asking why anyone should engage in philosophical reflection one question we need to address is what sort of results we can expect from it, and, in particular, whether they are the same sort of results we get from science, history and other subjects which deliver truths about the world. In Chapter 6 we consider challenges to the so-called representationalist notion that philosophical claims are straightforwardly true or false, especially the challenges formulated by Richard Rorty in defending his view of philosophy as edifying conversation. We discuss the worry that this would make philosophical works little different from other literary productions which do not invite the same kind of agreement or disagreement. We conclude by canvassing the possibility of a middle way between Rorty's position and representationalism – a way that preserves as much as possible of the traditional approach to philosophising.

If we ask how philosophy should be done we need to delineate the standards for good performance. More especially, we need to know what serious lapses from these standards would disqualify something from counting as philosophy at all. In Chapter 7, we discuss these questions by reflecting upon the criticisms that analytic philosophers have levelled at French post-structuralist Jacques Derrida and comparing them with those that Socrates directed at the Sophists. We consider the kinds of criticisms that might be made of philosophical style and method, and examine conceptions of the philosophical virtues and of the reflectiveness and seriousness the subject demands of its practitioners.

Finally, in Chapter 8, we take up Bertrand Russell's question about the value of philosophy in order to consider some reasons that might be offered for studying the subject. We distinguish the value of various sorts of product that philosophy may provide from the value of its practice, and we contrast the subject's possible value to individuals with its value to society at large. Among philosophy's products some seem valuable because they subtract erroneous notions from our store of ideas. Others perhaps add something worthwhile to it, and here we particularly consider the possible value of the world views philosophers may articulate. We ask if philosophy should be expected to effect moral improvement or to make for better judgements about social or political problems. We conclude quite optimistically by suggesting that the practice of philosophy may foster various intellectual virtues.

2   What is philosophy?

Introduction

Philosophy seems to have had a somewhat disappointing career. It was once hailed as the 'queen of the sciences', but more recently it has been demoted to their 'under-labourer', if not pronounced irrelevant or 'dead' altogether.[1] Yet philosophy soldiers on, if not entirely unscathed, then at most with minor cuts and bruises. The number of professional practitioners of philosophy has never been higher, and students continue to enrol in philosophy programmes. Despite its loss of prestige, then, philosophy apparently continues to appeal to human beings. But what *is* this thing called philosophy?

Tempting as it may be to start formulating one's reply straightaway, it is worth pausing to consider what, precisely, the question is we are supposed to answer. As G. E. Moore once wrote:

> [I]n Ethics, as in all other philosophical studies, the difficulties and disagreements, of which its history is full, are mainly due to a very simple cause: namely to the attempt to answer questions, without first discovering precisely *what* question it is which you desire to answer.[2]

As we shall see, Moore's implicit suggestion that most philosophical disagreements would go away if only philosophers would get clear on the

---

[1] Kant famously wrote: 'Time was when metaphysics was entitled the Queen of all the sciences' (1929: A viii). Kant's image, if not the precise wording, goes back to Aristotle, who called metaphysics 'the most authoritative of the sciences', 'most honourable' and 'most divine' (Aristotle 1984: 982b–983a). The conception of the philosopher as an 'under-labourer' – popular with logical positivists and many other twentieth-century analytic philosophers – can be traced back to Locke (1997: 11; 'The Epistle to the Reader'). In the next chapter, we discuss a recent defence of the view that philosophy has lost all relevance.

[2] Moore 1991: vii.

question they want to answer before setting about answering it is probably too optimistic. Yet at least the effort to clarify what the question is
might enable us to see which philosophers genuinely agree or disagree in
their answers to that question and which philosophers simply debate a
different question altogether. The question 'What is philosophy?' is very
much a case in point.

As mentioned in Chapter 1, there are two ways to understand the
question: as a *descriptive* question and as a *prescriptive* one. Understood as
inviting a descriptive reply, the question is what philosophy *actually*, or in
fact, is. Taken prescriptively, the question is what philosophy *ought* to be.
Allen Wood, who calls the prescriptive the 'apologetic' question, and who
speaks of the 'analytic' rather than the descriptive question, illustrates the
difference between the two sorts of questions in the following way:

> 'What is Christianity?' asked by a committed Christian, and 'What is
> the American Way?' asked by a patriotic American, are usually framed
> as apologetic questions. Because in human life what exists is very seldom
> perfect ... to ask an *analytical* 'What is *x*?' question about something
> human is often to invite an openly critical or even deflationary answer. No
> investigation of (really existing) Christianity can afford to ignore the roles
> moral hypocrisy and religious intolerance have played in this religion's
> practices ... But for this very reason, apologetic treatments of Christianity
> will represent self-honesty and tolerance as among the Christian virtues.[3]

As Wood emphasises, it is no objection to the prescriptive account of what
Christianity is that the religion as it is actually practised often fails to
correspond to it. Correspondingly, a prescriptive answer to 'What is philosophy?' is not refuted by the discovery that philosophers' actual practice
is very different. Although the prescriptive question is arguably the (philosophically) more interesting one – and indeed the one most philosophers
have in mind when they talk about what philosophy is – we begin this
chapter by briefly surveying some replies to the descriptive question.

What is (really existing) philosophy?

Philosophy as it is now practised at Western universities is in one sense
a very ancient field. 'Why', Wittgenstein asks, 'do I wish to call our

[3] Wood 2001: 98–9.

present activity philosophy, when we also call Plato's activity philosophy?' 'Perhaps', he continues, 'because of a certain analogy between them, or perhaps because of the continuous development of the subject'.[4] Philosophy is ancient in the sense that most of what philosophers *now* do – the sorts of general questions they raise and the ways in which they try to resolve them – derives from what Plato and Aristotle did almost two and a half millennia ago and has close similarities to it.[5] Obviously, some special branches of philosophy – say, philosophy of quantum mechanics or philosophy of film – are of necessity more recent additions to the family. But in general, the sorts of things that now occupy philosophers were matters of concern to the ancient Greeks as well.

There is, however, a sense in which philosophy as we now know it is a fairly recent invention, less than two centuries old. Plato and Aristotle – and for that matter, Descartes, Locke and Kant – regarded some questions as paradigmatically philosophical that today would not be considered the philosopher's business at all. (Their philosophical wonder was also aroused by certain questions that today we would simply find a lot less gripping. Socrates, for example, seems to have found it deeply puzzling that a person might become shorter than another person without 'losing anything in bulk' – that is, simply because the latter person has grown.[6]) 'Philosophy' used to mean roughly the same thing as 'rational inquiry' or 'science', as we now understand these terms. Descartes, for example, held that philosophy 'encompasses everything which the human mind is capable of knowing', 'both for the conduct of life and for the preservation of health and the discovery of all manner of skills'.[7] Only during the nineteenth century did people begin to distinguish between science and philosophy, and indeed the mathematics department at the University of Oxford still has a chair of 'Natural Philosophy'. The origin of the universe, the nature of living things or the smallest constituents of matter are no longer questions examined by the philosopher *qua* philosopher, but rather by physicists and biologists. While what we now call philosophy existed

---

[4] Wittgenstein 1979: 28.

[5] The adjective 'general' is of course important here. Plato and Aristotle did not discuss Gettier cases, trolley problems or disjunctivism (at least not under those names), but they did discuss the nature of knowledge, perception and the good.

[6] Plato 1989: *Theaetetus* 155b–c.

[7] Descartes 1985: 180, 179.

under that name two millennia ago, philosophy then included much that we now consider the subject matters of the special sciences.

What, then, is 'really existing' philosophy *now*? At first blush, one would have to say: many, quite different things. It may be hard to see what, if anything, unites the efforts of the logician, the political philosopher, the metaethicist, the epistemologist and the feminist philosopher. This seems to invite a *deflationary* response: philosophy, it might be said, is whatever the people who are employed *as* philosophers at universities and other institutions do, or whatever material librarians catalogue as such – end of story. On this sort of view, nothing important unites the efforts of philosophers and sets these apart from what psychologists, mathematicians and literature professors do. In the words of Quine, 'philosophy' is simply 'one of a number of blanket terms used by deans and librarians in their necessary task of grouping the myriad topics and problems of science and scholarship under a manageable number of headings', and the fact that two people's topics 'are grouped under "philosophy" makes neither man responsible for the other's topic'.[8]

Perhaps, though, such a deflationary view ought to be a last resort not accepted straight off. Yet the prospects of the opposite extreme – *essentialism* – do not seem very good either. Hoping, in Simon Blackburn's words, 'to lay down a definition, an eternal fence, so that what lies within is philosophy, and what lies without is not',[9] essentialist views are in tension with the fact that, as already mentioned, the fence has seemingly been erected in different places in the course of philosophy's history. Moreover, it is highly unlikely that a definition can be formulated that will allow us to include all and only those activities we *currently* think of as philosophical.

Essentialist attempts to define philosophy can be either *topical* or *methodological*, but both sorts have their problems. Take a candidate methodological 'fence': philosophy, let us say, is distinguished by its a priori – or 'armchair' – methods. Clearly, this will not do, as mathematics and other formal sciences meet the 'armchair' requirement.[10] But any attempt to offer a narrower characterisation of the method – for example 'conceptual analysis' – will almost certainly exclude too much. The suggestion that

---

[8] Quine 1975: 228.

[9] Blackburn 2004: xiii. Note that Blackburn does not endorse essentialism.

[10] Perhaps the definition also *excludes* something that should have been included: after all, there is such a thing as 'experimental philosophy'.

the method of conceptual analysis is what is distinctive of philosophy thus excludes not only most or all of so-called continental philosophy, but significant parts of contemporary 'analytic' philosophy as well.

One response to this objection has been to claim that, in reality, philosophers practise philosophy in the way suggested – they just don't realise it. In this vein, some argue that 'philosophical statements are analyses of puzzling concepts', even if the philosophers who make them do not take this to be what they are doing.[11] Another famous example is Norman Malcolm's interpretation of G. E. Moore as an ordinary language philosopher *avant la lettre*, an interpretation Moore indignantly rejected. It is difficult to assess claims like these about what philosophers really do without realising it. Philosophers often seem to let their own prescriptive views of philosophy, for instance that it should analyse or revise our concepts, affect their descriptions of what others are actually doing. And perhaps it is safest to take what philosophers are doing at face value to arrive at a properly descriptive view.

Topical definitions do not seem to fare much better than methodological ones. Sellars's famous statement that philosophy aims 'to understand how things in the broadest possible sense of the term hang together in the broadest possible sense of the term' certainly seems to cover all parts of philosophy. This becomes particularly clear if one reads the rarely quoted next few sentences of Sellars's essay: 'Under "things in the broadest possible sense" I include such radically different items as not only "cabbages and kings", but numbers and duties, possibilities and finger snaps, aesthetic experience and death.'[12] This characterisation, however, is surely much too inclusive, covering all of natural science and the humanities, and is for that reason alone not very helpful. It could be suggested that what is distinctive of philosophy, however, is that philosophy tries to show how *all* these things hang together. Perhaps this is what G. E. Moore had in mind when he said that the most important and interesting job of philosophers is to give 'a general description of the *whole* of the Universe'.[13] But many philosophers do seem to have rather more limited concerns, for example asking what numbers or duties are.

Suppose it is said instead that philosophy deals with 'the "big questions" that we have regarding the world's scheme of things and our place within

---

[11] Ambrose 1992: 149. Ambrose is reporting the view, not adopting it.
[12] Both quotes Sellars 1991: 1.   [13] Moore 1953: 1.

it'[14] – including, presumably, the nature of truth, knowledge, meaning, the good and so forth. This again seems to cast too wide a net. It is not clear that, say, fine art and literature cannot with equal right be said to concern themselves with the 'big questions'.

To avoid subsuming fine art under the heading of philosophy, one might add a set of methodological requirements to the topical definition. Philosophy, say, approaches these questions by way of reason and argument, broadly conceived, and because of its discursive nature its typical physical manifestation is the theoretical essay, as opposed to novels, plays, paintings, sculptures and cinema.[15] Something certainly seems right about this hybrid characterisation; yet unfortunately, it seems to *exclude* certain parts of the philosophical family – not just recent additions such as, say, the philosophy of sport, but also more established areas of research, such as the parts of formal logic that shade off into mathematics. It is at the very least not obvious that such branches of philosophy can be said to deal with the fundamental questions about human beings and our place in the world. To mention one final possibility, it does not seem that the once celebrated idea that philosophy has some special interest in our 'concepts' (or 'conceptual scheme')[16] indicates a topic shared by all philosophers either. Not just so-called continental philosophers, but also prominent analytic philosophers reject the idea that philosophy has some special concern with 'concepts'.[17]

The truth, then, lies probably somewhere in the middle. There are no 'eternal fences' to be erected, nor should we assume without further ado that 'philosophy' is merely a convenient catalogue label for booksellers and librarians. In particular, the suggestion that philosophy has some special interest in the fundamental questions about the world and our place in it might perhaps point to a certain 'centre of gravity' of philosophy, then as well as now. As Stuart Hampshire once wrote:

> There are six words which, taken together, mark the principal interest
> of philosophers, as philosophy is understood in the Greek and Western

---

[14] Rescher 2001: 3.

[15] Though of course the essay is not philosophy's only physical manifestation. Conversations, lectures, radio and TV shows (as well as blogs, podcasts, TED talks and other recent inventions) are possible ways for philosophy to manifest itself.

[16] A claim also recently made by Searle (1999).

[17] See, for example, Williamson 2007: 21.

tradition. They are 'know', 'true', 'exist', 'same', 'cause', 'good'. No constructive philosopher has failed to have something to say about all, or most, of these notions … [T]hey are not the concern of specific positive sciences, but, being to the highest degree general, of philosophy.[18]

Hampshire appears to think his list is exhaustive insofar as the *principal* interest of philosophers is concerned, but this seems questionable. Certain branches of philosophy, arguably central to philosophy from the beginning, are hardly represented at all in Hampshire's list, including the philosophy of mind ('see', 'think' and so on), logic ('therefore') and philosophical aesthetics ('beauty', 'art'). But Hampshire's fundamental intuition that there is some relatively limited number of notions that are, and always have been, central to what concerns philosophers – some 'centre of gravity', as we put it before – seems right. It is just important to keep in mind that the philosophical body has more peripheral parts as well, such as those where notions that are fundamental within particular spheres of human life form the subject of discussion. To name just a couple of fairly peripheral parts, one might think of philosophy of food or philosophy of film.

If we add to this topical characterisation the methodological requirement that philosophers' way of approaching these notions is by reason and argument, broadly conceived, we seem to have the outline of an answer to the *descriptive* question of what philosophy is – an answer that is neither deflationary nor essentialist. This answer, indeed, is fully compatible with the anti-essentialist point that philosophy shades off into mathematics at one end, the natural sciences at another end and linguistics, politics, psychology and literature at yet other ends, and that it may not be possible to say precisely where philosophy ends and those other subjects begin. Yet the answer is, or at least need not be, entirely deflationary either, because, as Wittgenstein once remarked, the fact that the border between two countries is in dispute doesn't put the citizenship of all their inhabitants in question.[19] Some questions and ways of addressing them may just *obviously* belong to philosophy, rather than any of its neighbouring disciplines, and this is fully compatible with the fact that there may be no clear-cut demarcation line between philosophy and those other disciplines.

[18] Hampshire 1975: 89.   [19] Wittgenstein 1967: § 556.

Much more can be said in answer to the descriptive question of what philosophers *qua* philosophers actually do, and we should not overlook the fact that what philosophers are prepared to count as philosophy is often influenced by their view of what they themselves are doing, so that they see in others affinities with that or radical differences from it. But philosophers generally tend to be more interested in the *prescriptive* question of what philosophy *ought* to be. It is with this question that we will be concerned in the remainder of this chapter.

A continuum between two extremes

Philosophers have taken a great number of different views on what we have termed the prescriptive question of what philosophy is. At first blush, it might seem that a good way to carve up the field is to distinguish positions that conceive of philosophy (properly understood) as somehow part of science from views according to which philosophy is separate from science and constitutes a different enterprise altogether. Call the former 'philosophy-as-science' views and the latter 'philosophy-as-distinct-from-science' views. One complication immediately comes to the fore. Before we can begin to sort metaphilosophical positions into these two baskets, we need to know what is meant by 'science'. If science here means 'natural science' – very roughly, the attempt to determine the laws of nature by means of observation and experiment – most philosophers would presumably be committed to viewing philosophy as distinct from science. At least, only a minority of philosophers actually *do* philosophy as if it were an empirical or natural science (design experiments, etc.). Most, though not all, philosophers conduct the majority of their inquiries from the proverbial 'armchair'. It might of course be that, if asked explicitly to state their metaphilosophical views, many of those 'armchair philosophers' would belie their own practice. But the principle of charity commands that we presume philosophers innocent of such inconsistency until proven guilty.

If, however, we include what is sometimes called the 'formal sciences' (mathematics, formal logic, etc.) under the heading of 'science', the scales would perhaps tip in favour of philosophy-as-science views. On this understanding of 'science' a defender of complete separation would be forced to exclude logic from philosophy. As we shall see, this is a bullet some philosophers are fully prepared to bite and, perhaps, logic is something of an odd man out within the philosophical family. However that may be, one can take an even broader view of science and understand it as including such humanities subjects as history and language studies, which would surely commit the majority of philosophers to versions of the philosophy-as-science view. The right conclusion to draw here seems to be that we will need more than just two large groups of views – 'philosophy-as-science' versus 'philosophy-as-distinct-from-science' views. In fact, as we shall see, the most common metaphilosophical views vary along a continuum between two extremes: the idea of philosophy as literally a part of natural science at one end, and at the other the view that philosophy is an altogether different enterprise – not just separate from *natural* science, but not a cognitive discipline at all.

Later chapters address problems associated with most of these views. In the present chapter, our aim is merely to provide a rough overview of the metaphilosophical landscape, as it were. Nevertheless, for the purposes of distinguishing the views from each other, and to give at least a preliminary indication of their respective strengths and weaknesses, we confront each position with the following questions:

1. Just how revisionist vis-à-vis existing philosophy (past and present) is the view? We shall assume that it counts against a view if it has the implication that much of what is commonly regarded as philosophy should not be so regarded, or that most philosophers (past and/or present) have been doing philosophy in completely the wrong way.
2. How does the view explain the relative 'lack of progress' characteristic of philosophy relative to the natural sciences? We shall assume that, *ceteris paribus*, it counts against a view if it (explicitly or implicitly) suggests that philosophy should have made progress of a kind that it manifestly has not.

The reason for making the first assumption is that when someone suggests how philosophy ought to be done it is philosophy he or she is talking about, and this is different from the suggestion that we should do something that would not count as philosophy at all. So consider someone who suggested that football would be better played without goalkeepers. One's reply would be that this might be an interesting game, no doubt providing many more goals, but that it would not be football. Similarly with philosophy: overly radical departures from accepted practice would produce a different subject, not just a better way of pursuing the old one. Or, to put the same point differently, if the radical reformer insisted that what he was going to do was philosophy then he ought to disqualify what was done in the past from bearing the same label. While, as we noted, we can sometimes allow this (e.g. for what has passed into science), we cannot plausibly write off the bulk of the subject in this way. So while proposals for new methods may, of course, be made, they should not have the effect of disqualifying all that has gone before.

The reason for the second assumption is less obvious. After all, not so long ago, some philosophers heralded 'the revolution in philosophy',[20] which they hoped would overcome the alleged sterility of the subject. So it would be wrong to assume that philosophers always resign themselves to conceding that their subject never makes any progress. Rather, when they suggest how philosophy should be practised we expect them to be able to say why previous ways of practising it were unproductive. And, indeed, those who thought of the revolution offered by explicit conceptual analysis could offer an explanation in terms of their predecessors' lack of clarity about their aims and methods. Thus an account of how to philosophise aright needs to show either why a certain sort of progress should not be expected or how lack of progress can be overcome. And if it opts for the latter route, we need to know why it has taken so long for philosophy to make real progress.

Philosophy as part of science

A deflationary answer to the descriptive question is fully compatible with robust, positive views on what philosophy, properly conceived, is – on what philosophers *ought to* be doing. Quine seems to be an example of someone who holds such a combination of views. According to Quine, philosophy, properly conceived, is 'a part of science', though it 'lies at the abstract and theoretical end' of it.[21] Given Quine's celebrated attack on the synthetic-analytic distinction and his associated claim that no propositions are immune to revision in the light of experience, for him there can only be a difference in degree between 'natural' and 'formal' science. All of science is in principle empirical, but the propositions of mathematics or logic

---

[20] Ryle 1956.   [21] Quine, in Magee 1982: 143.

simply occupy a more central position in our network of beliefs and thus are less likely to be overturned by experience than, say, the propositions of chemistry.[22] Philosophy, Quine thinks, enjoys a similarly protected position in the web of science.

Some, however, go further than Quine. So-called experimental philosophers explicitly regard philosophy as a straightforward part of empirical science and they cheerfully embrace the consequence that philosophy should be done using the established methods of empirical science. (The challenge experimental philosophy poses to traditional analytic philosophy is a topic of Chapter 4.) That the views of the experimental philosophers differ from those of Quine becomes clear once we confront the two parties with our test questions. For the experimental philosopher, presumably the reason philosophy has failed to make much progress is that, at least until a few years ago, philosophers have generally adopted armchair methods inherently unsuited to the philosophers' field of research. But if this is what experimental philosophers think, then obviously they subscribe to the view that the majority of philosophers (past and present) have been practising philosophy in the wrong way.

Quine need not commit to this idea. It is possible that philosophers, working at the abstract, more 'protected' end of science, are perfectly entitled to pursue their inquiries from an armchair – as presumably are mathematicians, on Quine's view. So Quine can give a much less revisionistic reply to our first question than can the experimental philosophers. It is less clear how Quine would explain the lack of progress in philosophy. If logic and mathematics have made ample progress, despite being very abstract and theoretical, then certainly it cannot be because of its position in the total web of science that philosophy has failed to emulate the successes of its close cousins.

Philosophy as immature science

A slight adjustment of the Quinean view yields an interesting answer. The reason philosophy has not made progress, it might be said, is that it is a science that has not yet, or has only very recently, 'matured', that is, 'attained a clear view of its subject-matter and its goals'[23] and settled on a method

---

[22] See Quine 1953: 42–6.   [23] Dummett 1978: 457.

or a set of methods that permits it to achieve those goals in a systematic fashion. One interesting fact about the 'only recently' version of the view is that the claim has been made any number of times throughout the history of modern philosophy, by, among others, Descartes, Locke, Hume, Kant, Russell, Husserl and, more recently, Michael Dummett and Timothy Williamson.[24] Dummett, for example, writes that 'philosophy has only just very recently struggled out of its early stage into maturity'.[25] As an answer to the *prescriptive* question, this view is not refuted by the fact that so far, none of the alleged maturations has led to any substantial progress in philosophy comparable to what we find in the natural sciences. Philosophy, perhaps, really has been put on the path of science once (or indeed several times), only for this achievement to be immediately thwarted by philosophers' failure to follow through on it.

But the view has other disadvantages. For one, it seems revisionist in the extreme – not merely implying that most contemporary philosophers fail to conduct philosophical research in the right manner, but that they continue to do so despite the fact that it has already been shown how to make philosophy 'a rigorous science', in Husserl's expression. (Of course, there is a rejoinder to this objection: that all *previous* proclamations of philosophy having finally 'come of age' were premature and that really only now can such an announcement be truly made. Thus, one can hardly blame philosophers for not yet having fully absorbed this new development. But that philosophy has only recently come of age is precisely what has always been said. Why should we think it true *this* time?) Another dimension of the same problem is that if philosophy has now finally been put on the path of a science, then it seems that at least one practice most if not all philosophers engage in, and think they *should* engage in, now becomes obsolete: that of reading the works of (pre-scientific) philosophers such as Plato, Aristotle, Descartes, Hume, Kant, Russell, Husserl and so forth – depending on when you think the decisive step onto the path of science was taken. Neuroscientists usually do not read Descartes' musings on the function of the pineal gland, nor do physicists read Newton (or even Einstein), and it is hard to see why they would need to bother. If philosophy

---

[24] See Hacker 2009: 134, and Philipse 2009.
[25] Dummett 1978: 457. Dummett refers to the work of Frege as the decisive turning point.

has now been put on the secure path of science, why should philosophers continue to study the *Meditations on First Philosophy*? But wouldn't most philosophers be very reluctant to consider the practice of studying the work of the great philosophers of the past anything but *highly relevant* to doing philosophy?

Similar worries apply to the idea that philosophy has not yet come of age. Does this not imply that we are all doing philosophy the wrong way? Philosophy, on this view, ought to be a science, but one gets the impression from the way most philosophers continue to practise it that it is a very different enterprise. And just why has two millennia of concerted efforts by some of the greatest minds of humankind failed to change this unfortunate state of affairs?

Colin McGinn has defended a metaphilosophical position at the philosophy-as-science end of the spectrum, which has replies to these worries. According to McGinn, philosophical questions are straightforward empirical questions about the natural world; the reason we have not yet found scientific ways of resolving them is that 'we are not cognitively equipped to solve philosophical problems'.[26] In other words: 'We make so little progress in philosophy for the same reason we make so little progress in unassisted flying: we lack the requisite equipment.'[27] On this view, philosophy in the hands of humans will never move beyond its immature state, so the lack of progress is easily explained. And it makes scant sense to accuse philosophers past and present of doing philosophy the wrong way, given that there is no right way for *us* to do it. Yet these advantages come at a cost. For if McGinn is right, philosophising seems an utterly pointless activity. This is a bullet McGinn is prepared to bite, adding merely that since his view '*might* be false', it would be premature to start calling for the closure of philosophy departments worldwide.[28] But we suspect that most philosophers would find it hard to swallow the notion that the activity they engage in is utterly pointless. McGinn's view looks like a last resort. Furthermore, the view seems to fit the philosophy of mind much better than, say, ethics, political philosophy or philosophical aesthetics. There

---

[26] McGinn 1993: 10.   [27] Ibid.: 13.

[28] Ibid.: 153. McGinn also thinks that 'much of what is done under the name "philosophy" can still be done' even if his thesis is true, including 'conceptual analysis, the systematization of the sciences, ethics and politics' (ibid.).

would be something odd about the suggestion that questions concerning the nature of justice are straightforwardly empirical questions that we simply cannot answer because of our cognitive limitations. For these and other reasons, McGinn's view has not caught on.

Philosophy as 'midwife' and 'residue' of the sciences

There is another, much more popular, metaphilosophical position that still thinks of philosophy as continuous with natural science and accepts, in a way, McGinn's point that there are principled reasons why philosophy will never make progress the way science does, while at the same time maintaining that philosophising has a point. This is the very widespread notion that philosophy is the 'midwife' and 'residue' of the sciences. Austin famously offers the following image:

> In the history of human inquiry, philosophy has the place of the initial central sun, seminal and tumultuous: from time to time it throws off some portion of itself to take station as a science, a planet, cool and well regulated, progressing steadily towards a distant final state.[29]

The image suggests that philosophy 'shrinks' as problems hitherto considered philosophical are, in Austin's phrase, 'kicked upstairs'. Although Austin suggests that this is no cause for concern, as plenty of problems remain for philosophers to grapple with, Oxford philosophers in Austin's day did talk – in all seriousness – about 'how long it would take to "finish off"' the subject, equipped, as they thought they now were, with an effective method. P. F. Strawson recalls, for example, that a lecturer concluded his lectures on Hume's moral philosophy 'by remarking: "Had Hume shown the same acumen in logic [i.e. epistemology] as he showed in morals ... philosophy ... would have been over ... sooner"'.[30]

Numerous important philosophers have defended the residue view. Bertrand Russell, for example, held that there is no essential difference between philosophy and empirical science. Both are types of inquiry aimed at gathering knowledge about the world. The difference between philosophy and science is simply that we call an inquiry 'scientific' when 'definite knowledge' concerning its subject matter becomes possible. The 'residue'

[29] Austin 1979: 232.   [30] Both quotes Strawson 2011: 72.

of questions to which no definite, conclusive answers have yet been given, is, according to Russell, what we call 'philosophy'.[31] John Searle articulates essentially the same view: 'As soon as we can revise and formulate a philosophical question to the point that we can find a systematic way to answer it, it ceases to be philosophical and becomes scientific'.[32]

The attractions of the residue view are easily appreciated. For a start, the explanation for why philosophy does not make progress the way science does is wonderfully simple: as Jack Smart puts it, philosophy does not make progress 'for the same reason that treason never prospers. If it prospered, it would cease to be called "treason" and would become a glorious revolution'.[33] When real progress is made on a philosophical problem, all the credit invariably goes to a (new) science. The residue view can also afford to be fairly conservative when it comes to existing philosophical practice. If it is the proper role of philosophy to be this 'tumultuous sun' that once in a while 'throws off some portion of itself to take station as a science', then it seems perfectly possible that philosophy is, and always has been, more or less the way it ought to be. Depending on sympathies and temperament, some might also consider it a virtue of the residue view that it holds out the promise (or threat) of 'finishing off' philosophy at some point. The more worrying suggestion that we have already reached this point is examined in the following chapter.

For now, we shall note two potential objections to the residue view. The first was essentially already raised against McGinn's view: like the latter, the residue view cannot easily cover moral and political philosophy, as it is hard to see how these could be turned into sciences – and not because of cognitive limitations on our part.[34] A possible rejoinder might be that there is no reason why there could not be certain parts of philosophy that are more resistant to giving birth to sciences than others, and indeed perhaps there are essential reasons why some parts will remain at the 'tumultuous' stage forever. Another objection is perhaps harder to respond to. As Peter Hacker formulates it, as philosophy gives birth to new sciences,

> new areas of philosophical investigation [are] thereby generated, e.g. philosophy of physics or philosophy of the psychological sciences. But it would be misguided to suppose that questions in the philosophies of the

---

[31] Russell 1998: 87, 90.   [32] Searle 1999: 2069.
[33] Smart 1993: 81.   [34] Hacker 2009: 133.

special sciences remain philosophical only because they are insufficiently clearly understood to be handled by a new meta-science.[35]

If Hacker is wrong about the last bit, we open the door to an in principle infinite series of potential meta-sciences. When a new science S is created, the *philosophy of S* pops into existence as well, but if a systematic way is found to answer the questions of the philosophy of S, a new science *S(s)* emerges, thereby generating *the philosophy of S(s)*, which in turn can be turned into a science and so forth. As Hacker implies, something does seem odd about such a scenario; but perhaps some of the oddness would vanish if we considered the idea in less abstract terms. Maybe some questions that used to belong to the philosophy of science now belong to, say, the sociology of science; and maybe the latter generates its own set of philosophical questions, some of which may one day be addressed by a higher-level sociology. Surely, there is nothing obviously absurd or even implausible about this suggestion. Thus, none of the objections to the residue view seems conclusive.

Platonism

A different sort of proposal – typically associated with Plato – is that philosophy, properly conceived, is the study of some particularly 'deep' and intangible part of reality beyond reach of the empirical sciences. This view is suggested by Plato's allegory of the cave in the *Republic*. The empirical sciences study what Plato calls 'the region revealed through sight', which corresponds to the world of 'shadows' in Plato's allegory, and only the right sort of philosopher can extricate herself – with immense difficulty – from the preoccupation with shadows and eventually ascent to 'the intelligible region'.[36] The philosopher who has successfully reached the latter is able to contemplate the pure forms of, for example, beauty or the good, of which the instances in the empirical world are but pale and imperfect imitations. The difficulty of the philosophical exercise and the constant allure of the world of shadows may explain why philosophy has made scant progress, and the Platonist might regard the traditional project of conceptual analysis as fairly close to the sort of thing philosophers ought to be doing. So

---

[35] Ibid.: 132.   [36] Plato 1989: *Republic* 517b–c.

it seems the Platonist has little difficulty providing answers to our two questions.

Among contemporary philosophers, however, it is not easy to find anyone openly advocating Platonism, at least of the full-blown sort considered here. This has a lot to do with the fact that, as we will see in the next chapter, most contemporary philosophers are committed to 'naturalistic' views that imply the rejection of the 'Platonic Heaven' of pure forms. It is probably also to do with the Platonists' rather lofty pretensions. In Colin McGinn's words, Platonism regards the questions of philosophy as 'simply more profound – more elevated – than the questions of science, which is concerned merely with the ordinary empirical world of sensory observation'.[37] To many, such claims will sound cheeky at best and megalomanic at worst.[38] Perhaps the main area where Platonism has retained its attraction is in the philosophy of mathematics, where Frege and his followers have viewed numbers and so on as abstract objects. But here, as with other Platonist accounts, the problem is to explain how we can know anything about such objects which *ex hypothesi* have no causal influence upon us. If philosophy were concerned with Platonic objects, one might expect it to be quite unclear how it could discover anything about them.

Thus, 'Platonism' these days is more of an accusation made against others than a position anyone explicitly defends. A historically interesting example of the use of Platonism as a stick with which to beat other philosophers is found in Gilbert Ryle's paper 'Phenomenology versus "The Concept of Mind"'.[39] In this paper, Ryle accuses Husserl of espousing Platonism, since, so Ryle alleges, the founder of phenomenology was wedded to the idea of 'some super-inspections of some super-objects'.[40] More recently, advocates of experimental approaches to philosophical questions, intending to be provocative, have branded the traditional 'armchair' approaches as Platonistic.[41] Being of limited contemporary relevance, Platonism will not be considered further in this book.

[37] McGinn 2002: 201.
[38] Cf. Smart 1993: 68 and Popper 1975: 43.
[39] This was Ryle's contribution to the infamous Royaumont Colloquium of 1958 – a conference intended to create a dialogue between analytic philosophers and mainly French and Belgian continentalists. For a detailed account of this failed attempt at rapprochement between the two camps, see Overgaard 2010.
[40] Ryle 2009a: 187.
[41] Weinberg, Nichols and Stich 2008: 19.

Philosophy as the logic of science

Platonists, in Ryle's image, might think of philosophy as a sort of super-science of super-objects, and thus as continuous with empirical science, if science has to admit the existence of such objects in mathematics. The logical positivists, though very deferential to the empirical sciences, believed philosophy to be quite different from them. Moritz Schlick, for example, diagnoses what he calls 'a curious misunderstanding and misinterpretation of the nature of philosophy'. As he explains, the misinterpretation 'lies in the idea that the nature of philosophy and science are more or less the same, that they both consist of true propositions about the world. In reality philosophy is never a system of propositions and therefore quite different from science'.[42] While science is in the business of discovering truths about the world, philosophy, according to Schlick, is *the activity of finding meaning*'.[43] As such, philosophy is very important to the sciences, because they cannot investigate the possible truth (or falsity) of a proposition if its meaning has not been made clear. On the other hand, Schlick emphasises that scientific problems constitute the only genuine problems and thus all the so-called problems of philosophy will turn out to be either scientific (i.e. genuine) problems in disguise, or meaningless pseudo-problems.[44] In the words of another prominent member of the Vienna Circle, Rudolf Carnap, *Philosophy is the logic of science*, i.e., the logical analysis of the concepts, propositions, proofs, theories of science.'[45] For present purposes, we can regard Carnap as making essentially the same point as Schlick:[46] philosophy is not to be thought of as any sort of science (let alone a Platonic super-science), but is concerned to clarify and analyse the meanings of, and logical relations between, scientific concepts, propositions and theories.

Much like the 'residue' view, the metaphilosophical position defended by the logical positivists has little difficulty explaining the lack of

---

[42] Both quotes from Schlick 1992: 45.

[43] Ibid.: 50.   [44] Ibid.: 51.

[45] Carnap 1992: 54–5.

[46] One thing they seem to disagree about is whether there can be any philosophical propositions. Schlick here seems to have been influenced by Wittgenstein's *Tractatus* in arguing that there cannot, whereas Carnap explicitly takes issue with Wittgenstein on this point. There are other differences too, but they need not concern us here.

progress in philosophy. Analysing and clarifying the meanings of propositions and theories is very different from accumulating empirical knowledge, and one should therefore not expect to find in philosophy the sort of progress that characterises the empirical sciences. Arguably this is because we clarify meanings for particular purposes, so that it is unclear what any systematic and progressive task of clarifying meanings would come to. It is less easy to see how the idea that philosophy is, or ought to be, the 'logic of science' can avoid being excessively revisionistic vis-à-vis philosophy as it has been and continues to be practised. The logical positivists seem to reduce all of philosophy to a quite narrowly circumscribed approach to the philosophy of science (and maybe the philosophy of empirical knowledge more broadly), branding most of what other philosophers do as either nonsense or an intrusion into the proper domain of some empirical science. As we will see in Chapter 5, Carnap took the philosophy of Heidegger as a paradigmatic example of nonsensical metaphysics, but Carnap's verdict on current analytic metaphysics, had he lived long enough to become acquainted with it, would surely have been very similar. Indeed the positivists seem happy to think of themselves as playing a quite different game from the one from the past they disparagingly dismiss as metaphysics.

Philosophy as a contribution to human understanding

Although in other ways opposed to the logical positivists, the later Wittgenstein and his followers would agree with Schlick that philosophy is 'quite different from science'. Wittgenstein himself notoriously likened his philosophical methods to 'therapies' and declared: 'The philosopher's treatment of a question is like the treatment of an illness.'[47] This suggests that Wittgenstein regarded philosophical questions as intellectual diseases of some kind and that he thought philosophers' only legitimate task was to cure themselves (and each other) of their pathological urge to raise such questions. Yet Wittgenstein also, more positively, spoke of philosophy as providing a 'perspicuous representation' (*übersichtliche Darstellung*),[48] and his most prominent contemporary expositor, Peter Hacker, emphasises

---

[47] Wittgenstein 1958: §§ 133, 255.   [48] Ibid.: § 122.

that the negative, therapeutic analysis cannot be separated from a more positive, 'connective' analysis also present in Wittgenstein's work.[49]

As Hacker presents the Wittgensteinian metaphilosophical position, philosophy is not only not part of natural science, it makes no contribution to human knowledge whatsoever. That does not, however, mean that philosophy yields no positive gains. In Hacker's words, philosophy is 'the pursuit not of knowledge but of understanding. The task of philosophy is not to add to the sum of human knowledge, but to enable us to attain a clear understanding of what is already known'.[50] Philosophy is in this sense – and this, too, is something the logical positivists might agree with – a 'second-order discipline'.[51] It gives us no new information, but enables us reflectively to understand the information we already have. To see how this idea might work, consider a story told by Strawson:

> When the first Spanish or, strictly, Castilian grammar was presented to Queen Isabella of Castile, her response was to ask what use it was … For of course the grammar was in a certain sense of no use at all to fluent speakers of Castilian. In a sense they knew it all already. They spoke grammatically correct Castilian because grammatically correct Castilian simply *was* what they spoke. The grammar did not set the standard of correctness for the sentences they spoke; on the contrary, it was the sentences they spoke that set the standard of correctness for the grammar. However, though in a sense they knew the grammar of their language, there was another sense in which they did not know it.[52]

The speakers of Castilian, as Strawson puts it, had an *implicit* understanding of the Castilian grammar; but they did not have an *explicit* understanding in the sense of being able to state the grammatical rules they observed. In general, 'the practical mastery of our conceptual equipment in no way entails the possession of a clear, explicit understanding of the principles which govern it, the theory of our practice'.[53] That explicit, theoretical understanding is precisely what philosophy is supposed to deliver.

Strawson's story about the Castilian grammar is more than just an analogy, insofar as both he and Hacker emphasise the linguistic focus of their

---

[49] Although, as Hacker is fully aware, the term 'connective analysis' is Peter Strawson's (1992), not Wittgenstein's.

[50] Hacker 1996: 272–3.   [51] See e.g. White 1975: 104.

[52] Strawson 1992: 5.   [53] Ibid.: 7.

philosophical investigations. We are supposed to examine 'the uses of words',[54] or assemble grammatical 'reminders', as Wittgenstein famously held.[55] But the idea that the task of philosophy is to provide reflective, 'second-order' understanding of something we in a sense already know is independent of the so-called linguistic turn, and can be found in the work of continental philosophers who did not take that turn, as we will see in the next section. It is also closely related with the notion that philosophy is a *humanistic* discipline, which we examine in a bit more detail in the following chapter. For now, we wish to note that, like the logical positivists, Hacker has no problem explaining the lack of progress in philosophy. Philosophy is not a discipline that adds anything to our knowledge of the world, and thus one should not expect it to make progress the way science does.[56] And unlike the logical positivists' view, Hacker's view need not be overly revisionistic. At least for Hacker, the reflective, philosophical quest for understanding is not thematically restricted to science – or to anything else, for that matter. As Hacker says, philosophical questions 'can, in principle, be concerned with any subject matter at all'. Yet, on the other hand, Hacker also suggests that logic – striving as it does 'to produce theorems by means of proofs'[57] – is a formal science alongside mathematics and thus not part of philosophy, properly speaking.

Philosophy as transcendental inquiry

In continental philosophy, similar ideas have had considerable currency. The general notion that it is the task of philosophy to elucidate something that, in some sense, is already known to us is supported by many phenomenologists. Husserl, for example, stated that he was striving for a 'comprehensible *understanding* of what the real being of the world, and real being in general, *means* ... in natural life itself',[58] prior to all philosophising. The distinction between first-order and second-order inquiry seems relevant here too. As we ourselves are the subjects of the 'natural life' in question, we must, on some basic level, be familiar with the meaning or sense that the world has for us. Phenomenology, then, does not add to the

---

[54] Hacker 2009: 142.   [55] Wittgenstein 1958: § 127.

[56] Hacker does, however, outline three different senses in which there can be said to be progress in philosophy (2009: 151–3).

[57] Hacker 2009: 139, 130.   [58] Husserl 1959: 481–2.

sum of our (first-order) knowledge. Yet the understanding that phenomenology aims to provide is one we do not yet have, since we are wont to let our gaze pass through the meaning the world has for us – seeing straight through it to the objects we are interested in.[59] Only the phenomenological second-order inquiry yields an explicit understanding, Husserl thinks. The phenomenological reflection, as he puts it, transforms 'the universal obviousness [*Selbstverständlichkeit*] of the being of the world … into something intelligible [*eine Verständlichkeit*]'.[60]

A similar picture emerges in the writings of other phenomenologists. In the words of Merleau-Ponty, phenomenological reflection reawakens our 'basic experience of the world'[61]; it 'slackens the intentional threads which attach us to the world and thus brings them to our notice'.[62] But thereby it only makes explicit something we were already implicitly familiar with. The philosopher 'claims to speak in the very name of the naïve evidence of the world' and 'refrains from adding anything to it', limiting herself to reflectively 'drawing out all its consequences'.[63] It is no coincidence that Merleau-Ponty in this context refers to Augustine's famous remark on time: 'I know well enough what it is, provided that nobody asks me; but if I am asked what it is and try to explain, I am baffled.'[64] Our implicit familiarity with time, or world experience, does not make the philosophical task of reflectively clarifying these phenomena any easier. According to Heidegger, we all have an implicit, 'pre-ontological' understanding of the manners of being of the various sorts of things around us. Yet we might not be able to make this understanding explicit if asked to do so. Only phenomenological reflection gives us an explicit – 'ontological' – understanding of what we already know implicitly.[65]

Two things, however, set the phenomenologists' perspective apart from that of Hacker and most other followers of Wittgenstein. First, the former do not focus their investigations exclusively on language use, but tend, rather, to be at least as preoccupied with describing how we *experience*

---

[59] Cf. Husserl 1970: 105.

[60] Husserl 1970: 180. Unfortunately, this rare example of a Husserlian pun does not work in English.

[61] Merleau-Ponty 2002: ix.   [62] Ibid.: xv.

[63] Merleau-Ponty 1964a: 4.

[64] Augustine 1961: 264. Cf. Merleau-Ponty 1964a: 3.

[65] Cf. Heidegger 1962: 32.

things in everyday contexts. Merleau-Ponty, for example, explicitly rejects the reduction of philosophy 'to a linguistic analysis' and avers that the philosopher is 'not concerned with "word-meanings"' and should not 'seek a verbal substitute for the world we see'.[66] Second, many continental philosophers, including phenomenologists such as Husserl and (less markedly) Heidegger and Merleau-Ponty, understand philosophy as a *transcendental* sort of inquiry. A transcendental inquiry is, as Kant put it, one 'occupied not so much with objects as with the mode of our knowledge of objects in so far as this mode of knowledge is to be possible *a priori*'.[67] To phrase it slightly differently, transcendental philosophers reflect on our (first-order) knowledge with a view to unveiling the 'conditions of possibility' of such knowledge. On the views of many continental philosophers, what sets philosophy fundamentally apart from the empirical sciences is precisely that the former essentially is – that is, ought to be – transcendental inquiry into the conditions of possibility underlying ordinary and scientific experience and inquiry.

Like other views that portray philosophy as distinct from science, this view is not embarrassed by the apparent lack of progress in philosophy in comparison with science. To be sure, we are owed an answer as to why transcendental research has apparently failed to reveal any generally agreed upon 'conditions of possibility' of experience or knowledge – and this goes in particular for a phenomenologist such as Husserl who believed he was turning philosophy into a 'rigorous' *transcendental* science. But on the other hand, the mere fact that philosophy is a fundamentally different enterprise from empirical science suggests that there is no obvious reason to expect the former to be characterised by the same sort of progress as the latter.

Less clear is whether the view that philosophy is transcendental inquiry can avoid being fairly revisionistic. It seems more obviously suited to what Kant might call 'theoretical' philosophy than to, say, political or moral philosophy. Not that there cannot be such a thing as inquiring into the 'conditions of possibility' of moral behaviour, for example – perhaps this is indeed what phenomenologist Emmanuel Levinas was trying to do[68] – but it seems very unlikely that this is an adequate characterisation of what

---

[66] Merleau-Ponty 1964a: 96, 4.   [67] Kant 1929: B 25.
[68] For an articulation and defence of this claim, see de Boer 1986.

people working in, say, applied ethics or the philosophy of law are up to. The naturalism prevailing in mainstream philosophy probably also contributes to making the majority of contemporary philosophers wary of the transcendental conception of philosophy.

World views

One of the philosophical movements that sprang, in part, from phenomenology was existentialism, the cluster of ideas associated with Jean-Paul Sartre, Simone de Beauvoir and Albert Camus in the mid twentieth century. Their leitmotiv is an affirmation of our total freedom. 'We are condemned to be free'[69] because neither do we have an essential nature nor is there a purpose in life beyond the one we give it: our life is 'absurd'. Sartre offers phenomenological evidence for such supposed insights, but the point of reporting them here is to illustrate a further view of the aim of philosophy which can best be summed up by saying that it is to provide a *Weltanschauung* or world view.

The idea that philosophy aims at articulating and arguing for world views was itself a reaction against attempts to find a role for the subject as a contribution to science or as modelled on science in its account of the world. Such attempts led, in the words of Wilhelm Dilthey, who developed a philosophy of world views, to an 'attitude to the world as something other, alien and terrible'.[70] Instead a philosophical world view is intended to capture what it is actually like to live a human life in the world – an approach which explains a possible affinity with phenomenology. The point of a world view, however, is not just to describe our experience of the world but to do so in a way that can shape our attitude to it and inform our practical decisions. In this respect world views address the question of the meaning of life, traditionally thought of as one of the tasks of philosophy, at least until logical positivists cast doubt on whether this question itself was meaningful. But to address the question is not necessarily to find a positive answer, as the existentialist view of life as absurd illustrates. Thus a contemporary advocate of the world view approach to philosophy writes:

> The worldviews of Christians and positivists, of Spinoza and John Stuart
> Mill, of Marxists and existentialists ... differ not only because they would

---

[69] Sartre 1966: 34.   [70] Dilthey 1976: 136.

assign different importance and truth-value to the same propositions, but also because to accept one rather than the other is to feel one way rather than another about reality and man's place in it.[71]

World views, as we understand the notion here, aim to integrate the way the world is taken to be with the stance we should take to it and the way we should act in it. In this regard the idea that philosophy provides world views can potentially better explain the relationship between ethics and the more metaphysical aspects of the subject than philosophy-as-science accounts. It also offers a plausible criterion of why the 'big questions' are big – they are big because the answers matter to us in our lives.

Philosophers in the analytic tradition, by contrast with the continental one,[72] have not commonly embraced the world view approach, though one time positivist Friedrich Waismann is a possible exception. '[W]hat is characteristic of philosophy,' he wrote, 'is the piercing of that dead crust of tradition and convention, the breaking of those fetters which bind us to inherited preconceptions, so as to attain a new and broader way of looking at things'.[73] This is what Waismann calls 'vision', and he attributes it to every great philosopher, referring to their *Weltanschauungen*. Richard Rorty interprets Waismann as championing '*proposals* about how to talk', rather than '*descriptions* of the nature of things'.[74] But while this might be the right way to gloss Waismann's account it is no necessary feature of the world view conception. However, rather than seeking explicit adherents, we might better look for approaches which presuppose it. Much recent feminist philosophy might be cited as an example. Philosophers like Susan Mendus have argued that many philosophical systems, such as Kant's, are androcentric, reflecting the experiences and expectations of men rather than women. This seems to implicitly regard philosophy as offering world views which philosophers should evaluate by seeing whether they work for women, that is to say, whether they can claim validity in virtue of working for people generally. Here it is worth reminding ourselves that de Beauvoir saw existentialism as liberating for women precisely because it denied a fixed female nature and promised a free

[71] Kekes 1980: 67.
[72] Although Husserl criticised the philosophy of *Weltanschauung* in his essay 'Philosophy as Rigorous Science' (Husserl 1965: 122–47).
[73] Waismann 1959: 375.   [74] Rorty 1992b: 34–5.

choice of identity. To that extent it attempted to offer them, and others, a satisfactory world view.

There is nothing obviously revisionist about the world view account of philosophy, as we have seen by the variety of philosophers and systems cited by its proponents. Yet the credibility of attributing the provision of world views to philosophers of the past depends upon being able to read them in this way whatever their stated intentions, and, as noted earlier, this is always perilous. Moreover it is far from clear that recent Anglo-American philosophy can be viewed in this way. 'Edification', writes Ryle, 'is not palatable to colleagues. Nor is the space of an article or a discussion-paper broad enough to admit of a crusade against, or a crusade on behalf of, any massive "Ism"'.[75] Yet these are the typical forms that this sort of philosophy takes. A not implausible reply would be that individual philosophers contribute to some collective contemporary world view such as materialism.

The idea of philosophy as providing world views, to which we return in Chapter 8, can arguably explain the apparent lack of progress in the subject by showing why we should not expect it. 'Some problems', it is said, 'endure, endlessly persist, and solving them consists in making a continued effort of coping',[76] and the problems with which philosophy deals, such as the meaning of life, are of this enduring kind. There will always be a variety of answers to such problems and which will prevail at any time will depend upon those specific circumstances. Thus, 'if one faction succeeds in presenting its side victoriously, the argument is only temporarily resolved. For the relevant considerations will change and the merits of competing claims will be pressed again'.[77] This kind of explanation of the lack of progress chimes in with next type of prescriptive account of philosophy we consider. But it is not the only one available to world view philosophers, who could also hold either that the problems philosophers face themselves change over time or that the resources philosophers bring to enduring problems from other areas of culture change in a non-cumulative way, as, for instance, with the decline in religious belief or a widening of moral sympathies. None of this implies that world views cannot be compared as better or worse at a given time. Our example from feminist philosophy illustrates this. It only implies that the sort of succession of world views

[75] Ryle 1956: 4.   [76] Kekes 1980: 36.   [77] Ibid.: 40.

we witness across time does not represent the kind of progress manifest in the march of scientific theory or mathematical formalisation.

Philosophy as 'edifying conversation'

The final metaphilosophical view we consider here is commonly associated with important figures of continental philosophy, perhaps Nietzsche and Derrida in particular, though arguably its clearest and most consistent advocate is Richard Rorty. According to the latter, 'philosophy is not a name for a discipline which confronts permanent issues, and unfortunately keeps misstating them, or attacking them with clumsy dialectical instruments. Rather, it is a cultural genre, a "voice in the conversation of mankind"'.[78] This view of philosophy is characteristic of what Rorty calls 'edifying philosophers', supposedly exemplified by Dewey, Heidegger and Wittgenstein, among others. As Rorty explains, 'the point of edifying philosophy is to keep the conversation going rather than to find objective truth'.[79] He is well aware that this is a far cry from how philosophers generally like to think about what they do, and he admits that edifying philosophy seems to be on the way to 'dispensing with philosophy' as a discipline.[80] At the same time, Rorty assures us that edifying philosophers 'can never end philosophy'; what they can do is 'help prevent it from attaining the secure path of a science'.[81]

Rorty would agree with Hacker, then, that philosophy is not – that is, ought not to be – a cognitive discipline. Philosophy should not aim to 'find objective truth'. But whereas Hacker believes philosophy has the positive aim of reflectively understanding the truths already found, Rorty thinks it should just keep 'the conversation of mankind' going. That such activity should not lead to progress along the lines of the natural sciences is hardly surprising – from Rorty's point of view, indeed, such progress would be *detrimental* to philosophy, for it would mean that it was 'on the secure path of a science' and thus had ceased to perform its proper task. It is less clear that the time and energy philosophers spend constructing rigorous arguments and detecting the faults in those of others would be compatible with them having cancelled the search for objective truth, as Rorty's edifying

[78] Rorty 1979: 264.   [79] Ibid.: 377.
[80] Ibid.: 179.   [81] Ibid.: 372.

philosopher has. But Rorty could maintain that, whether we realise it or not, 'keeping the conversation going' is really all that we *are* doing. He might further point out that the endemic philosophical disagreements, and the attending lack of real progress, are at least indications that we are not getting any closer to objective, universally agreed upon truths about the matters we are discussing. Moreover, Rorty's conversation metaphor obviously makes no restrictions on the conversational topics, so that there is no obvious problem about including all members of the philosophical family – although the logician's case for refusing to accept the idea of 'talk unanimated by the desire for truth'[82] would seem particularly good. In Chapter 6, we return to Rorty's challenge to the self-image of mainstream philosophy and examine it more closely.

Conclusion

In this chapter, we have surveyed various answers to what we called the 'descriptive' and 'prescriptive' questions concerning the nature of philosophy. We argued that both 'essentialist' and 'deflationary' replies to the former were problematic, and tentatively suggested that perhaps an account in terms of family resemblances might be able to home in on a certain set of issues and characteristic ways of dealing with them, which are central to philosophy as it is actually practised. The prescriptive question, we then went on to suggest, has been answered in myriad ways, a number of which we attempted to locate on a continuum between the view that philosophy is literally part of science, at one end, and the idea that it is not a cognitive enterprise of any sort, at the other. Along the way, we briefly suggested some problems the various views might face, but most of the metaphilosophical theses broached will be subjected to more in-depth discussion in later chapters.

---

[82] This is Charles Griswold's (2002: 157) description of what Rorty and Derrida's recommendation amounts to from a Socratic perspective. But while Rorty seems happy enough to accept such a rendering of his views (2003: 21), there may in fact be reason to think Derrida's philosophy *is* animated by the desire for truth (see Plant 2012).

3 Philosophy, science and the humanities

Introduction

Recently, Stephen Hawking boldly declared that philosophy is dead. 'Philosophy', he explains, 'has not kept up with modern developments in science, particularly physics. Scientists have become the bearers of the torch of discovery in our quest for knowledge'.[1] As a result, he claims, philosophical discussion has become outdated and irrelevant. If Hawking is right, philosophy belongs to a past we have finally put behind us; it has no future.

Of course, despite itself, Hawking's claim voices a philosophical view, one based on a number of contentious and unacknowledged assumptions about the nature of philosophy.[2] It appears to be a 'residue' view of philosophy which conceives of philosophy as a cognitive enterprise and an earlier, unsystematic and failed attempt to explain the natural world, in competition with physics and the special sciences. On this view, as explained in Chapter 2, incrementally (over the years and bit by bit), philosophy has found its subject matter become the business of natural science until it has been

---

[1] Hawking and Mlodinow 2010: 5.

[2] In fact, despite their scornful dismissal of philosophy, Hawking and his co-author go on to argue for a thesis in a manner that can only be described as philosophical. Moreover, neither their thesis nor their arguments will be new to anyone familiar with the history of ideas. So, for example, in chapter 3 of *The Grand Design*, they flirt with a form of idealism and come around to a view they call 'model-dependent realism', in which the brain is said to form models of the world from sensory input and what we take to be 'reality' is the model most successful at explaining events. This then leads them via a quick road to a straightforwardly instrumentalist view of science in which, they argue, there is no point in asking which model is 'actually real'; what is important is which model best fits the observational evidence. We leave it to others to assess the cogency of these views (e.g. Norris 2011).

left with the 'gaps'; that is, those questions, such as 'Why does the universe exist?', to which natural science has found difficulty offering an answer. But now, or so Hawking thinks, even this sort of inquiry is susceptible to scientific treatment, leaving philosophy outmoded and its purpose usurped.

This declaration was bound to ruffle philosophical feathers, but in reality it may not be that remote from views propounded by some prominent *philosophers*. Two decades ago, Hilary Putnam complained that philosophy had become

> increasingly dominated by the idea that science, and only science, describes the world as it is in itself, independent of perspective …
> [T]he idea that science leaves no room for an independent philosophical enterprise has reached the point at which leading practitioners [of analytic philosophy] sometimes suggest that all that is left for philosophy is to try to anticipate what the presumed scientific solutions to all metaphysical problems will eventually look like.[3]

If Putnam is right, leading philosophers essentially agree with Hawking: science has progressed to a point at which there are no 'gaps' left for philosophers to call their own.

One twentieth-century philosopher who was not shy about his naturalistic and scientistic sympathies – Wilfrid Sellars – famously stated that 'in the dimension of describing and explaining the world, science is the measure of all things, of what is that it is, and of what is not that it is not'.[4] The question raised in this chapter is to what extent it follows from Sellars's claim – which Putnam is probably right to think would command widespread assent in the philosophical community – that science leaves 'no room for an independent philosophical enterprise'. But before addressing this question, we need to tackle a prior one: what reason is there to think it is true, as Hawking, Sellars and the philosophers Putnam refers to apparently all do, that only science describes the world as it is, because it describes it 'independent of perspective'?

Science: a tough act to follow

It is a commonplace in the history of ideas that the natural sciences, as we now understand them, grew gradually out of philosophy during the

---

[3] Putnam 1992: ix–x.   [4] Sellars 1991: 173.

Renaissance and early modern period, when systematised observational and experimental methods were brought to bear on what were hitherto, at least in large part, empirically uncorroborated speculations on the nature of things. Thus problems in natural philosophy slowly became the subject of inquiry for the new sciences. For a long period during this development, however, philosophers or – more correctly, given that they would not have thought of themselves as doing something distinct from the emerging sciences – figures in the history of philosophy continued to make important contributions to the development of natural science: we might think here of Gassendi's molecular theory, Diderot's contribution to the idea of natural selection or Kant's suggestion that the Milky Way and nebulae were distinct 'island universes' (i.e. galaxies). Of course, these contributions did not always prove successful – and here we might consider Descartes' vortex theory of planetary motion or his pneumatic physiology, with its reliance on 'animal spirits' – but it is an honourable history, nonetheless.

Thus, when William Whewell proposed the term 'scientist' in 1833, in a famous debate with Samuel Coleridge in a meeting of the British Association for the Advancement of Science, he intended it to be mildly satirical, drawing an analogy to 'artist', and comparing its form to established terms such as 'economist' and 'atheist'. Whewell lamented what he saw as an increasing fragmentation in the field of knowledge, where 'philosopher' had become regarded as 'too wide and lofty a term' to describe what he labelled 'cultivators of science'.[5] However, as Hawking would no doubt be eager to stress, this fragmentation and the decline in philosophers' contributions to the growth of scientific knowledge has perhaps been inevitable given the increase and specialisation of knowledge over this period and the professionalisation that has necessarily accompanied this.

Most contemporary philosophers accept the trajectory traced out by this history and defer to natural science in the discovery of new facts and the development of explanations of natural phenomena. As already suggested,

---

[5] The Whewell–Coleridge debate was reported anonymously by Whewell in a review of Mary Somerville's *On the Connexion of the Physical Sciences* in the *Quarterly Review* in 1834. Despite Whewell's intentions, use of the term 'scientist' became established, but only very slowly and often extremely reluctantly. He used 'scientist' again (here alongside the phrase 'cultivators of science') in his 1840 book *Philosophy and the Inductive Sciences* (See Yeo 1993 and Holmes 2008).

they may agree with another unspoken assumption in Hawking's claim: that science is uniquely effective as a way of finding out how things stand and that that no other forms of inquiry are capable of producing comparable results. And even those inclined to dispute this cannot dispute the success of the natural sciences, both intellectually and practically. The immense technological achievements made possible by natural science – the fruits of which we enjoy every day – alone are enough to clinch the case. Science is, as the saying goes, a hard act to follow and this success may cause anxiety for academics who are not scientists. This is especially so in a sociopolitical context where the paymasters of those academics increasingly see the value of knowledge in instrumental terms only.

Progress in philosophy?

Even if the enormous success of the natural sciences is indisputable, however, perhaps the unflattering comparisons usually made with philosophy's alleged lack of success can be questioned. Philosophy, by comparison with the sciences, is characterised by a veritable deficiency of results and an absence of progress – so the story usually goes. But is this story actually true?

On the one hand, it might be pointed out, philosophers appear capable of achieving a consensus, if not unanimity (even if this consensus mainly concerns positions to which they do *not* assent). There are nowadays few substance dualists in the Cartesian mould, for example; most philosophers working in the philosophy of mind would consider themselves materialists of one stripe or another and many will be working on refining one or other of a set of widely held theories. In other words, many philosophers look very much as if they are working within something akin to what Thomas Kuhn, with respect to the history of science, called a 'paradigm' – a framework for theoretical and experimental work consisting of an 'entire constellation of beliefs, values, techniques and so on shared by members of a given community'.[6] Furthermore, it may be argued, the process of refining those philosophical theories itself yields results, so that knowledge within the philosophical community has increased. For example, Timothy Williamson expresses just such a view when he writes:

---

[6] Kuhn 1962: 175.

We know much more in 2007 than was known in 1957; much more was known in 1957 than in 1907; much more was known in 1907 than was known in 1857. As in natural science, something can be collectively known in a community even if it is occasionally denied by eccentric members of that community. Although fundamental disagreement is conspicuous in most areas of philosophy, the best theories in a given area are in most cases far better developed in 2007 than the best theories in that area were in 1957, and so on.[7]

What is known is various; it may include such things as greater clarity on the nature of a problem, what difficulties certain argumentative moves encounter and how they may be avoided and what distinctions and other conceptual tools are useful in formulating an answer. In the case of some branches of philosophy, such as logic, this sort of progress has perhaps been more evident. Indeed, Michael Dummett has recently suggested that advancements in logic amply demonstrate that agreement is possible in philosophy, though it may be exceedingly slow: 'That philosophy does make progress, and even achieve assured results, is shown by the fact that what perplexed medieval logicians is now a five finger exercise for beginners.'[8] Even though logic might be considered a special case, there is some justice in Dummett's claim, for surely the formalisation of modern symbolic logic must stand as one of the great intellectual achievements of the nineteenth and twentieth centuries.

David Lewis has suggested that even the typical philosophical debate results in some sort of progress. To be sure, the result is rarely universal agreement on a particular theory or position, he observes, but philosophical arguments do tend to make clear the price of maintaining the various views on offer. The resulting picture of the characteristic problems these views face is something philosophers can often agree upon – though again, they will typically disagree on the seriousness of the various problems, and therefore often continue to hold different views.[9] Still, achieving widespread agreement on the price to be paid – the problems that must be addressed – by anyone who wishes to defend a particular philosophical position is one kind of progress.

Philosophers may be tempted by these considerations to offer a *tu quoque* argument against a scientist who scoffs at philosophers' inability

---

[7] Williamson 2007: 280.   [8] Dummett 2010: 14.   [9] Lewis 1983: x.

to agree for, on the other hand, one can easily enough point to examples of conspicuous disagreement over fundamentals in science, and sometimes consensus is the best science can achieve. Even well-established scientific theories have their maverick opponents. So, to cite notable examples, astronomer Sir Fred Hoyle, who coined the term 'big bang', always considered the big bang theory a damp squib and championed his own 'steady state' theory instead, and in evolutionary biology, Stephen J. Gould advocated his own theory of punctuated equilibrium, despite quite vociferous opposition from orthodox gradualists.[10] And science also has its current controversies, which often generate more political heat than scientific illumination: so, for example, some notable scientists, such as Freeman Dyson, remain sceptical of or deviate from the consensus view on global warming.

Nonetheless, the scientific maverick is usually an individual nonconformist and, although one can overplay disagreement in philosophy in contrast with a convergence of views in science, it is still true that science is capable of delivering a surety of outcome that eludes philosophy. Many scientific discoveries cannot now be sensibly regarded as contentious, tentative or provisional: Harvey's discovery of the circulation of the blood, say, or that the Earth does orbit the Sun, or that water molecules consist of two hydrogen atoms and one oxygen atom, or that elements exhibit a periodicity of properties, as described by Mendeleev, or that the Earth's crust consists of drifting plates, as originally proposed by Wegener. These, and many more besides, count as 'real results' in science, secured by the sedimentation of all subsequent discoveries in their fields to the point where it is unthinkable that they might be challenged: that is to say, everything speaks for them and nothing against.[11] It is not just that philosophy does not, as a matter of fact, achieve this degree

[10] Opponents labelled punctuated equilibrium, in which evolution proceeds in fits and starts, 'evolution by jerks'. Gould responded by calling gradualism 'evolution by creeps'.

[11] *Pace* what has become a post-Popperian dogma that *all* scientific statements are tentative and provisional and always open to revision. These discoveries have secured a cardinal position for themselves, not just in their respective branches of science but in our thinking more generally, that is significantly different from more speculative or less established empirical claims. One might say they have become 'hard' and now perform a different role in our thinking from other empirical claims (see Wittgenstein 1968).

of security for its conclusions but that such security is so alien to the subject that it would appear distinctly odd if a philosophical thesis were to claim it. One might well wonder if such a thesis were a *philosophical* thesis after all. Disagreement and debate seem endemic in philosophy to an extent that appears pathological from the point of view of the natural sciences.

Why should this be so? It is certainly not the case that philosophical modes of argument are uniquely adversarial or open-ended or are of a kind that foster endless conflict. They should, however, facilitate disagreement. It has been suggested, for example, that 'philosophical discussion is, in effect, a collaborative effort to maintain the conditions under which disagreement is possible'.[12] The point here is that a conclusion is only philosophically worthwhile if reached freely. That is to say, in a philosophical debate, persuasion should consist in the free assent of one's interlocutor and not come about as a result of one deliberately employing rhetorical sleights of hand. Philosophers, in other words, have an obligation to be open in argument and allow space for disagreement; an obligation that arises if we take philosophical debate to be pursuing something like the truth of the matter. But this, in itself, does not account for the persistence of disagreement in philosophy, as it is true for all academic discussion, including that in the natural sciences. One might similarly argue that a conclusion is scientifically useful only if one has not persuaded one's peers by falsifying data, covering up experimental mistakes, making personal attacks on one's opponents and so on. A conclusion established by any of the latter means may have other uses – advancing one's career, for example – but it would not be scientifically useful and the reason for this is, as Richard Feynman famously reminded us, that 'Nature cannot be fooled'.[13]

One slightly uncomfortable suggestion is that philosophers themselves, rather than their arguments, foster endless conflict.[14] The way philosophers conduct themselves prolongs actual disagreement and does not simply maintain the conditions under which disagreement is possible. Mathematicians and scientists, it is claimed, appear to make progress because they are trying to agree. Philosophers, on the other hand, try not to agree. This is not a question of individual psychology but a matter of

[12] Johnstone 1978: 19.   [13] Feynman 1986: F 5.   [14] Weber 2011.

professional temperament: philosophers as an academic profession, one might say, suffer from an excess of criticality. Thus, in apparent contrast to questions in a mathematics seminar, those in a philosophy seminar 'are inherently critical and antagonistic, even if the questioner is polite'.[15] This echoes a reproach made by Alistair MacIntyre of the way subjects in the humanities and social sciences are pursued in the modern university. One aspect of their current practice that he criticises is an incessant disputation that manifests itself in what he calls 'unconstrained and limitless disagreement', something he contrasts with the 'creative rational disagreement' characteristic of the pre-liberal university.[16] Sure enough, philosophers do like to 'test the argument' and discussion can be adversarial and disagreement widespread; but, without falling into the trap of taking issue with these claims solely for the sake of dispute, this is as much a question of rhetorical style as substance. We have already suggested that agreement in philosophy is actually more prevalent than superficial considerations of behaviour would suggest and that, from a different angle, philosophical debates may be seen as a form of collaborative disagreement where a consensus may be slowly achieved and issues clarified.

Aristotle goes to college: a thought experiment

Whatever the reason for philosophy's very modest advances, however, it does seem that they do contrast sharply with the almost limitless achievements of the natural sciences. To gauge just how sharp the contrast is, consider a thought experiment devised by philosopher and cognitive scientist Eric Dietrich. We are to imagine that Aristotle encounters a time warp and is propelled forward into the twenty-first century, where he ends up in a campus somewhere in the English-speaking world, endowed with the ability to speak English. None of this drives him mad or even upsets him, and he decides to attend a physics lecture to check out what the weird-looking people around him know about the world.

[15] Ibid.: 199. Taking a more positive view on what may be the same phenomenon, Graham Priest suggests that philosophy is defined by its spirit of 'unbridled criticism' (2006: 207).
[16] MacIntyre 1990: 225.

What he hears shocks him. A feather and an iron ball fall at the same
rate in a vacuum; being heavier doesn't mean falling faster, something
he doesn't understand. Aristotle along with the rest of the class is shown
the experimental verification of this from the moon (*from the moon*?!?!?)
performed by Commander David Scott of Apollo 15. The very same
equations (*equations*?!?!?) that explain why an apple falls to the ground
explain how the moon stays in orbit around Earth and how Earth stays
in orbit around the sun (*orbits*?!?!?). He learns of quantum mechanics
strangenesses. The more he hears, the more shocked he gets.[17]

The pattern repeats itself in the cosmology and biology classes. Hearing for
the first time of the Big Bang, galaxies, dark matter, genetics and evolution,
Aristotle is in a constant state of shock and repeatedly faints. Confused
and disoriented, he wanders around campus and eventually ends up in a
metaphysics class, where things take a different turn. For here

> he hears the professor lecturing about essences, about being qua being,
> about the most general structures of our thinking about the world. He
> knows exactly what the professor is talking about. Aristotle raises his
> hand to discuss some errors the professor seems to have made, and some
> important distinctions that he has not drawn. As the discussion proceeds,
> the metaphysics professor is a bit taken aback but also delighted at his
> (older) student's acumen and insight.[18]

Afterwards, this pattern is repeated in an ethics class. The lecturer's
discussion of something she calls 'virtue ethics' is immediately grasped
by Aristotle, who again feels that the lecturer ignores some important
details.

The point of Dietrich's thought experiment is not to show that nothing
philosophy professors lecture about would baffle Aristotle at all – a lot of
what goes on in current philosophy of mind, for example, would surely
sound strange and unfamiliar to him. Rather, the point is that a surprisingly large portion of the issues and arguments covered in philosophy
lectures *would* make sense to him, whereas hardly anything that goes on
in a science lecture would. As Dietrich explains, 'From our twenty-first
century perspective, we see that Aristotle was not even in the ballpark
with most of his scientific ideas, theories and conclusions … But he is a
giant to this day in philosophy. We can *learn* by reading his philosophical

[17] Dietrich 2011: 334.   [18] Ibid.

works.'[19] Perhaps, contra Dietrich, the thing to conclude from this is not quite that philosophy 'has not progressed one iota',[20] for as we saw earlier, there are plausible examples of progress in philosophy. But at least it does indicate that the prospects for showing that philosophy has made progress comparable to the natural sciences are very dim indeed.

Yet do the manifest achievements of the natural sciences – and the lack of anything even approaching them in philosophy – force us to acknowledge that, as Sellars put it, science 'is the measure of everything' in the domain of describing and explaining the world as it is in itself? Surely not. But other considerations do seem to point in that direction, as we shall see next.

Naturalism

Most contemporary philosophers – like the vast majority of natural scientists – accept some version of a view we can call 'ontological *naturalism*'. Notoriously, there is an abundance of different 'naturalisms' in circulation in current philosophy. Some three decades ago, Peter Strawson usefully distinguished between two broad conceptions of naturalism: what he labelled a 'hard (strict or reductive) naturalism' on one hand and a 'soft (catholic or liberal) naturalism' on the other.[21] A similar distinction occurs more recently in John McDowell's work, under the slightly different labels of 'bald' versus 'relaxed' naturalism.[22] What they mean by 'hard' or 'bald' naturalism is a form of thinking that accepts that reality is, as McDowell puts it, 'exhausted by the natural world, in the sense of the world as the natural sciences are capable of revealing it to us'.[23] 'Soft' naturalism stops somewhere short of such a claim while rejecting the idea of 'mysterious gift[s] from outside nature'.[24] However that may be, what interests us here is something with which most philosophers who would describe themselves as 'naturalists' would agree. This minimal ontological naturalism is expressed in Ernest Nagel's characterisation of the naturalist view:

> In the conception of nature's processes which naturalism affirms, there is no place for the operation of disembodied forces, no place for an

[19] Ibid.: 335.   [20] Ibid.: 333.
[21] Strawson 1985: 1.   [22] McDowell 1996: 88–9.
[23] McDowell 1998: 173.   [24] McDowell 1996: 88.

immaterial spirit directing the course of events, no place for the survival of personality after the corruption of the body which exhibits it.[25]

Nagel adds some further commitments of naturalism, most of which would probably also garner widespread assent: that organised matter has an existential and causal primacy; that there are no trans-empirical substances; that the manifest nature of things does not conceal an 'ultimate reality'; that the nature and relations between things is amenable to rational inquiry; that nature is not teleologically organised; that human beings are 'at home' in nature and should be understood in this framework; that philosophy offers no cosmic consolation. Nagel presents us here with principles he describes as 'guides'[26] and this is the best way to understand his or any characterisation. Indeed, the term 'naturalism' is a cluster concept or a family resemblance term; that is, a concept defined by a medley of qualities, none of which are essential. Naturalism in philosophy may be distinguished by a variety of shared aims, beliefs, principles, assumptions, methodological procedures, attitudes and values. Of course, this does not mean we cannot discern a typical or paradigmatic naturalism and Nagel's guides seem to offer a characterisation of just that.

Nagel's characterisation mostly concerns itself with what is and is not, and thus voices a general version of ontological naturalism. On this view, the natural world is, so to speak, all that is the case, and human beings are thus part of the natural world. Of course, that bare statement can be unpacked in different ways; but, essentially, it is to say that an accurate and complete description of the world makes – or would make – reference only to natural categories (entities, events, properties, processes, laws, practices, social relations) and does not – or would not – include any reference to supernatural entities or powers.[27] So a naturalist ontology does not include

---

[25] Nagel 1955: 8–9.   [26] Ibid.: 8.

[27] Ontological naturalism is itself not merely descriptive but is prescriptive (i.e. it tells us what sort of things should or should not be included in our ontology) and thus circumscribes what we should regard as 'real'. As we do not have an accurate and complete description of the world (and, of course, probably never will have – hence the phrases 'or would make' and 'or would not' used previously), it tells us to what sort of categories one should refer. Therefore, if someone claims something exists, but that it cannot be described in terms of natural categories, it may be ruled out as real. Where does this leave putative phenomena that are presently not well understood (e.g. apparently supernatural entities such as, say, poltergeists or powers such as telekinesis)? The answer is that, *if they are real phenomena*, they will turn out to

supernatural entities such as the gods, Platonic forms or Cartesian mental substance, nor any supernatural powers such as those exercised by gods, angels or mediums. This is a negative account of ontological naturalism: it says what a complete natural description of the world excludes. A very general positive account might be to say that the natural world – the order of things accessible to us through everyday observation or the methods of the empirical sciences – is all that exists.

This sort of general ontological naturalism, viewed against the background of the impressive ability of the natural sciences to describe, explain and predict events in the world precisely in strictly natural terms, yields a powerful motivation for adopting the Sellarsian view that only science describes the world as it is. Philosophical naturalism thus tends to bend its knee to science when it comes to answering questions of what exists. 'At the very least', writes Huw Price, 'to be a philosophical naturalist is to believe that philosophy … properly defers to science, where the concerns of the two disciplines coincide'.[28] Indeed, according to Quine, naturalism just is 'the recognition that it is within science itself, and not in some prior philosophy, that reality is to be identified and described'.[29]

We can now conclude three things. First, the achievements of (natural) science are indisputable. Second, philosophy – though perhaps not in quite as bad a shape as is often assumed – has very few comparable successes. Third, given the widespread and not implausible naturalistic view that the natural world accessible to us through everyday observation and the methods of natural science is all there is, it does seem plausible that it is to natural science, and not to 'some prior philosophy', that we have to look for a description of the world as it is in itself, independent of perspective. A corollary would seem to be that the speculative metaphysics prevalent in much of philosophy's history is to be regarded as suspect and redundant – unless, presumably, it is the sort of speculative metaphysics

have a naturalistic explanation – that is to say, an explanation that refers to natural categories and which 'fits' with our explanations of other natural phenomena. Is this just an act of faith like the various beliefs with which it comes into conflict? Not just an act of faith, naturalists would contend, because it is based on the continuing success of science.

[28] Price 2004: 71.

[29] Quine 1981: 21. We should note that Quine construes 'science' broadly and includes under this heading fields of inquiry such as economics, sociology and even history (Quine 1995: 49).

offered so often nowadays by cosmologists and theoretical physicists such as Hawking.

But does it also follow that there is nothing left for philosophy to do, as Hawking believes? Arguably, this might only follow if the sort of (soft) ontological naturalism we have outlined brings with it a commitment to what we might call *methodological* naturalism (or scientism): the view that the *only* way to say something meaningful or important about the world is by employing the methods of the natural sciences.

Quine and Wittgenstein

That methodological and ontological naturalism might perfectly well go hand in hand is illustrated by the fact that implicit in Quine's statement that it is 'within science that reality is to be identified and described' is a commitment to methodological naturalism. As we saw in the last chapter, Quine thinks of philosophy as 'continuous with science, and even as part of science … Philosophy lies at the abstract and theoretical end of science … through being very general'.[30] For methodological naturalists such as Quine, then, any worthwhile philosophy would be continuous with science because the only genuine knowledge we have of the world is yielded by science. But is this true?

We begin to appreciate the radical nature of Quine's naturalism by seeing that any answer must itself be based on the methods of science. He is aware of the threat of circularity inherent in this approach but argues that circularity is only a problem if we insist that philosophy is a normative project able to offer a validation of science, instead of seeing the task as simply to describe science as an institution. The only resources we have for the assessment of knowledge claims are those we find in the sciences, so that epistemology is 'contained in natural science, as a chapter of psychology'.[31] This is not the place to evaluate this so-called project of 'naturalising epistemology', however one might go about it. Rather, we want to suggest that the work of another towering figure of twentieth-century analytic philosophy – the later Wittgenstein – shows that one *can* advocate ontological naturalism without thereby committing to methodological naturalism.

[30] Magee 1982: 143.   [31] Quine 1969: 83.

Wittgenstein's later work more generally may be construed as naturalistic because his subject matter is everyday human practices, especially our linguistic practices (what he famously calls 'language-games'). In this way, Wittgenstein's descriptive exploration of human practices and, in particular, the close attention to concrete uses of language has something of an anthropological flavour about it,[32] and this certainly gives his work the air of naturalism.

Furthermore, Wittgenstein states that there may be some 'very general facts of nature' (*sehr allgemeinen Naturtatsachen*) – facts so general that we might not usually pay attention to them – that underlie the formation of our concepts and thus our ways of acting and speaking[33] and, that if these were different, our concepts and practices might be different also. Thus, there is a contingency to the concepts and practices we have: they are what they are, but they could have been different if certain facts of nature had been different – including facts about human nature. Language, after all, though infinitely variable and plastic, fits in with our lives, which in the broadest sense includes such general facts about us and the world in which we live: 'And to imagine a language means to imagine a life-form', as Wittgenstein contends.[34] Our 'life-form' – this 'whirl of organism', as Cavell revealingly calls it – is what 'Human speech and activity' ultimately rest upon, on Wittgenstein's view.[35]

However, it would be quite wrong to think of his approach as some sort of idiosyncratic version or extension of an empirical field of study such as linguistic anthropology or any other natural science. Whereas Quine argued that epistemology should give way to psychology, Wittgenstein did not think philosophy should give way to linguistics or anthropology. Wittgenstein insisted that philosophy should avoid theorising, so that 'we must do away with all explanation and description alone must take its place'.[36] But despite his instruction 'don't think, but look!'[37] he does not

---

[32] As Cavell writes, 'Wittgenstein's motive … is to put the human animal back into language and therewith back into philosophy' (1979: 207). See also Padilla Gálvez 2010.

[33] Wittgenstein 1958: 195.   [34] Ibid.: § 19.

[35] Cavell 2002: 52. Though perhaps we should add that for Wittgenstein, there is no strong dependency here such as we find in a supervenience relation. It might be therefore better to say that these very general facts of nature form a background to our concept formation rather than underlie our concepts.

[36] Wittgenstein 1958: § 109.   [37] Ibid.: § 66.

arrive at his descriptions by engaging in empirical field observation of ordinary language use (say, on the Clapham omnibus or in the launderette or supermarket), nor do his remarks look like the sort of detailed accounts one might expect to find in a work of linguistics. When he introduces the term 'language-game' as a way of understanding how language works,[38] Wittgenstein is not offering a hypothesis in linguistics that stands in need of corroboration or refutation by means of empirical investigation. To think his insights are somehow empirically testable would be to miss the point entirely.

Nothing about the Wittgensteinian method of describing grammar or language games requires us to leave our armchairs (or, in Wittgenstein's case, his deck chair). Rather, he drew upon an understanding and intuitions that should be available to any competent speaker of the language (say, German and English) and his method of describing involved the use of imaginative similes, analogies and metaphors alongside the employment of techniques familiar to the philosopher, such as thought experiments. In the foregoing passage from the *Investigations* where he speaks of the *Naturtatsachen* he is also adamant that 'we are not doing natural science, nor yet natural history' and elsewhere reminds us that in doing philosophy 'our considerations could not be scientific ones'.[39] Our interest, as philosophers, does not lie with these facts of nature and, though it may be awakened by the correspondence, it is not as a set of possible causes. Nothing makes Wittgenstein bristle more than the idea that philosophical problems – which, after all, do more than provide the occasion for his explorations but which are their focus and primary concern – can be solved by the sort of causal explanations provided by science. He insists that these problems are conceptual in nature, and so require resolution through clarification rather than through the discovery of new facts or by revealing something previously unknown to us. In this light, it is hardly surprising that Wittgenstein emphasises that we can invent cases or fictitious natural histories for our purposes.[40]

If Wittgenstein's philosophy can be described as, in some sense, naturalistic, it must also be recognised that it was one where philosophy is not 'continuous with' science, either methodologically or in terms of its aims.

---

[38] Ibid.: § 7.   [39] Ibid.: § 109.
[40] Ibid.: § 122 and p. 195.

In this respect, his position differs fundamentally from that of Quine.[41] Unless Wittgenstein's position is incoherent – and at least it is not obvious that it is – it would therefore seem perfectly possible to embrace onto- logical naturalism and yet reject the idea that only through the methods of natural science can we say anything interesting or important about the (natural) world in which we live.

The scientific image versus the manifest image

It may be useful here to consider a modified version of a distinction Wilfrid Sellars famously makes between what he calls the 'scientific image' and the 'manifest image'. For our present purposes, we might say that the 'manifest image' refers to the picture of the world with which sci- entifically enlightened common sense presents us. As Sellars writes, 'the manifest image is, in an appropriate sense, itself a scientific image'.[42] But it is not *the* scientific image – the latter being the sort of picture of the world we get from, say, molecular biology, chemistry and, in particular, physics.[43] As Sellars himself suggests,[44] the difference between the two images might be illustrated by the famous Cambridge astrophysicist A. S. Eddington's 'two tables' problem. In the preface to his book *The Nature of the Physical World*, Eddington wrote:

> I have settled down to the task of writing these lectures and have drawn
> up my chairs to my two tables. Two tables! Yes; there are duplicates of every
> object about me – two tables, two chairs, two pens. One of [my two tables] has
> been familiar to me from earliest years. It is a commonplace object of that
> environment which I call the world. How shall I describe it? It has extension;
> it is comparatively permanent; it is coloured; above all it is *substantial* … It is a

---

[41] See Arrington and Glock 1996: xiii–xiv.

[42] Sellars 1991: 7.

[43] This is not quite the contrast Sellars had in mind. On his view, there is 'one type of reasoning which [the manifest image], by stipulation, does *not* include, namely that which involves the postulation of imperceptible entities, and principles pertaining to them, to explain the behaviour of perceptible things' (1991: 7). We are not sure this is a helpful place to draw the line. Enlightened common sense surely has room for, say, bacteria and viruses having effects on people's behaviour. Moreover, sensa- tions and thoughts play significant roles in our commonsense understanding of each other's behaviour; and it is at least not obvious that such things are perceptible.

[44] Sellars 1991: 35–6.

thing; not like space, which is a mere negation; ... Table No. 2 is my scientific table. It is a more recent acquaintance and I do not feel so familiar with it. It does not belong to the world previously mentioned – that world which spontaneously appears around me when I open my eyes ... My scientific table is mostly emptiness. Sparsely scattered in that emptiness are numerous electric charges rushing about with great speed; but their combined bulk amounts to less than a billionth of the bulk of the table itself ... There is nothing *substantial* about my second table. It is nearly all empty space ... I need not tell you that modern physics has by delicate test and remorseless logic assured me that my second scientific table is the only one which is really there – wherever 'there' may be.[45]

In the last analysis, only the table considered as a mostly empty slice of space, with electrical charges rushing about, is *real*, according to Eddington. The table *as it appears to us* – the solid, coloured thing on which we place our coffee cups and so on – is ultimately just a subjective appearance without reality. But, importantly, the manifest image of the table does not appeal to supernatural forces or to entities like fairies, gods or disembodied spirits; it refers to ordinary objects, the ways they look and feel to us, the sorts of things we habitually do with them and so on. That is to say, nothing about the enlightened commonsense view of the table offends against the sort of (soft) naturalism sketched in the previous sections. Yet the picture of the table that we get here is undeniably different from the picture a hard naturalist like Eddison insists is the only true one.

According to what Sellars calls 'the perennial philosophy', the manifest image 'is the measure of what really is'.[46] In light of the considerations amassed previously in this chapter, many might be inclined to join Eddington and Sellars in rejecting this claim, conferring the status of 'measure' on the scientific image instead. On this view, only the scientific description of the table describes it as it is, 'independent of any perspective', to use Putnam's phrase again. We shall make no attempt to pass judgement on the view here. For our present purposes, what is important is that the view is compatible with maintaining that the description of the table as a solid, coloured *thing* (that, as Heidegger or a pragmatist might add, is useful for various purposes, including supporting books and coffee cups) is valid too – as a description of the table as it appears in, let us say,

---

[45] Eddington 1928: xi–xiv.   [46] Sellars 1991: 32.

a *human* perspective. Perhaps it is not true *sub specie aeternitatis* – or rather, from *no* point of view – that Eddington's table is coloured or solid, but it would certainly seem true *sub specie humanitatis.*

Nothing said so far in this chapter implies that only a 'perspective-free' description is true or valuable. Perhaps a description of a table as coloured or solid (or useful for putting things on) has only a relative value, essentially dependent on us being the sorts of creatures we are, with the sort of sensory and cognitive apparatus, the sorts of needs and interests and so on that we have. But what we count as 'truths' of this very sort are generally quite important to us in our everyday lives. (The absentminded physicist who buys the wrong colour of curtains can look forward to being reprimanded, and few people would regard the rejoinder that 'in reality nothing is really coloured' as anything but a lame excuse.)

The idea, then, that philosophy has some special concern with the manifest image leaves room for an 'independent philosophical enterprise', in Putnam's words, and the room it leaves would seem to be of the sort that does not shrink, regardless of the advances of the natural sciences. This idea has the added advantage of including central parts of the 'philosophical enterprise' that cannot be plausibly construed as striving for a description of the world as it is in itself, 'independent of perspective'. As A. C. Grayling emphasised in a radio discussion on Hawking's biting epitaph for philosophy, one must not overlook the diversity of philosophy's 'pursuits'; it has always been as interested in moral matters and aesthetics as in scientific or quasi-scientific issues.[47] Perhaps there is some sense in which there are objective truths about what it is right or wrong to do, or about the nature of a just society, but surely they are not likely to be of the completely 'viewpoint-independent' sort. Presumably, they are still relative to certain very broad facts about the sorts of creatures we (and other of Earth's inhabitants) are, the things that matter to us and so forth.

Moreover, the truths (if that is what they are) of the manifest image are arguably indispensable if we want a theoretical account of the world that bears some relation to the world as we know it. The difficulty with some hard naturalist positions is not just that we like to think of ourselves as special in ways ruled out by the naturalist, but that we do not easily recognise ourselves in their descriptions at all, as we shall illustrate. There is

---

[47] Grayling and Greenfield 2010.

something of an anti-humanist strain in the uncompromising hard natur-alist's accounts, such that we might easily feel something important about what it is to be human is lost. For example, Lynne Rudder Baker argues that naturalistic theories, being 'relentlessly third personal', miss out the first person perspective: that is, 'the perspective from which one thinks of oneself as oneself'.[48] Similarly, Charles Taylor, perhaps philosophical natur-alism's most trenchant contemporary critic, argues that reductive explana-tions of social institutions and practices, including the making of ethical and aesthetic judgements, are simply implausible – because understanding these requires us to take up *the perspective of the agent*, a notion that has no counterpart in natural science.[49] This thought, that something import-ant appears to be missing in the hard naturalist's descriptions, suggests an alternative view of philosophy's role and its relation to science.

Philosophy and the humanities

Perhaps, in the light of the foregoing considerations, philosophy, as Bernard Williams urges, 'should not try to behave like an extension of the natural sciences (except in the special cases where that is what it is)', but instead should 'think of itself as part of a wider humanistic enterprise of making sense of ourselves and of our activities'.[50] As we have noted, the principal reason for thinking of philosophy as continuous with science is the belief that whatever can be known can be known by means of science alone, a view Quine certainly seems to defend.[51] But a long-standing trad-ition denies this and thus emphasises philosophy's differences from the sciences in order to maintain a distinctive role for the subject. The story starts as soon as the natural sciences develop their own observational and experimental methods during the sixteenth century. At roughly the same time, theology, previously intertwined with Western philosophy, begins its break from it. The sort of world picture possible in the Middle Ages, which unifies God, nature and mankind, dissolves, and one concomitant

---

[48] Baker 2007: 203.
[49] Taylor 2007. Putnam makes the interesting suggestion that the fact that hard natur-alism leaves no room for ethical judgements and the like is precisely what some find *attractive* about it. The appeal of naturalism, he suggests, 'is based on *fear* ... of the normative' (2004: 70).
[50] Williams 2006: 197.   [51] See e.g. Quine 1960: 22–3.

of this is a conception of philosophy as principally the study of man. This is, indeed, the conception the Renaissance humanists adopt as a result of their desire to see human beings as neither just part of nature nor different from other parts simply because of their special relationship to God. Conceptions of philosophy like this continue to flourish through the idea that there is a distinctive type of study corresponding to the distinctive features that human beings are taken to have. Collectively instances of this have become known as the humanities and it is as one of the humanities that we are considering alternatives to the conception of philosophy as continuous with science.

It will be objected straightaway that it is not only humanities subjects like history that study human beings but sciences like psychology too. So what distinguishes the humanities from them? One answer which now has few adherents is that, while science collects evidence about bodies and their behaviour, the humanities seek evidence about non-bodily mental items. Descartes is, of course, the paradigm of this way of thinking, so that it is because we have non-observational knowledge of our own mental states that we can infer those of others from their behaviour. The problems with this dualistic view are too well known to recapitulate here, yet it is worth turning back to Descartes' starting point for his assertion that he is a thinking thing. It is his taking up a certain standpoint: this, he asserts, is how things are for me, whatever else may be the case. Again and again we find Descartes telling us how things seem to him – the way he is struck by the sweetness and scent of the beeswax taken from the hive and so forth. He tells us, that is, about his experiences of the world, and we can find in his approach a way of thinking about human beings arguably not available to the sciences. It is to think of ourselves as having ways of experiencing the world, or, as it was phrased earlier, first person perspectives. Then the difference between the humanities and the sciences would be that the former present first person perspectives on the world and the latter a third person one, in the sense of one available to any humans independently of the sort of conscious states they have. But what we earlier termed the human perspective is irremediably first personal. It is the perspective in which the world is presented to all of us as human beings.

From thinking about human beings as a special sort of item in the world, as Descartes did, we move to considering them as creatures with their own sort of outlook on the world. This leads to a particular way of viewing the humanities, though arguably one that these subjects implicitly accept. The rise of the novel, for example, is a factor which has influenced historians to conceive explicitly of their task to be that of describing the world as historical actors would have perceived it – a process for which the philosopher Herder coined the term *einfühlen* – feeling oneself into their situation. Thus he declares, 'you must enter the spirit of a nation before you can share even one of its thoughts and deeds'.[52] Much later Wilhelm Dilthey systematised these ideas about how the humanities should be conducted by contrast with the sciences. He enunciates the celebrated principle: 'We explain nature, but we understand the life of the soul'.[53] And we achieve this understanding by being able to imaginatively reconstruct another's experience of the world.[54] There is much that requires clarification and examination here, but the general thrust of this account of the humanities should be enough for us to use it to test the view that philosophy should be regarded as one of them. First, however, we should ask why we might want to.

Science aims to be objective, in the sense that it relies as little as possible 'on the specifics of the individual's makeup and position in the world, or on the character of the particular type of creature he is'.[55] It accounts for events, including human behaviour, from what we called the third person perspective. Consider, for example, a sociobiologist's account of sexual love as a form of pair-bonding which has evolved to give a female male support over her long period of gestation and nursing in return for exclusive sexual access. It is the kind of account that might be offered for species quite different from our own. Grasping it does not rely upon our being members of the species it concerns or feeling the passions and pangs of love ourselves. But the problem with this objective account is evident. We just cannot think of our own loves in these terms. And this is not just a defect in the particular account in terms of pair-bonding. It infects any account which substitutes, in place of the reasons for love we

---

[52] Barnard 1969: 181.   [53] Quoted in Bowie 2003: 200.

[54] Martha Nussbaum sees this as provided by literature through 'narrative imagination', as she calls it. It is one of three capacities she sees as cultivated by the humanities, the others being knowledge of other cultures and the critical examination of one's own culture, which she thinks of as undertaken primarily by philosophy. See Nussbaum 1997 and 2010.

[55] Nagel 1986: 5.

take ourselves to have, a scientific explanation. For we think of our loves as explicable by the reasons we have for thinking of our beloved as beautiful, charming and so forth, and these are reasons anyone who responds in similar ways to ourselves can see the force of. They provide a subjective understanding rather than an objective explanation of love, and it is to love stories, poetry and so on that we turn for illumination of the place of love in our own lives, not to sociobiology and the like.

Of course we do sometimes rationalise our own behaviour, so that, for example, we may take ourselves to be in love when we are only acting out of sexual attraction. Perhaps we might even be persuaded to give up talk of romantic love altogether as some feminists have urged. But it is surely inconceivable that we should relinquish our commitment to the first person perspective altogether. This would, for instance, force us to give up talking about the colour of things in the way we do, for only certain species perceive such colours, so that from an objective standpoint all we could say would be that things reflected light of various wavelengths. But from a human perspective things are coloured, as in our manifest image of them, and it is impossible for normally sighted people to think of the visible world otherwise. If this line of argument is right then, as Thomas Nagel puts it, 'there are things about the world and life and ourselves that cannot be understood from a maximally objective standpoint',[56] so that 'any attempt to give a complete account of the world in objective terms detached from these perspectives inevitably leads to false reductions or to outright denial that certain patently real phenomena exist at all'.

If philosophy is to be regarded as more than merely nominally one of the humanities, then the way it tries to answer questions about what it is for us to be the human beings we are may be by capturing distinctively human perspectives on the world. The way this is to be done will evidently be different from the methods employed by historians, say, since philosophy does not seek facts about how people in different times and places have reacted to their situations. Its purpose is, we may suggest, more general, and in this generality we can see how philosophical claims might be evaluated, namely by chiming in with people's own experiences of the world. It is up to us to either agree or disagree. There is no other arbiter.

[56] Ibid.: 7.

How might this human perspective be described? Different philosophers have had different ideas about this and we shall investigate some of them. One way, which Herder and other German Romantic philosophers initiated, is by describing the language in which the perspective is expressed. Leaving Herder's own unsavoury linguistic nationalism aside, what is important for us about his account is that he sees language as articulating the way its speakers interact with the world, so that what they pick out and what they distinguish reflect their practical involvement with things. This view, which anticipates both Heidegger's and the later Wittgenstein's, denies that the world is already carved at the joints, in Aristotle's phrase, only awaiting our recognition of its structure in language. Rather, to describe our language is to describe our particular way of understanding the world, not to describe the world in the way science aims to classify its contents and explain their interactions.

The sort of view sketched here would seem to have a lot in common with the idea of philosophy as a second-order inquiry, mentioned in the previous chapter. And while this idea has often been associated with a focus on language, this is not necessarily so. As Hans-Johann Glock suggests, 'the Kantian idea that philosophy is a second-order discipline which reflects on the way we represent reality' can take several forms, depending on whether we reflect on 'language, conceptual thought, or non-conceptual perception', for example.[57] Indeed, even a paradigmatic 'ordinary-language' philosopher such as Austin was clear that when we reflect on 'what we should say when', we don't look 'merely at words (or "meanings", whatever they may be) but also at the realities we use the words to talk about: we are using a sharpened awareness of words to sharpen our perception of, though not as the final arbiter of, the phenomena'.[58]

On this kind of account, philosophy, for example in the form of conceptual analysis, can be viewed as one of the humanities because it seeks to show how our language expresses a specifically human perspective on the world. Writing of the relation between science and philosophy in the nineteenth century, A. J. Ayer notes the impact of such questions as whether scientific determinism is compatible with free will. 'These problems', he remarks, 'troubled the Victorians, and well they might. The solution of them is, I think, to be found in a logical analysis'.[59] The logical analysis

[57] Glock 2008: 128.   [58] Austin 1979: 182.   [59] Ayer 1949: 213.

of free will is meant to show how we can operate with the concept in our everyday lives despite living in a largely deterministic world. It is meant to remove the 'trouble' the Victorians experienced without the benefit of an analysis. So, even though Ayer thought of what he was doing in terms that recognised the supremacy of science, his practice betrays a concern with the humanistic project of making sense of the world as one in which we can live and act as we do. This is, apparently, a very different conception of analysis from that which sees it as a clarificatory part of the scientific endeavour to explain events in the world.

The humanistic approach regards philosophical problems as essentially problems of life. The problem of free will, as we have just seen, is a problem about how to continue to live as we do. On the scientific conception, by contrast, it is a problem about whether or not, given determinism at the relevant level, we can continue to apply a folk theory of choice and decision. The humanistic approach, however, seems quite consistent with ontological naturalism. Indeed the free will problem presupposes it, as there would be no problem if some interruption in the natural order were possible. Naturalism is, indeed, an expression of a distinctly modern idea that is difficult to deny without abandoning the modern world view in its entirety; viz. that human beings are part of the natural order. On the other hand, nor is it easy to claim that our everyday view of ourselves is simply an illusion, as hard, scientific naturalists sometimes imply. We have here a clash of outlooks, the resolution of which is a problem at the heart of contemporary philosophy.

Conclusion

The natural sciences, as we have seen, make progress in a way that dwarfs whatever advances may be found in philosophy. Coupled with ontological naturalism – roughly the view that the natural world is all that exists – this might seem to leave philosophy out of a job, precisely as Hawking suggests. As we have seen, however, things are a bit more complicated. While the sciences may be uniquely able to describe and explain the world 'from nowhere', such perspective-free accounts may not be the only valuable ones. In particular, it could be maintained that philosophy is part of the 'humanistic' enterprise of making sense of ourselves and of the world as it appears in what we called 'a human perspective'. To use Sellars's terms, it might be part of philosophy's special responsibilities to offer an articulation of the 'manifest' as opposed to the 'scientific image'. Most naturalistically inclined philosophers would no doubt wish to deny, with Sellars, the traditional philosophical prioritising of the manifest image at the expense of the scientific image. Yet one could do so, we suggested, without depriving the articulation of the manifest image of all value. Nevertheless, there remains a tension here between two outlooks that are not easily reconciled.

4 The data of philosophical arguments

Introduction

In the previous two chapters, we have been concerned with the descriptive and prescriptive variants of what we have called the 'What' question. But the question of what philosophy is or ought to be is, of course, not independent of the question of how it is (to be) done – whether you think philosophy is part of natural science may be relevant to the sorts of methods you think philosophers ought to employ. In this chapter, our focus shifts to the methodological 'How' question. As before, our main focus will be on the prescriptive version of this question. Our question, then, is not how philosophers actually go about justifying their claims, but how they *ought* to justify them.

There is more than one way to approach the How question. One way is to examine the various patterns of argument characteristically endorsed and employed by philosophers.[1] Although this is doubtless an important task, we shall not attempt it here. Instead of inquiring into the characteristic argument patterns of philosophers, we examine the sorts of considerations that usually function as *data* in such arguments. A helpful notion in this context is Timothy Williamson's idea of an academic discipline being *disciplined* by something. As Williamson explains, 'To be "disciplined" by X is not simply to pay lip-service to X; it is to make a systematic conscious effort to conform to the deliverances of X.' What, then, should discipline philosophy? The answer seems to be: all sorts of things! As Williamson writes, philosophy must be disciplined by 'semantics, ... syntax, logic, common sense, imaginary examples, the findings of other disciplines (mathematics, physics, biology, psychology, history ...) or the aesthetic

---

[1] Passmore 1961 is an excellent example of this approach, though some aspects of his discussion (for example, the 'paradigm case argument') now seem somewhat dated.

evaluation of theories (elegance, simplicity)'.[2] Nicholas Rescher lists the following as among the 'data' of philosophy:

> Commonsense beliefs, common knowledge and what have been 'the ordinary convictions of the plain man' since time immemorial;
>
> The facts (or purported facts) afforded by the science of the day; the views of well-informed 'experts' and 'authorities';
>
> The lessons we derive from our dealings with the world in everyday life;
>
> The received opinions that constitute the worldview of the day; views that accord with the 'spirit of the times' and the ambient convictions of one's cultural context;
>
> Tradition, inherited lore and ancestral wisdom (including religious tradition);
>
> The 'teachings of history' as best we can discern them.[3]

Clearly it is impossible to address all these potential sources of philosophical discipline within the confines of a single chapter. We propose, therefore, to focus on two sources of philosophical discipline: phenomenological description and conceptual analysis. There are two closely related reasons for this choice. First, although neither source of discipline is unique to philosophy, we believe they may be more characteristic of philosophy than of other academic disciplines. Second, phenomenology and conceptual analysis are arguably more central to philosophical argumentation than any other source of discipline. To the extent that there is any method that most continental philosophers agree is valid, at least within certain limits, it is the method of phenomenological description. And, although conceptual analysis has come under pressure in recent years, it is still the standard procedure in mainstream analytic philosophy, to the extent that there is a standard procedure.

Phenomenology

Phenomenology is a philosophical movement[4] which can be traced back to the beginning of the twentieth century. In fact, its inception can be

---

[2] Both quotes Williamson 2007: 285.

[3] Rescher 2001: 15–16. We doubt that Rescher intends to recommend all these as data that philosophers *ought* to rely upon ('the worldview of the day', 'inherited lore', etc.), or attribute equal weight to them.

[4] Which has, however, inspired the establishment of phenomenological movements in a host of other disciplines, including psychiatry, psychology and sociology.

dated precisely to 1900, the year the first volume of Edmund Husserl's *Logical Investigations* was published. Husserl was originally a mathematician whose interest in the foundational problems of mathematics had led him to logic and philosophy. Despite the title, *Logical Investigations* does not merely address logical problems narrowly conceived. Rather, Husserl advocated what he believed to be the right approach to philosophical problems in general: instead of resorting to system building and speculation, philosophers should consult the 'the things themselves', or that which 'manifests itself' or 'gives itself' (Greek: *phainomenon*).

One can say that phenomenologists advocate letting philosophy be disciplined by everyday *experience*, but it is important that this is understood in the right way. First of all, the notion of 'experience' in play here encompasses a lot more than just sensory experience or perception. A phenomenologist might take a descriptive interest in all sorts of mental phenomena, including thinking, dreaming, imagining, expecting, hoping, remembering, fearing, feeling anxious, feeling pain and, of course, perceiving. In fact, the phenomenological category of 'experience' is even broader than such mental phenomena. Having a conversation with an old friend, negotiating one's way through a crowded room, humming a pop tune, picking up a hammer and using it to drive a nail into a wooden board: all these actions and activities, too, are experiences in the phenomenological sense.

What all these things have in common is not easy to articulate, but at a first pass we might say that in all our examples something 'shows up' or is presented (or represented) to a subject in a particular way. Or, to put it differently, in all our examples a subject is having an experience *of* something, or a number of such experiences, whether the something in question is a toothache, a flower, the solution to a mathematical problem, an old friend or hammers and boards. To use a technical term that Husserl picked up from his teacher Franz Brentano, in all these cases,[5] a subject is having one or more 'intentional experiences'. An intentional experience is an experience 'of' or 'about' something or 'directed at' something.

---

[5] Perhaps not all of them. Is being in pain having an intentional experience? Opinions differ. Perhaps, too, you can be anxious without being directed at, anxious about, anything in particular. Does that mean this isn't an intentional experience or that it is, but simply has diffuse objects (say, you are anxious about existence as such)? Again, opinions differ.

To watch a soccer game, to want a new bicycle and to recall last year's summer holidays are examples of experiences that have the character of 'intentionality', of being directed at something (the soccer game, a new bicycle and last year's holidays, respectively).

Second, it is essential to distinguish between phenomenology in a *narrow* and a *broad* sense. To appreciate the difference between these two senses, we must keep in mind phenomenologists' special interests in intentional experiences – experiences 'of' or 'about' something or other. When it comes to such experiences, there are two 'poles' a description might focus on: the experience as a subjective phenomenon, on the one hand, and that which the experience is 'of' or 'about', on the other. A description that takes the first sort of focus aims to capture 'what it is like'[6] to have the experience in question. When analytical philosophers appeal to the 'phenomenology' of an experience, they usually mean phenomenology in this narrow sense. Thus, when analytical philosophers talk of the phenomenology of visual perception, they usually mean to refer to what it is like, subjectively, to see.

But all philosophers in the phenomenological tradition, pretty much without exception, have the broad sense in mind. The broad sense of phenomenology encompasses phenomenology in the narrow sense, plus the object pole of the experience (that which the experience is 'of' or 'about'). An example from Husserl might help to make this difference clear. Suppose you are sitting in a garden on a lovely spring day, admiring an apple tree in bloom. The narrow phenomenological description might include something about your shifts of attention, your tacit awareness of moving your eyes, the feelings of joy that accompany your looking and so on. The broad description adds something about the colours of the blossoms, how the tree stands out against a background of other things (the lawn, hedges, a garden shed and so on) and how it is presented as having sides and profiles not currently seen (the rear side of the trunk, minute details of the blossoms that can only be seen close at hand, etc.), and the aesthetic qualities the tree is experienced as having (it is beautiful, the very picture of spring and so on).

---

[6] The terminology here isn't found in the work of the classical phenomenologists themselves, but is due to Thomas Nagel's influential paper, 'What is it like to be a bat?' (Nagel 1979: 165–80).

Most phenomenologists, in fact, tend to prioritise the 'objective' side of the experience – the description of 'the way things strike us', as Gregory McCulloch has usefully put it.[7] Thus, although Husserl has quite a lot to say about what it is like to perceive, his analyses of perception invariably start with a phenomenological description of some perceived *object*. And while Heidegger has a lot to say about how a hammer shows itself in the activity of hammering, he has very little to say about what it is like, subjectively, to hammer. The reason for this prioritisation of the object pole of our experience is the following: paradoxical as this may seem, phenomenologists are generally not all that interested in subjective experience as such. The reason they focus on experience is that it is in experience that the world manifests itself to us, and it is that dimension of manifestation or 'givenness', as well as the structure of the manifested world, that interest phenomenologists. (We shall return to this point shortly.)

Connected with this point is another one. Contra the claims of some critics of phenomenology, phenomenologists do not usually rely on introspection.[8] If their primary concern were to offer phenomenological descriptions in the narrow sense, this might seem very odd. But given that phenomenologists are mainly concerned to describe the world as it manifests itself to us, it should come as no surprise that introspection plays a rather modest role in their work. To attend to material things 'as they strike you' is to engage in reflection, but it is still a reflective attending to *material things*, not (*pace* Dennett) to 'the things that swim in the stream of consciousness'.[9]

It is important to note that describing the object pole of an experience is not quite the same as describing the object that figures in the experience. To return to our apple tree example, the tree as such, considered as a thing of nature, 'can burn up, be resolved into its chemical elements, etc.', whereas none of this can be said of our *'perceived tree as*

---

[7] McCulloch 1995: 131.

[8] Dennett (1991: 44), for example, claims that phenomenologists rely on 'a special technique of introspection'.

[9] Ibid.: 45. The phenomenologist's description of the ways various things such as hammers, trees, people and so on strike us in various contexts is sometimes said to add up to a description of 'the life-world' (Husserl 1970: § 34). The life-world is the world we ordinarily take for granted: the experientially given, meaningful world in which we live our lives.

perceived'.[10] The latter has aesthetic properties, but not chemical properties. This is of course not to say that the object pole of an experience
never has such properties. Perhaps there are (obsessive) professors of
chemistry who can never look at a tree without its chemical properties
leaping out at them. And it is very likely that a person in desperate need
of firewood would perceive the tree as combustible. The point, however,
is that the object that interests phenomenology is the object strictly as
it is presented in the experience, regardless of the extent to which the
object thus described matches the 'real object' as described by natural
science, say. Two more examples may help to make the difference completely clear. If lighting conditions are manipulated in such a way as to
make a white object look pink, then the 'perceived object as perceived'
in this experience is pink, not white (because you don't *see* the object
as white; you see it as pink). If it is right that the human body consists
of eighty per cent H_2O this does not mean that when you meet a friend,
she *ever* strikes you as composed largely of hydrogen and oxygen. But
again, the fact that your friend, described strictly *as she appears to you* in
your normal interactions with her, isn't H_2Oish, doesn't mean that when
you offer this phenomenological description, you aren't really describing *your friend*, but only something 'swimming in the stream of your
consciousness'.

A third important point about the phenomenological interest in experience is the following. There is, for phenomenologists, a class of intentional experiences that is particularly important. This is the class of what
Husserl calls 'originarily giving' experiences; we might also speak of *presenting* experiences, as opposed to *re*presenting experiences. If you imagine
your mother – visualise her face, say – then this is an intentional experience and its object is of course none other than your mother. It is not, for
example, a picture of your mother that you are imagining (although you
can obviously do this as well: you can imagine her passport photo, for
example); it is your mother herself. Nevertheless, your mother is merely
*re*presented in such an experience: she isn't, as we might put it, presented
'in the flesh'. When you *see* her, on the other hand, she is present in the
flesh, or in person. Perception, in other words, is a presenting experience
in a way imagination is not. However, sense perception is not the only

[10] Both quotes from Husserl 1982: 216.

presenting experience. For example, although sense perception may be an aid to achieving insight in logical and mathematical matters, logical and mathematical truths are 'given' as such in purely intellectuals acts or experiences.[11]

Even so-called material things may be given or presented in other sorts of experiences than sense perception. If Heidegger's analysis is correct, a hammer may not present itself in its being-a-hammer – in its being 'equipment', as Heidegger puts it – in an act of disinterested observation. Rather, its 'hammer-hood' presents itself most originally in the activity of hammering. As Heidegger writes, 'the less we just stare at the hammer-Thing, and the more we seize hold of it and use it, the more primordial does our relationship to it become, and the more unveiledly is it encountered as that which it is – as equipment'.[12] Similarly, it might be that other people aren't originally presented *as people* in detached, theoretical observation. Perhaps their 'personhood' is rather presented in social interactions with them – in conversations, for example. Claims to this effect have been made by numerous phenomenologists, including Merleau-Ponty and Levinas. In a very recent formulation of the point, Matthew Ratcliffe contrasts his phenomenologically informed view with what he calls 'naturalism':

> Naturalism involves an epistemological assumption to the effect that the world is best disclosed from a standpoint of theoretical detachment (through which it is resolved as a collection of objective entities, processes, properties, and relations, extricated from one's own concerns and practical engagements). But other people are disclosed as people through a very different stance. People can only be appreciated as what they are through a bodily, affective receptivity that is constitutive of our sense of the personal. Hence, in the case of people, at least, the naturalistic standpoint is not the way in which we access the way things are.[13]

The reason presenting experiences are of particular interest to phenomenologists is simple. In such experiences we do not construct

---

[11] To give another sort of example, phenomenological reflection on our experiences is itself a presenting sort of experience – one that 'gives' our experiences 'in the flesh' – at least according to the phenomenologists. In his 'principle of all principles', Husserl directs phenomenologists to be faithful to what thus presents itself to phenomenological reflection: *'everything originarily* (so to speak, in its "personal actuality") *offered to us in "intuition" is to be accepted simply as what it is presented as being, but also only within the limits in which it is presented there'* (Husserl 1982: 44).

[12] Heidegger 1962: 98.   [13] Ratcliffe 2007: 242.

representations of the world around us: the world *presents itself* to us. A moment ago we explained how it is this dimension of presentation or manifestation, as well as the structure of the presented or manifested world, that primarily interests phenomenologists. The best way to unveil the structure of the world, phenomenologists believe, is to turn to the experiences in which the world presents itself. This, one could say, reveals phenomenology's kinship with 'empiricism' and 'positivism'. Phenomenologists have a much broader notion of experience – and of 'presenting' or 'giving' experience, in particular – than the British empiricists or the logical positivists. However, phenomenologists endorse the empiricist programme of grounding philosophy (and science) on what is given in experience.[14]

Armchair phenomenology

Do phenomenologists appeal to armchair evidence? They do in the sense that they obtain their phenomenological data without conducting polls or experiments, without providing statistical analyses and so on. They seem, instead, to appeal to their own experience, assuming that others' experiences will be similar. (More on this in a moment.) And reflecting on one's own experience is certainly something that one can do in an armchair. Of course, unless the phenomenologist occasionally left her armchair and engaged in various practical, social and cultural activities, there wouldn't be much for her to describe. Phenomenology is in this way 'parasitic' on our non-philosophical life outside the armchair. Nevertheless, phenomenological description may be described as a type of armchair evidence.

Some have questioned the suitability of such evidence to the phenomenologists' project. Since phenomenologists are obviously interested in articulating 'our' experience (as they sometimes, rather vaguely put it) and not merely their own individual experience, then their first person, armchair method seems problematic. Should we not rather conduct surveys and polls to find out what 'we' experience? Isn't this the only way to secure 'a method of phenomenological description that can (in principle) do justice to the most private and ineffable subjective experiences, while never

---

[14] As Husserl writes, 'If "*positivism*" is tantamount to an absolutely unprejudiced grounding of all sciences on the "positive", that is to say, on what can be seized upon originaliter, then *we* [i.e. the phenomenologists] are the genuine positivists' (1982: 39).

abandoning the methodological scruples of science'?[15] Isn't the phenomenologist's attempt to unveil 'our' experience by simply describing his or her
own experience hopelessly amateurish and in urgent need of replacement
by scientific methods?[16]

Now, as already indicated, phenomenology isn't particularly interested
in the 'most private and ineffable subjective experiences', but much more
interested in how objects strike us in various contexts. There isn't anything
particularly private about Heidegger's hammer as it manifests itself in our
use of it, for example. Also, phenomenologists are mainly concerned to
delineate the general structures of the manifested or experienced world.
The unique features of *this* particular experience of an angry person may
safely be ignored; what interests phenomenologists is what this experience has in common with countless other encounters with angry (or even
sad, happy and so on) people. On this level of generality, phenomenologists would argue, we all – at least all normal, socially competent adult
people[17] – have the same sorts of experience. And if so, there is of course
no problem in using oneself as an exemplar. Besides, phenomenologists
are not (in general) hermits; they *don't* just have their own descriptions
of their experience to go by. They present papers at conferences, publish
books, read what other phenomenologists write, discuss with them and so
on. If one phenomenologist really has a very idiosyncratic way of experiencing other people, for example, then surely this would emerge in the
course of such critical encounters.[18]

Moreover, phenomenologists are trained and experienced when it
comes to articulating experience in a way most people are not. Surveys
and polls would not tell us what people experienced if people were apt
to misdescribe their experiences. Most phenomenologists agree that it
isn't such an easy matter to capture one's experience faithfully – some

---

[15] Dennett 1991: 72.

[16] As Dennett writes elsewhere, 'Lone-wolf autophenomenology, in which the subject
and experimenter are one and the same person, is a foul, not because you can't do it,
but because it isn't science' (2003: 23).

[17] Evidence shows autistic subjects do not experience other people's emotional and
other mental states in the direct way the rest of us (often) do. See Hobson 2004.

[18] See Gallagher and Zahavi 2008: ch. 2 for a discussion of the role of intersubjective
validation of phenomenological findings. See Cerbone 2003 and the essays collected
in Noë 2007 for extensive discussions of Dennett's critique of phenomenology.

even believe that special methodological measures are needed. Husserl emphasised repeatedly that the methods he termed '*epoché*' (Greek for restraint or abstention) and 'phenomenological reduction' constituted a necessary 'gate of entry' to phenomenology.[19] According to Husserl, the epoché should 'bracket' our ordinary or 'natural' beliefs about the world and ourselves so that we don't rely on these when doing phenomenology. And while it is disputed to what extent later phenomenologists such as Heidegger, Sartre and Merleau-Ponty agreed with Husserl's methodology – which may be why Dennett charges that 'Phenomenology has failed to find a single, settled method that everyone could agree upon'[20] – virtually everyone agrees that some conscious effort to 'bracket' what we believe, or think we know, about some matter is important to ensure an unbiased description of our experience of it. Although the beliefs we hold may often reflect our experience, there is no guarantee that they do, so it is a good idea to abstain from relying on them – and thus to that extent subject them to an '*epoché*' – when trying to capture our experience. Of course, the ideal of an unbiased description of our experience may be just that: an ideal we will never fully realise; but presumably the phenomenologists' commitment to doing a conscious effort to approach the ideal gives them some edge over the average person filling in a questionnaire. At the very least it is not obvious, phenomenologists would argue, that polls could give us what we get from the concentrated efforts of phenomenologists to capture their experience and then subject their findings to the criticism of other, similarly dedicated phenomenologists.

The 'first-person plural assumption'

But do we all share the same phenomenology? In other words, is the phenomenologist's 'first-person plural assumption', as Dennett usefully terms it,[21] actually justified? To appreciate the full force of this objection, let us consider a classical example of philosophers offering fundamentally opposed phenomenological descriptions. When you move away from an object – say a table – you are usually not under any impression that the table is shrinking; rather, you are aware that the table retains its original size. Similarly, when you observe a coin or plate from an angle, you are

[19] Husserl 1970: § 71.   [20] Dennett 1991: 44.   [21] Ibid.: 67.

typically not tempted to think you are faced with an elliptical object; rather, you are aware that the coin or plate is round. Psychologists of perception term these phenomena 'size constancy' and 'shape constancy', respectively. Yet do you *perceive* the table as constant in size and the coin as constant in shape, or do you simply *judge* that they are – based, say, on your intimate knowledge of coins and tables? Empiricists from Locke onwards have maintained that, as far as our perceptual *experience* is concerned, the table seems to shrink and the tilted coin seems elliptical. And they have used these supposed phenomenological observations to establish a particular account of perception: the so-called sense-datum theory. As Hume argues:

> The table, which we see, seems to diminish, as we remove farther from it: but the real table, which exists independent of us, suffers no alteration: it was, therefore, nothing but its image, which was present to the mind.[22]

In the twentieth century, C. D. Broad offered essentially the same argument, based on the tilted coin example:

> When I look at a penny from the side I am certainly aware of *something*; and it is certainly plausible to hold that this something is elliptical in the same plain sense in which a suitably bent piece of wire, looked at from straight above, is elliptical ... it is clear that this something cannot be identified with the penny, if the latter really has the characteristics that it is commonly supposed to have. The penny is supposed to be round, whilst the sensum is elliptical.[23]

In other words, if a coin seems elliptical (a table seems to diminish), there is something of which you are aware, which is elliptical (diminishes). That something cannot be the coin (the table), for the coin remains round (the table 'suffers no alteration'). Therefore, it must be something else: a sense datum.

There are, of course, many things one could say in response to this argument. The first premise – the claim that if something *seems F*, then there must be something that *is F* – will strike many as particularly suspect. But Merleau-Ponty has suggested, along with others, that the argument simply

---

[22] Hume 1975: 152.
[23] Broad 1927: 240. Other classical examples of this argument are found in Locke 1997: book II, chapter ix: § 8; and Russell 1998: 3.

gets the phenomenology wrong. 'It is frequently said that I restore the true size [of a perceived object] on the basis of the apparent size by analysis and conjecture. This is inexact for the very convincing reason that the apparent size of which we are speaking is not perceived by me.'[24] Who is right? Those who claim that tilted coins look elliptical or those who deny this? Or should we perhaps abandon the 'first-person plural assumption' and admit that different people experience things in different ways?

Against the latter suggestion, phenomenologists might say that the fact that there are some cases where different people seem to have different phenomenologies doesn't undermine the claim that, in the vast majority of cases, people *do* experience things in the same way. This is particularly so, the phenomenologist might continue, when the structures of the experienced *objects* are what is at stake, rather than the finer details of 'what it is like' subjectively. In fact, if we didn't all experience things in *roughly* the same ways we would be in trouble. If other people didn't strike *all* of us – or very nearly all of us[25] – as fundamentally different from trees or lampposts, then our societies would surely collapse. On some fundamental level, we must experience things in the same way. That there are some marginal cases where our experiences differ does not detract from the value of phenomenology in all those cases where we experience things in the same way.

But in fact, it is not even clear that our example *is* a case of diverging experiences. After all, it is very rarely the case that someone mistakes a tilted plate for an elliptical object or wonders whether a table is shrinking or just receding into the distance. Surely, we all agree on this. The question is, however, whether we *see* the table as shrinking and simply *judge* that it remains the same – based, say, on our knowledge of tables and their usual (lack of) behaviour – or whether we *see* it *as* remaining the same, and thus have no need to draw on our knowledge of tables. Now, a case can be made for the claim that this dispute need not, in the end, interest phenomenologists a whole lot. For arguably, the dispute is more about where to draw the line between what is 'given to the senses' and what is 'added by the intellect' than it is about how tables and coins 'show up' in our experiences in

---

[24] Merleau-Ponty 1964b:14. See Smith 2002: 172, 180-5, for a similar critique of the notion that a tilted coin looks elliptical.

[25] Oliver Sacks describes a man who has lost the ability to recognise people as people, and as a consequence mistakes his wife for a hat (1986: 9-24).

the broad phenomenological sense of 'experience'. And perhaps we can all agree that, in our usual dealings with them, coins and tables don't strike us as the sort of things that change shape and size all the time.

Phenomenological disputes

Suppose a critic is willing to concede what we have so far said on behalf of phenomenology. All of us (or nearly all of us) experience things in much the same way, and the armchair methods of the phenomenologist are well suited to the task of revealing what that way is. Nevertheless, the critic may say, our example has drawn attention to a significant problem in the way the phenomenologist tries to establish philosophical theses. For if someone denies that a phenomenological description is adequate, there is nothing the phenomenologist can do to convince him or her otherwise, except shouting and foot stomping.

Arguably, there is something to this criticism, and it might spell trouble for 'purist' phenomenologists – those who believe phenomenological description is *all* that ought to discipline philosophy.[26] But it need not be the case that the phenomenologist is entirely without means to settle such disputes – at least if his or her opponent doesn't 'feign anaesthesia' or pretends to have discordant experiences. One strategy for resolving phenomenological conflicts involves the attempt to find contrasting cases.[27] Suppose a phenomenologist claims, along with Merleau-Ponty, that a distant object doesn't, in general, look smaller than its actual size, and her opponent claims that it does. If the former could point out an unusual case where all would agree that things *do* look smaller than their actual size, and if all would agree that part of what *makes* this case unusual is the fact that things look smaller than normal, this would tell against the view that distant objects generally look smaller than their real sizes. Such a case might be available. Arguably, part of what makes it a very striking experience to look down from the roof of a skyscraper is the fact that there is a sense in which things below look smaller than their actual sizes: cars look like toy cars, people like 'ants'. But surely this illustrates that it isn't the

---

[26] Contemporary phenomenologists are rarely, if ever, purists. And amongst the 'classical' phenomenologists, Merleau-Ponty drew heavily on the findings of psychologists and psychiatrists.

[27] See Kriegel 2007 for a discussion of ways to settle phenomenological disputes.

case that cars in the distance normally look like tiny toy cars; for if they did, how could this very fact be what makes the skyscraper experience so special?

Even if this strategy works in some cases, however, it will hardly work in all cases. What, for example, might be a suitable contrasting case to show that a tilted coin does not look elliptical? Indeed, it is not clear what is to prevent a follower of Broad from suggesting that what is special about seeing a coin full face is precisely that it looks round; so surely it cannot be maintained that it also looks round when it is tilted. The phenomenological standoff, then, remains a real threat. The only way phenomenologists can remove it entirely is by appealing to other types of evidence. These may be scientific, or they may be other types of armchair evidence. This, we suspect, points to a more general lesson: that philosophy cannot accomplish very much if it is only subjected to *one* sort of discipline.

Conceptual analysis

So much for the phenomenological method. Although Anglo-American philosophers occasionally and perhaps increasingly appeal to phenomenology, arguably the main source of discipline in English and American philosophy to this day is (conceptual) analysis. Now, saying this isn't necessarily saying very much, for, in the course of the twentieth century (and the first decade of the twenty-first), adherents of philosophical analysis have taken themselves to be doing very different things.[28] We shall, however, concentrate on a relatively simple model of analysis which we believe captures the practice of a great many philosophers, whether or not they like to advertise the fact.[29]

As we mentioned in Chapter 3, prominent ordinary language philosopher J. L. Austin described his procedure as that of 'examining *what we should say when*'.[30] Austin's idea was that we can shed light on a philosophically interesting concept[31] – say, the concept of *knowledge* – by looking

---

[28] See Beaney 2009.

[29] Perhaps, as Frank Jackson surmises, 'There is a lot of "closet" conceptual analysis going on' (1998: vii).

[30] Austin 1979: 181.

[31] It is a very delicate question what, precisely, concepts are. Most would agree that the concept 'horse' is what the words 'horse', 'Pferd' and 'cheval' all express (in English,

at the sorts of situations in which we would say (or would not say) that someone knows something (or doesn't know something). Whilst ordinary language philosophy has long since fallen out of favour, a workable model of analysis can be developed in a few simple steps if we take our point of departure in analysis as understood by Austin and his Oxford colleagues. One of these colleagues, H. P. Grice, offered the following characterisation of conceptual analysis:

> To be looking for a conceptual analysis of a given expression E is to be in a position to apply or withhold E in particular cases, but to be looking for a general characterization of the types of cases in which one would apply E rather than withhold it ... the characteristic procedure is to think up a possible general characterization of one's use of E and then to test it by trying to find or imagine a particular situation which fits the suggested characterization and yet would *not* be a situation in which one would apply E.[32]

A majority of the current community of philosophers would probably reject a couple of explicit and implicit assumptions in this quote. First of all, most philosophers would be wary of the linguistic emphasis discernable in Grice's passage. As we might put it, philosophers aren't, or ought not to be, particularly concerned with *expressions*. Philosophers should pose questions about knowledge, perception, the good or perhaps the 'concepts' of knowledge, perception and the good, but not about the expressions ' ... knows ... ', ' ... sees ... ', 'good'. As Frank Jackson puts it, 'our focus is on getting clear about the cases covered [by a particular word] rather than on what does the covering, the word *per se*'.[33]

Second, Grice speaks of situations in which 'one would (or wouldn't) apply E', which indicates a further problem. For, as Grice himself has taught us,[34] there might be a number of reasons why an 'expression' wouldn't be used on a particular occasion. We wouldn't say of a freshly mowed lawn in broad daylight that it 'looks' green, because doing so would insinuate that there are reasons to think appearances misleading. But that doesn't mean that the statement 'This lawn looks green' is *false*. Or, to pick another

---

German and French, respectively), but beyond that, things get tricky. Some, such as Frege, take a Platonist view of concepts, while others, perhaps a majority, think of concepts as mental representations.

[32] Grice 1989: 174.   [33] Jackson 1998: 33.   [34] See Grice 1989: 1–57.

example, we would very rarely say of someone that she knows her own name; but again, that isn't because it would be false were we to apply the expression 'knows' in this case. Whereas ordinary language philosophers were very alert to the question whether we *would* or *wouldn't* apply a particular concept in a particular case, arguably they should have paid more attention to the question of whether or not such an application would result in a statement that was *true*. Taking these points into account, we can revise Grice's characterisation of the analytic procedure:

> The characteristic procedure is to think up a possible general characterisation of the cases falling under some concept C and then to test it by trying to find or imagine a particular situation which fits the suggested characterisation and yet would *not* be a situation to which C could be truthfully applied.[35]

The analytic procedure, thus understood, is as old as philosophy itself. In the *Republic*, for example, Socrates counters Cephalus' suggestion that justice is 'to tell the truth and return what one has received' by questioning whether it would be just to return to a mad person his weapons, or 'speak nothing but the truth to one who was in that state'.[36] A suggested characterisation of the necessary and sufficient conditions for justice is tested by finding or imagining a situation in which all those conditions are met, but which it would be wrong to describe as an instance of justice. In the case of Cephalus' suggested analysis of justice, such a case isn't hard to find, and thus the analysis must be rejected.

Appealing to intuitions

To take a much more recent example, which we will be concerned with throughout the remainder of this chapter, Edmund Gettier proceeds in precisely the same way in his famous paper 'Is Justified True Belief Knowledge?'[37] Some philosophers (including Ayer and Chisholm) had suggested the general characterisation mentioned in the title of Gettier's paper,

---

[35] Of course, philosophers also use imagined (or real) possible cases to show that something may be an instance of C *without* fitting the suggested general characterisation, as well as, more positively, to show that a particular characterisation is able to capture all the known problematic cases.

[36] Plato 1989: *Republic* 331c–d.   [37] Gettier 1963.

and Gettier attempted to refute it by imagining cases in which people have justified beliefs that happen to be true, but where, so Gettier thought, it would be *false* to say that the people in question had knowledge.

The following is an example of the type of cases to which Gettier drew attention. Suppose John drives along a countryside road. The pasture by the side of the road is crowded with white animals that look exactly like sheep. Unknown to John, however, all but two of these animals are dogs cleverly disguised to look exactly like sheep; and the two genuine sheep are surrounded by fake sheep in such a way as not to be visible to John as he drives along the road. John believes there are sheep in the pasture, and so there are. Also, John is justified in so believing, as he has visual information to the effect that there are sheepish-looking animals all around and no reason to think those creatures aren't sheep. Does John know there are sheep in the pasture? No, said Gettier, and most philosophers agreed with this verdict.

Note that it isn't obvious what we (or anyone) *would* say if we experienced this sort of thing. John, if he discovered his mistake, would surely be more likely to exclaim, 'Why in Heaven's name would someone dress up dogs to look like sheep?!' than to say, 'Gosh; so although I was right about there being sheep there, I couldn't have *known* this given that I didn't actually see any genuine sheep'. Nor is it given that the lack of knowledge despite justified true belief is what the prankster responsible would draw John's attention to. In other words, Gettier's point isn't obviously a point about ordinary usage: he isn't speculating about what we might be inclined to say were we actually to find ourselves in John's shoes. Rather, his point is that we, *as philosophers interested in evaluating the correctness of a particular account of knowledge*, must recognise that the concept doesn't apply in John's case. Gettier, as philosophers sometimes put it, appeals to our *intuitions* about this case:

> We find it *intuitively* obvious that there could be a situation like that described and in such a situation the person would not know that there is a sheep in the pasture despite having a justified true belief. This *intuition* – that there could be such a situation and in it the person would not know – and other intuitions like it are our *evidence* that the traditional theory [of knowledge] is mistaken.[38]

---

[38] Bealer 1998: 204–5; our emphases.

Such philosophical intuition, on Bealer's view, is a sort of 'intellectual seeming'.[39] By this he means that philosophical intuition is, as phenomenologists might put it, a putative *presenting experience*.[40] Rival views, however, hold that intuitions are 'immediate unreflective judgments', or 'some sort of spontaneous mental judgments'.[41] While it is not our purpose to adjudicate this issue here, it seems to us that the latter sort of view underdescribes what is going on when a philosopher agrees with Gettier's intuition about cases like the one we have been considering. Surely, it is not *simply* that you 'spontaneously judge' that John does not know about the sheep in the pasture – although of course you do that too – but that you '*see*' or *realise* that he does not know. Or take another case Bealer mentions: when you have an intuition that if P then not not P, this phenomenon is not captured by the observation that you spontaneously judge that if P then not not P. Rather, you *see* it; you see that it *must be so*. It seems, in other words, that the 'spontaneous judgment' view cannot fully capture an aspect of the phenomenology (in the 'narrow' sense defined earlier) of philosophical intuition.[42]

Experimental philosophy

The model of analysis outlined in the previous section has, in recent years, come under considerable pressure. The emergence of so-called experimental philosophy, in particular, has been thought to spell trouble for the standard procedure of analytic philosophy. What unites the experimental

[39] Ibid.: 208.
[40] There are some interesting parallels between (Husserlian) phenomenology and Bealer's take on philosophical intuition. Phenomenologists, as we have seen, work with a broad notion of presenting experience – broad enough to include the realisation of a mathematical truth, for example. Moreover, Husserl's important notions of 'eidetic variation' and 'eidetic intuition' seem to place him in very close proximity to traditional conceptual analysts. An 'eidetic intuition' of the essential properties of X, Husserl thinks, is achieved through a process of 'freely varying' a paradigmatic example of X until it is no longer an example of X. That way, we 'intuit' or 'see' (*erschauen*) the essential boundaries of X-hood (1973: § 87).
[41] Foley 1998: 245; Goldman and Pust 1998: 179.
[42] Bealer is explicit that his arguments against construing philosophical intuitions as beliefs, judgements, hunches and the like, to a large extent turn on the different phenomenologies of these (1998: 210). This seems another illustration of the need to have more than one source of philosophical discipline.

movement is that it seeks to replace or supplement traditional analysis with empirical, experimental data, specifically collected for the purposes of illuminating some philosophical question.[43] As the word 'supplement' in our last sentence indicates, not all experimental philosophers are out to criticise the method of analysis,[44] but our interest here concerns those who are.

In an important paper, Jonathan Weinberg, Shaun Nichols and Steven Stich aimed to determine whether Gettier's intuitions about knowledge ascription were universal. They found that a majority of Westerners of low socio-economic status, East Asians and people from the Indian subcontinent did not share philosophers' intuition that people in Gettier cases do not have knowledge.[45] Simply to ignore these findings and return to business as usual, Weinberg et al. argued, would display an intolerable intellectual arrogance. For surely, the intuitions of a few Westerners of high socio-economic standing cannot, without further ado, be allowed to outweigh the intuitions not only of East Asians and people from the Indian subcontinent, but also of Westerners of lower socio-economic status. Why should we think the intuitions of a few well-educated Westerners count for more than the intuitions of the majority of the world's population?[46]

This criticism raises an important question about the scope of 'our' in appeals to 'our' intuitions about possible cases (or 'we' in 'what we should say when'). A fairly widespread assumption is that the traditional analytic philosopher makes appeals to 'people's intuitions' taking it 'that we all know what people's intuitions are' so that 'there is no need for more rigorous attempts to quantify them'.[47] The idea, then, is that analytic philosophers enlist support from the intuitions of 'ordinary people' – 'lay intuitions'[48] – in their attempts to justify or criticise philosophical theories, thinking it obvious what those intuitions are. Plainly, if this account of the analytic enterprise were correct, then there would be something

[43] Arguably, this is what is special about experimental philosophy. Philosophers have always read science articles and used scientific data when and where they thought these relevant to a philosophical discussion. Experimental philosophers, however, *design* and *conduct* experiments with the explicit aim of answering philosophical questions (see Prinz 2008).

[44] See Nadelhoffer and Nahmias 2007.

[45] Weinberg, Nichols and Stich 2008.

[46] Ibid.: 38.   [47] Knobe 2007: 81.

[48] Prinz 2008: 201.

seriously wrong with that enterprise. Philosophers' persistent failure to employ standard empirical procedures would be breathtakingly irrational. In his defence of conceptual analysis, Frank Jackson has this to say:

> I am sometimes asked – in a tone that suggests that the question is a major objection – why, if conceptual analysis is concerned to elucidate what governs our classificatory practice, don't I advocate doing serious opinion polls on people's responses to various cases? My answer is that I do – when it is necessary. Everyone who presents the Gettier cases to a class of students is doing their own bit of fieldwork, and we all know the answer they get in the vast majority of cases. But it is also true that often we know that our own case is typical and so can generalize from it to others. It was surely not a surprise to Gettier that so many people agreed about his cases.[49]

It is doubtful whether this reply will do. First of all, if the aim is to discover 'our', or 'people's', intuitive responses to various cases, then it is hard to see how Jackson can be justified in implying that serious opinion polls aren't necessary *all the time*. Jackson suggests, of course, that we sometimes know that our own case is typical and thus are able to generalise from it to others. But he gives our intuitions about Gettier cases as an example of this, and Weinberg et al. have (apparently) shown that it is quite problematic to generalise these intuitions. Besides, the practice of asking classes of philosophy students questions about Gettier cases hardly counts as conducting 'serious opinion polls'. Just to mention one problem, the sample is bound to be biased: philosophy students surely differ in significant ways from the general population. So Jackson's response to the problem only heightens the impression that we are dealing with a 'major objection' to the analytic practice.

Jackson is surely right about one thing, though. It was hardly surprising to Gettier that many people agreed with his intuitions about his cases. Why wasn't he surprised? Had he conducted polls himself, perhaps? For all we know, he might have. But we doubt that this was his reason for feeling confident that others would see his cases the way he himself saw them. For it seems fairly obvious that, generally speaking, analytic philosophers don't intend to pronounce on what intuitions people in general, or lay people in particular, would have about various cases. As explained earlier,

---

[49] Jackson 1998: 36–7.

analytic philosophers aren't generally concerned with what anyone *would* say about the applicability of a certain concept C in various cases, but rather with what it would be true to say – what one *ought* to say. And they rely on their intuitions to determine what it would be true to say. This entails a *prescriptive* claim about the intuitions all other users of C ought to have, and so the scope of 'our' is indeed all users of C; but it doesn't entail any prediction about what other people's actual responses would be.[50] Thus, we suspect that Gettier was confident that others would agree, not because he had collected information about other people's responses to his cases, but because he believed he had '*seen*' – in the way one 'sees' that Q follows from (P→Q) & P – that his cases weren't cases of knowledge.

Let us now return to Weinberg, Nichols and Stich's argument. One thing the defender of the traditional analytic approach could draw attention to in response to it is that, strictly speaking, philosophical appeals to intuition involve more than just the description of a possible case and then voicing one's intuitions about the case. Philosophers also highlight particular important aspects of those cases. So, in the case of John's justified true belief that there are sheep in the pasture, a philosopher seeking to elicit our intuitions about the case might draw attention to such things as the fact that John has not actually seen a single sheep in the pasture (the two genuine sheep being hidden from his view), although he thinks he has; and they may highlight the fact that, if the two genuine sheep weren't there, this would not affect John's forming his belief, nor would it affect the justification he has for his belief – his seeing lots of animals he takes to be sheep – since he never even saw the genuine sheep to begin with.

To be sure, philosophers do not always spell out the crucial features of the scenarios they envisage in the way we have just done here, but that is usually because they expect their fellow philosophers to be good at picking out those features, given the way such scenarios are typically designed. Gettier, for example, designed his cases in such a way that his protagonists had true beliefs as well as justifications for those beliefs, but were ignorant of the fact that something important was wrong with their justifications. Philosophers at the time had little difficulty focussing on

---

[50] But perhaps the prescriptive claim implies a prediction about the response of a *maximally competent* concept user in an *ideal* situation. See Kauppinen 2007 for a much more detailed discussion of these issues than we can give here.

the justification problems Gettier called attention to. This ought to be no surprise, as philosophers are experts when it comes to detecting conceptually important features of actual and possible situations. This ability is a central aim of the education of a philosopher.

Having made this point, it would probably be wise of the defender of the analytic project to accept that such widespread divergence from the standard intuitions of philosophers as displayed by East Asians and Indians in the experiments of Weinberg et al. gives us reason for caution in the way we handle our intuitions in this area.[51] The traditional philosopher might, for example, propose that the findings ought to make us look for unnoticed or insufficiently appreciated features of Gettier cases. He or she could suggest that a somewhat fuller idea of what features the East Asian and Indian subjects respond to when they claim that Gettier cases are cases of knowledge would be helpful in this regard, and he or she might call for more research in this area. Indeed, the traditional philosopher might also concede that if the East Asian intuitions were offered not simply as 'naked' intuitions, but together with an account of important yet insufficiently attended to features of the cases, we might be forced to rethink our conclusions about the Gettier cases altogether.[52] None of this, however, departs in any significant way from the traditional method of analysis. Careful weighing of intuitive responses, searching for unnoticed features of possible cases, exploring possible important differences between cases usually treated alike and challenging the orthodox view on any of these grounds: all of these are familiar, indeed standard moves in the game of traditional analytic philosophising.

In fact, the traditional philosopher might argue that critics such as Weinberg, Nichols and Stich face a dilemma.[53] Either they are suggesting modifications of the traditional practice along the lines sketched in the previous paragraph – in which case their criticism stays well within the bounds of the traditional method. Or else they are recommending that we avoid relying on intuitions altogether. The latter, indeed, seems to be the position of Weinberg et al. It is, they write, 'hard to see why we

[51] See e.g. Williamson 2007: 192.

[52] And if significant divergences between our intuitions and the East Asians' still remained after such careful rethinking, the traditionalist might conclude that perhaps their concept of 'knowledge' simply differs from ours.

[53] See DePaul 1998.

should think that [philosophers'] intuitions tell us anything at all about the modal structure of reality or about epistemic norms or indeed about anything else of philosophical interest'.[54] Obviously, if intuitions can't tell us anything about anything of philosophical interest, then the method of traditional philosophy doesn't need amending: it needs abandoning altogether. But what are the consequences of doing so?

One question that is undeniably of philosophical interest is the question whether justified true belief suffices for knowledge. How do Weinberg et al. propose that we go about attempting to answer this question? Surely their suggestion isn't that we conduct polls on Gettier cases and let the majority decide the answer. At least one of the authors (Nichols) is explicit about this: philosophical inquiry isn't, and shouldn't be, a 'popularity contest', he states.[55] The trouble, however, isn't that Weinberg et al. leave us without a positive suggestion about how to conduct philosophical inquiry. For after all, we cannot require that any criticism be accompanied by a positive suggestion if it is to be taken seriously. Such a requirement would sink many important contributions to philosophy (including Gettier's own, for he offers no constructive account of knowledge in his famous paper). The trouble is, rather, that their negative conclusion might seem to require that we simply *stop thinking* about such matters. The great value of Gettier cases is that they bring to the fore the features we are interested in. John has a true belief about the presence of sheep in the field, and he also has a justification for this belief: his seeing sheep-like animals in the field. So does John have knowledge that there are sheep in the field? According to Weinberg et al. we aren't allowed to appeal to our intuitions in deciding this question. But surely, the traditional philosopher might respond, this amounts to disallowing us the right to *think* about the question at all. For what could thinking about John's predicament be if it must not involve carefully drawing attention to important features of the case and eliciting intuitions about the applicability, in those circumstances, of the concept of 'knowledge'? As the traditional analytic philosopher might point out, this looks like a *reductio ad absurdum* of the position advocated by Weinberg et al.

So, one set of natural reactions to the data of Weinberg et al. is fully compatible with the traditional way of proceeding in philosophy. This is the

---

[54] Weinberg et al. 2008: 38.   [55] Knobe and Nichols 2008b: 6.

first horn of the dilemma. Another set of reactions – including the conclusion that intuitions cannot tell us anything philosophically important and therefore should be ignored – seems to lead to the seemingly absurd conclusion that we must give up thinking about possible cases altogether. This is the second horn of the dilemma that the intuition critic seems to face.

Intuition scepticism

Even if the defender of the traditional analytical approach is right that critics such as Weinberg, Nichols and Stich face the dilemma just outlined, the latter might not be too impressed by any of this. One possibility is to embrace the first horn of the dilemma and concede that some of the more radical conclusions Weinberg et al. drew were premature. There is, on this proposal, no reason to think that the findings about differing epistemic intuitions call for more than caution and self-critical reflection in the way the traditional philosopher uses his or her epistemic intuitions about Gettier-style cases.[56] Since this brings the apparent intuition critic back in line with the defender of the traditional way of proceeding we shall not consider this option any further.

Alternatively, and perhaps more naturally, the intuition critic might opt for the second horn of the dilemma and maintain that 'thinking', at least as this is usually understood by philosophers, really *is* philosophically useless – and that saying this is anything but absurd. For the link the traditionalist tries to forge between philosophical thinking and the appeal to intuitions is a double-edged sword: the traditional philosopher uses this to try to force his or her critics to acknowledge the indispensability of

---

[56] This may be David Papineau's position. On the one hand, Papineau repeatedly denies that he is recommending that philosophers change their methods (2009: 2, 13, 22); on the other hand, he stresses that there is no reason to think our intuitions about possible cases particularly reliable (e.g. ibid.: 23). In fact, Papineau maintains that 'philosophical intuitions need a posteriori backing before we can place any confidence in them' (ibid.: 28). It is not clear that this is consistent with Papineau's official view that philosophy is fine as it is conducted now; for surely, the way philosophy is typically conducted, intuitions are not first appealed to when we have obtained 'a posteriori backing' for them. Indeed, it could be argued, that to the extent that we have obtained such a proteriori backing for our intuitions, there is no need to appeal to the intuitions themselves. This is the essence of Cummins' 'calibration' objection, which we discuss later in this chapter.

intuitions, but of course the critic might infer, rather, that the very notion of (philosophical) thinking is problematic. If 'thinking' is identified with the procedure of considering possible cases and eliciting intuitions about them, or if the latter is thought to be an essential component in 'thinking', then indeed we need to abandon 'thinking' in favour of the methods of empirical science. But surely, this is no great loss. After all, the scientific method has proven remarkably successful in terms of its ability to produce consensus whereas the standard methods of philosophy have given us, in William Lycan's words:

> a disgusting mess of squabbling, inconclusion, dogma and counter-dogma, trendy patois, fashionable but actually groundless assumptions, vacillation from one paradigm to another, mere speculation, and sheer abuse.[57]

Intuition sceptics such as Lycan, Hilary Kornblith and Robert Cummins adamantly argue that philosophy needs a complete methodological over-haul,[58] and they would hardly be very impressed by the suggestion that they advocate giving up thinking. To the extent that 'thinking' means the sort of thing philosophers have traditionally done, then we precisely *ought* to stop thinking and start doing serious scientific research.

Traditional analytic philosophers have a number of counterarguments available to them, some more promising than others. At the very weak end of the spectrum is the suggestion that intuition sceptics simply replace philosophy with science, possibly retaining the word 'philosophy', but using it to refer to a sort of inquiry very different from philosophy as we have all been taught to do it. The obvious problem with this suggestion is that it begs the question, assuming as it does that philosophy should be done in the traditional way – that is, precisely what the intuition sceptic denies.

A potentially more promising strategy for the traditionalist is to attempt to refine the dilemma argument in such a way as to make the

---

[57] Lycan 1996: 149.

[58] 'Appeals to intuition, and attempts at their systematization', writes Kornblith, 'con-stitute ... a procedure which we should abandon' (2006: 11). 'Philosophical intuition', writes Cummins, 'is epistemologically useless' and 'cannot support any conclusion worth drawing' (1998: 118, 125, 126). According to Lycan, 'philosophical intuition is and always will be *laughably un*reliable' (1996: 144).

second horn less palatable for the intuition sceptics. The aim would be to show that appealing to intuition is involved in all rational inquiry – or at least in certain sorts of inquiry considered respectable by the sceptics themselves. Thus, if appeals to intuition are a necessary part of methods of justification sanctioned by the intuition sceptics – or indeed part of all rational methods of justification – then abolishing the practice of appealing to intuitions means abolishing justification altogether; and *this*, surely, is a conclusion not even intuition sceptics can want to embrace. If such a refinement of the second horn of the intuition critic's dilemma can be made to work, then the intuition sceptic seems in serious trouble. However, it is not clear to us that any such attempts at refinement have been successful thus far.[59]

A related, but not identical, line of attack the traditionalist might try out consists in attempting to show an inconsistency in the intuition sceptic's position – specifically of the variety that Karl-Otto Apel has dubbed 'performative self-contradiction'.[60] While explicitly recommending the abolishment of appeals to intuition, so the traditionalist might maintain, the intuition sceptic tacitly continues to employ the method – including when he or she makes the case for its very abolishment.

A possible case of such self-contradiction is found in a paper by Stephen Stich critiquing the use of the method of 'reflective equilibrium' in epistemology. For Stich, 'reflective equilibrium theories' belong to a family of epistemological theories, characteristic of which is the procedure of testing our judgements 'against our "pretheoretic intuition"'.[61] Reflective equilibrium theories, in other words, take intuitions as data or input, possibly alongside other sorts of data (namely when the strategy pursued is that of 'wide' reflective equilibrium). Stich suggests that such theories have difficulties handling what he calls 'the problem of cognitive diversity'. For suppose that 'patently unacceptable rules of inference would pass the reflective equilibrium test for many people'.[62] When they appeal to *their* intuitions, it seems clear to them that certain classical fallacies – say, affirming the consequent – are perfectly valid inference rules. He subsequently goes on to consider the objection that perhaps no flawed rules of

---

[59] Attempts in this direction are found in DePaul 1998 and Pust 2001.
[60] See for example Apel 2001.
[61] Stich 1998: 105.   [62] Ibid.: 100.

inference *would* pass the reflective equilibrium test for anyone and replies that the mere possibility of this happening is enough to clinch his case. As Stich writes:

> [I]f it is granted, as surely it must be, that the gambler's fallacy (or any of the other inferential oddities that have attracted the attention of psychologists in recent years) could possibly pass the reflective equilibrium test for some group of subjects, this is enough to cast doubt on the view that reflective equilibrium is constitutive of justification as that notion is ordinarily used. For surely we are not at all inclined to say that a person is justified in using any inferential principle – no matter how bizarre it may be – simply because it accords with his reflective inferential practice.[63]

The details are not important here. For our present purposes, all that interests us about Stich's reply is that it seems a fine example of the traditional philosophical use of intuitions – that is, precisely the procedure Stich wants to cast doubt on. Stich's uses of 'surely' in the last quote mark the two places where he makes intuitions do argumentative work. He relies on intuition to determine the possibility of someone having bizarre inferential principles in reflective equilibrium. He appeals to intuition again when he concludes that we should not say of someone using such bizarre principles that she was justified in so doing simply because those principles are in reflective equilibrium for that person. This is right up Grice's street and just about as traditional as a philosophical argument can get. First, use intuition to determine that a certain scenario is possible. Then use intuition to determine whether a concept of interest ('justification', 'knowledge') should be applied or withheld in such a scenario.

If all this is right, then it seems Stich actively uses the very argumentative strategy he sets out to criticise. He is thus entangled in what Apel calls 'performative self-contradiction'. Two things should be noted about this sort of critique of intuition scepticism. First, this sort of argument is much easier to make than the argument we considered previously, a version of which turned on the idea that one cannot abandon intuition without abandoning justification altogether. For all we need in order to make the present case is an intuition sceptic who actually *does* rely on intuition, and, as our discussion of Stich suggests, such people may not be too hard

---

[63] Ibid.: 100–1.

to come by. This might make the argument very attractive to defenders of the traditional analytic approach. Second, and rather less encouraging for the traditionalist, the argument we have just outlined is a mere *tu quoque*. It accuses a particular intuition sceptic of not practising what he is preaching. And while this is certainly uncomfortable for Stich, and should lead to some serious critical reflection on his part, it does nothing to show which bit of his position should be abandoned: is the problem what he practises or what he preaches?

In fact, intuition sceptics could resist the suggestion that this *tu quoque*, even if on target, renders their position in any way uncomfortable. As Cummins argues, if, by appealing to intuitions, you can show intuitions to be philosophically 'useless', then what you have is a *reductio ad absurdum* of the practice of appealing to intuitions.[64] In other words, assume (for *reductio*) that the method of appealing to intuition is reliable. Rely on this method to conclude, by a series of steps all of which are intuitively correct, that the method is *un*reliable. Finally reject the initial assumption about the reliability of the method which generated this contradiction. For the intuition sceptic, surely, there is nothing at all uncomfortable about this sort of argument, even if at first blush it might appear to involve a 'performative self-contradiction'.

The traditionalist has to concede that if the sceptic only relies on intuitions in order to demonstrate the unreliability of the method, then the *tu quoque* has no bite, while the *reductio* might well have. However, the traditionalist may suspect that the intuition sceptic is a lot more committed to the method, in his or her actual practice, than he or she lets on. And if, outside the contexts in which the sceptic is trying to offer a *reductio* of the method, he or she relies on intuitions to prove and disprove other philosophical theses, then indeed the sceptic's position *is* incoherent and something has to give: the intuition sceptic must either change his or her practice or stop preaching its abolishment.

Sceptical rejoinders

So far, we have mainly focussed on the traditionalists' arguments against the intuition sceptic. But the latter also has a variety of arguments against

---

[64] Cummins 1998: 127, note 8.

the former. One type of response focusses on the nature of intuition. What, precisely, is 'intuition' supposed to be? Is it a form of introspection, a form of 'mental judgment', an intellectual 'seeming' or what? As we mentioned earlier, philosophers do not agree on this. Nor is it obvious that there must be widespread agreement on the precise description of a source of evidence before it can be defensible to rely on it. Sosa makes this point by comparing intuition to perception and introspection. He writes: 'Why require knowledge of the specific processes and mechanisms involved [in intuition], things that remained undiscovered for much of our perceptual and introspective repertoire?'[65] The point is not only that the basics of perception were unknown for millennia,[66] during which people, quite sensibly and *highly* conducive to their survival, nevertheless relied on perception as a source of evidence. In addition, one should note that even today the correct philosophical account of perception is hotly disputed: representationalists, disjunctivists and sense-datum theorists don't just disagree about the details, but defend fundamentally different accounts of perception. But, again, none of this leads anyone to place less trust in perception as a source of evidence about the world, nor should it. So whilst a comprehensive account of intuition that enjoys widespread philosophical support is most certainly a *desideratum*, Sosa is surely right to point out that the absence of such an account doesn't in itself do anything to undermine the idea that intuition can be a source of evidence.

Why, though, should we think that intuition is a *reliable* source of evidence about anything – except, perhaps, about what our intuitions are? Cummins suggests that while scientists only rely on observational techniques and 'calibrated' instruments, philosophers never attempt to calibrate their philosophical intuitions. The procedure of calibration is nicely illustrated by an example Cummins gives:

> When Galileo pointed his newly devised telescope to the moon and saw mountains – earthlike blemishes on what should [according to contemporary wisdom] have been a perfect celestial object – it was

---

[65] Sosa 1998: 267.

[66] Some ancient Greek thinkers, for example, favoured an 'extromission' theory of vision, according to which vision occurs when a particular type of outward emission from the eye encounters an object. See Robinson for a brief description of this theory (1994: 4–5). Incidentally, Robinson is one of the few contemporary defenders of the sense-datum theory.

legitimate for the opposition to inquire whether the apparent mountains were artifacts [i.e. were distortions caused by the telescope and thus not features of the surface of the moon]. The proper response was to point the telescope at something of known size, distance, color, and so on to determine what distortions it introduced; to calibrate it, in short.[67]

According to Cummins, it is no coincidence that philosophers don't calibrate philosophical intuition. For, as the Galileo example illustrates, you can only calibrate a procedure or instrument if you have some sort of independent access to the target (for example, Galileo could have pointed the telescope at a smooth, white wall, the smoothness and whiteness of which could be ascertained by unaided perception). And, in standard uses of philosophical intuition such as Gettier's argument, it is far from easy to see what might constitute such independent access to the target ('knowledge', say).[68] Moreover, Cummins maintains that if we did have such independent access to the targets of philosophical discussions, our philosophical intuitions would no longer be needed. He concludes: 'Once we are in a position to identify artifacts and errors in intuition, philosophy no longer has any use for it. But if we are *not* in a position to do this, philosophy should not have any faith in it.'[69]

How worried should this argument make defenders of the traditional method? Both Bealer and Sosa liken intuition to introspection and perception. The latter is, in Bealer's terminology, a *basic* source of evidence, and the same goes, Bealer claims, for intuition.[70] Now, we do not want to enter into the details of Bealer's complex discussion of basic sources of evidence, but at least it seems plausible that one sense in which perception is basic is that it is not the sort of thing we need to calibrate before it becomes legitimate to rely upon its deliverances. Indeed, it is hard to see how perception *could* be calibrated without the calibration also relying in some way on perception. The traditionalist might hold that the same goes for intuition: is it really plausible to suggest that your intuition that Q follows from $(P \rightarrow Q)$ & P needs to be 'calibrated' before you can rely upon it? Intuition, on this view, should not be likened to a new instrument or

---

[67] Cummins 1998: 116–17.

[68] In fact, this might not be so obvious. Kornblith, for example, argues that knowledge is a natural kind (like gold, cats, etc.) and, as such, can be investigated empirically (2006). We will return to this suggestion shortly.

[69] Cummins 1998: 118.   [70] Bealer 1998: 217.

procedure, but is our most basic source of insight into abstract and conceptual matters.

Timothy Williamson has suggested a similarly short way with the intuition sceptic's objection. According to Williamson, intuition sceptics, just like traditional external world sceptics, commit 'the fallacy ... of psychologizing evidence'.[71] A sceptic about our knowledge of the external world might challenge the view that we have such knowledge by drawing attention to the fallibility of sense perception. You think that among the things of which you have evidence are such facts as that you have two hands and that there is a book on metaphilosophy in front of you. But you think you have evidence for the latter because you *see* the book, and as we sometimes see (or it seems to us that we see) things that aren't there, all you are really justified in saying is that *it seems* to you that there is a book in front of you (or that you are having a visual experience 'as of' a book on metaphilosophy). We started out with an evidence base that included facts about the external world (the presence of a book on metaphilosophy), but end up with factual evidence restricted to our own experiences. Our evidence has thus become 'psychologised'.

As anyone familiar with the literature on scepticism will know, once this psychologised set-up is accepted, it is very difficult to regain any evidence about books and hands. In the case of intuition scepticism, we start out thinking that we have evidence that a person in a Gettier scenario doesn't have knowledge. But the reason we think this is that we have certain intuitions to that effect; and as our intuitions sometimes mislead us, we are only left with evidence that we have those intuitions. And why should we think that the fact that we have these intuitions tells us anything about knowledge as such? According to Williamson, the correct response in both cases is simply to reject the psychologisation of our evidence.[72] Among the things for which you have evidence are such facts as that you have hands and that people in Gettier cases have justified true belief without knowledge.

In response to such arguments, as well as those of Bealer and Sosa, the intuition sceptic is liable to return to the question of what this special source of evidence into the abstract is supposed to be. Aren't the traditionalists equipping us with an utterly mysterious ability about which

---

[71] Williamson 2007: 274.   [72] Ibid.: 234–41.

they then say precious little – and, in particular, nothing that suggests how this ability might be fitted into a naturalistic picture of the world? Someone who attributed telepathy to us and then refused to say anything about the underlying mechanism wouldn't be taken very seriously; why should the traditionalists be treated any differently? Analogies between intuition and perception break down here, the intuition sceptic might suggest, for at least we have a rough idea of what perception is and of how it can be fitted into a naturalistic picture of the world. At this point, the naturalist might offer his or her own account of what intuitions might be – bits of tacit theory made explicit, for example – and argue that, on such an account of intuition there is exactly *no* reason to think intuitions particularly reliable.[73] If the traditionalists want to counter this, it seems they have little choice but to offer more details about what they take intuitions to be and what the underlying mechanisms might be. Without this, it seems that the charge of mystery mongering will be hard to shake off completely.[74]

Concepts, conceptions and phenomena

Let us briefly consider one final objection to the practice of appealing to intuitions. This objection is closely related to the objection we have just discussed, but takes the form of a backhanded compliment, so to speak. First, it is granted that our epistemic intuitions, for example, do inform us, quite reliably, about our concept of knowledge. But then, in a second step, it is maintained that our concept of knowledge might be 'a product of ignorance and error' and thus could 'mischaracterize the very phenomena which they are concepts of'.[75] Thus, as reliable as our intuitions may be when it comes to determining our *concept* of knowledge, this counts for nothing if we are interested in knowledge, rather than our concept of it. And although philosophers in the twentieth century have been very interested in concepts, the ambition of philosophy throughout most of its history has been to better understand the world. If we want to retain this ambition, we have to acknowledge that appealing to intuitions will get us nowhere.[76]

[73] See e.g. Cummins 1998: 118–24.

[74] See Gutting (2009: ch. 4) for more discussion and a qualified defence of the analytic practice of appealing to intuitions.

[75] Kornblith 2006: 14.   [76] Ibid.: 11–14, 17, 24.

In attempting to evaluate this argument, it is worth noting that Kornblith follows Jackson in identifying 'our concepts' with 'our ordinary conceptions'.[77] This seems problematic, because if concepts are conceptions or theories, then it is obvious that 'our concepts' may be wrong. But traditionalists would not necessarily accept this (nor should they). One *conception* of knowledge – perhaps not an 'ordinary' one, but certainly a philosophical one – is that knowledge is justified true belief. Another conception, more likely to be an ordinary one, is that knowledge is a true belief held with a high degree of subjective confidence. Any such conception can be erroneous, as both these certainly are. When we test the former conception against our intuitions about Gettier cases, we might say we test whether it captures the (not 'our') concept of knowledge.

But might this concept itself turn out to be incorrect – to fail to map onto knowledge itself? Kornblith certainly thinks so, and this is connected with his view that knowledge is a natural kind. But we confess that we find it hard to make sense of this. On Kornblith's view, it seems it might turn out that the following is true:

> John knows that there are sheep in the pasture if and only if (a) he feels certain that there are sheep in the pasture and (b) there are sheep in the pasture [i.e. his belief is true].

On the face of it, this seems absurd. Surely, this *cannot* be the correct analysis of *knowledge*. Suppose, as before, that John hasn't seen a single sheep (though he thinks he has). Along comes Jane, who is aware that there are sheep impostors about and carefully investigates the situation, eventually singling out the two genuine sheep as the only real sheep in the pasture. Jane, however, is a philosopher, and she doesn't feel *absolutely* certain that even these two sheep are the genuine article. So John knows there are sheep in the pasture and *Jane doesn't*? Surely, this cannot be right. The idea that 'our' concept of knowledge might be erroneous and something like the conception just discussed might capture the real phenomenon 'knowledge' seems absurd.

[77] Ibid.: 18. According to Jackson, a conceptual analysis of X reveals our 'ordinary conception' or 'folk theory' of X (1998: 31). This seems to run together 'our concept (or better, *the* concept) of X' with 'our ordinary *conception*' of X (ibid.). But whereas 'conception' might refer to some sort of theory, 'concept' does not – at least not obviously. See Papineau (2009: 11–12) for a similar criticism of Jackson.

Perhaps it might be said that the view that our concepts could fail to map on to the phenomena need not involve commitment to the idea that our concepts could need as radical revision as in our example. Perhaps, in the case of knowledge, it might turn out that something like the conception Gettier criticised adequately captures what knowledge is, whereas 'our' concept of knowledge seems to impose stricter – hence too strict – requirements on knowledge. But, given Kornblith's strict dichotomy of concept and phenomenon, on what basis are we supposed to determine how radically one might deviate from the other? If our concepts can mischaracterise the phenomena, why can't they also radically mischaracterise them? Besides, the supposedly less radical suggestion that knowledge might after all turn out to be justified true belief contra our more demanding concept of knowledge still seems pretty absurd. Of course, when we respond in this way we are relying on our *intuitions* about when it is appropriate to ascribe knowledge and when it is not. Thus, we use 'data' that Kornblith would consider impermissible, and it is hence unlikely that our objections would sway him in the least.

Before we bring this discussion to a close, let us mention one more point. As we have seen, Kornblith draws a sharp distinction between concepts and the world. He is not, of course, alone in doing so. But it should be noted that not all philosophers would accept this dichotomy. According to some, to say something about the concept of knowledge is to say something about what counts as knowledge and what doesn't. That is, it is to say something about the *phenomenon* of knowledge in the phenomenological sense of the word 'phenomenon': about what knowledge is in the context of human life or, perhaps, in the context of human life within a certain (viz. our) culture. There is no dichotomy between concepts and the world if the world is understood as the world of meaning and significance in which we live our lives: the world of 'phenomena', or what phenomenologists sometimes call the 'life-world'. As A. J. Ayer remarks, 'the distinction between "about language" and "about the world" isn't all that sharp, because the world is the world as we describe it, the world as it figures in our system of concepts'.[78] On this sort of view, to study concepts is not to abandon the project of understanding the world. On the contrary, it is part and parcel of that project, if 'world' is understood to refer, not to the world as described by particle physics, but to the life-world.[79]

---

[78] In Magee 1982: 104.
[79] For a perceptive discussion of related points, see Wild 1958.

Conclusion

In this chapter, we have looked at two highly influential styles of philosophical argumentation: appeals to phenomenology and appeals to intuitions about possible cases. In recent years, both of these have come under pressure from methodological naturalists who argue that the time is ripe for philosophy to leave behind such 'armchair' methods in favour of the universally accepted canons of empirical science. As we have seen, it is not obvious that the traditional methods are quite as problematic as their critics maintain. On the other hand, these are live debates and it would be premature to offer a confident verdict on the outcome of them. One conclusion that does seem to emerge from our discussion, however, is that methodological 'purism' – the idea that philosophy should only be disciplined by one thing, whether that thing is conceptual analysis or phenomenological description or whatever – looks like a bad idea. Philosophy, it seems, benefits from being 'disciplined' by more than one sort of data.

5 Analytic and continental philosophy

Introduction

Describing the state of philosophy in the late 1980s, Michael Dummett remarked:

> It is obvious that philosophers will never reach agreement. It is a pity, however, if they can no longer talk to one another or understand one another. It is difficult to achieve such understanding, because if you think people are on the wrong track, you may have no great desire to talk with them or to take the trouble to criticise their views. But we have reached a point at which it's as if we're working in different subjects.

Dummett is referring to the split between so-called analytic and continental philosophy, a split he argues has widened continuously throughout the past century to the point at which 'It's no use now shouting across the gulf'.[1] This in spite of the fact that the founders of the two traditions – according to Dummett: Frege and Husserl – were 'remarkably close in orientation, despite some divergence of interests'. Consequently, Dummett can compare the development of analytical and continental philosophy with 'the Rhine and the Danube, which rise quite close to one another and for a time pursue roughly parallel courses, only to diverge in utterly different directions and flow into different seas'.[2]

No introduction to the central questions of metaphilosophy can be complete without a survey of the different directions allegedly taken by analytic and continental philosophy and of the 'seas' into which these currents flow. If Dummett is right, it looks as if there is not one answer to the question 'What is philosophy?', but two 'utterly different' ones. Indeed,

---

[1] Both quotes Dummett 1993: 193.
[2] Both quotes Ibid.: 26.

as C. G. Prado puts it, the respective positions taken by analytic and continental philosophers 'have tended to be seen, not as divergent positions within philosophy, but rather as positions that define incommensurable conceptions of philosophy'.[3] Of course, as we saw in Chapter 2, there are numerous 'conceptions of philosophy' out there – not just one or two. But Dummett and Prado are not talking about what we called in the introduction 'explicit metaphilosophy' – the sorts of replies philosophers give when they explicitly address the question of the nature of philosophy. What Dummett is suggesting, rather, is that the sorts of positions analytic and continental philosophers take when discussing other philosophical questions, the ways in which they defend those positions or the topics they consider important betray their (implicit) allegiance to two radically different visions of philosophy. In this chapter, we examine the extent to which such views are right and attempt to determine just what the differences are between analytic and continental philosophy.

The labels and their extensions

As many philosophers have noted, the labels 'analytic' and 'continental' themselves are unhelpful. In Bernard Williams's words, they involve 'a strange cross-classification – rather as though one divided cars into front-wheel drive and Japanese'.[4] 'Analytic' seems to refer to a method and 'continental' to a place (the European mainland), and there is surely no reason in principle why a philosopher from continental Europe couldn't employ the method of analysis. Capturing the opposition in purely geographical terms, as some have attempted – opposing 'Anglo-American' philosophy to continental or 'modern European' philosophy – does not make things any better. Not only is the work of many philosophers active on the European mainland actually 'Anglo-American' (i.e. analytic) in anyone's book, but, as Dummett has emphasised, the roots of Anglo-American philosophy, no less than those of continental philosophy, are found on the European mainland: 'The sources of analytic philosophy were the writings of philosophers who wrote, principally or exclusively, in the German language.'[5] Moreover, probably the majority of work in so-called modern European philosophy is now done outside

---

[3] Prado 2003b: 13.   [4] Williams 2003: 23.   [5] Dummett 1993: ix.

continental Europe: in the United Kingdom, Asia, Latin America and above all North America.[6]

Although the labels are clumsy and unhelpful, there is widespread agreement about their *extensions*. Almost everyone will agree that analytic philosophy is the sort of philosophy expounded by Frege, Russell, Moore, Wittgenstein, Carnap, Ryle, Ayer, Quine, Davidson, Dummett, Putnam, Kripke and many others, plus most of the philosophers discussing the views and arguments of these thinkers. One can also be fairly confident that if an article is published in, say, *Analysis*, *Mind* or *Philosophical Studies*, then it is a piece of analytic philosophy. Continental philosophy, on the other hand, is what we find in the works of Husserl, Heidegger, Sartre, Merleau-Ponty, Levinas, Derrida, Foucault, Lyotard, Deleuze and Irigaray, say, and most of their commentators and followers. To be sure, there may be some borderline cases that are hard to place, such as, perhaps, Cavell, Feyerabend and Rorty; but here, too, Wittgenstein's remark that a dispute about the precise border between two countries doesn't put the citizenship of all their inhabitants in question seems apposite. And in general, there is seldom disagreement about how to classify a philosophical author, book or paper.

Nor is there reason to doubt what we might term the 'institutional reality' of the divide. That is, in terms of reading and citation patterns, conference organisation and attendance and so on, most analytical philosophers hardly engage with continental philosophers at all, nor do most continental thinkers cite the papers of analytic philosophers or attend their symposia.

Much less clear is what the *intensions* of the terms 'analytic' and 'continental' are supposed to be. In other words, there is little general agreement about what it *means* to say of a philosophical work that it is 'analytic' or 'continental'. Do these terms reflect real differences in terms of method, doctrine or topics addressed? Or are these mainly historical traditions – trails of influence, handed down ideas about who to cite and who to ignore and so on? Or is the difference mainly one of literary style? Or, finally, is the very idea that there is any interesting distinction to be drawn between

---

[6] For this reason, refining the geographical designations – contrasting 'Anglo-Austrian' philosophy (Dummett 1993: 2) with, say, Franco-German philosophy – is of no help either.

two types of philosophy – corresponding to the extensions of the labels 'analytic' and 'continental' – spurious? As we shall see, the positions taken on these issues differ markedly, even amongst philosophers supposedly belonging to the same 'camp'.

The usual suspects

There are, however, fairly widespread ideas in each 'camp' about what characterises the work of those from the other 'camp'. Gary Gutting, whose own work straddles the divide, articulates some of these ideas in a passage intended to capture the weaknesses of both camps:

> [C]ontinental philosophy is typically sexier than analytic, promising the excitement of novelty and iconoclasm. This very feature is also responsible for the continentalists' characteristic weakness of pretentious obscurity. When the effort to move creatively beyond old categories fails, as it usually does, the result may well be little more than self-important gibberish or, marginally better, an excruciating restatement of the obvious. Correspondingly, analytic philosophy's characteristic faults are the plodding clarity and misplaced rigor of someone who, in a glorious meadow that calls for exuberant roaming, crawls along as through a minefield.[7]

Many analytic philosophers will nod their heads approvingly at characterisations of continental philosophy as consisting mainly of a species of 'self-important gibberish' that tends, regrettably, to appeal more to students than do the plainly written and rigorously argued texts in the analytic canon. In Kevin Mulligan's words, continental philosophy 'is inherently obscure and obscurantist, often closer to the genre of literature than to that of philosophy; it is devoid of arguments, distinctions, examples and analysis; it is *problemarm* [i.e. lacks a set of clearly defined problems]'.[8] As Anthony Quinton opines, all varieties of continental thought 'rely on dramatic, even melodramatic, utterance rather than sustained rational argument'. Thus, for analytic philosophers, it can at most

---

[7] Gutting 1998: 10.
[8] Mulligan 1991: 115. Mulligan presents this as a description of 'the analytical clichés about Continental Philosophy' (ibid.), but he adds in a footnote that, to him, these clichés seem 'to be one and all true' (ibid.: 119).

be 'the object of occasional startled observation, like that of a nasty motor accident viewed from a passing car'.[9] Finally, rivalling Quinton's verdict in terms of harshness, Jack Smart declares: 'I have moments of despair about philosophy when I think of how so much phenomenological and existential philosophy seems such sheer bosh that I cannot even begin to read it.'[10]

Continentalists, on the other hand, will regard Gutting's description as confirming their impression of the sterility and tediousness of much work in analytic philosophy. The analytic philosopher 'seeks precision by total mind control, through issuing continuous and rigid interpretative directions'. She or he 'tries to remove in advance every conceivable misunderstanding or misinterpretation or objection, including those that would occur only to the malicious or the clinically literal-minded'.[11] As a consequence, much of what is published in the main analytic journals 'looks like bombination in a pseudoscientific vacuum' to most continental philosophers.[12] And most often the point of it all is not to rethink some fundamental aspect of the human condition or sociopolitical reality, but merely to 'come up with a hitherto unsuspected twist in the dialectic, earning a few more citations in one or another of the on-going games of fashionable philosophical ping-pong'.[13]

Of course, neither party is likely to accept that such characterisations capture the core of their favoured brand of philosophy. No analytic philosopher will accept that it is defining of analytic philosophy that it reduces philosophy to an idle game of argumentative ping-pong; nor will continentalists agree that it is characteristic of their work that it promulgates pretentious obscurities. If we want an adequate grasp of the nature of the 'gulf', such prejudices – however apt they may be as descriptions of the characteristic *dangers* faced by each camp – will obviously not do. Yet since such prejudices are doubtless in great measure responsible for maintaining what we called the 'institutional reality' of the gulf, it is useful to cast a brief glance at a decisive point in the history of their formation.

---

[9] Quinton 2005.

[10] Smart 1975: 61. As Lee Braver comments on a similar pronouncement Smart makes elsewhere, 'It is an impressive repulsion, indeed, which needs no exposure to that which repels it' (2011: 235).

[11] Both quotes Williams 2006: 183.

[12] Rorty 2003: 20.   [13] Mulligan et al. 2006: 65.

The role of Heidegger

In the last decades of the nineteenth century, Frege and Husserl were both working on issues in logic and the foundations of mathematics. It is well known that they corresponded and discussed each other's work. Frege wrote a critical review of an early book of Husserl's, and the former has been credited with influencing Husserl to reject the psychologism he had espoused in his early writings. So at this point in time, as Dummett and many others have documented, it does not make sense to distinguish a 'continental' philosophical tradition from an 'analytic' one. Nor was the split imminent. Around the turn of the century, Russell was familiar with the work of Brentano and Meinong and discussed it in print. He also read some of Husserl's works, including *Logical Investigations*, which he was supposed to have reviewed for the journal *Mind*. Two decades later, at Oxford, Gilbert Ryle gave courses on Husserl and other Austrian thinkers, and during the 1920s, 1930s and 1940s Ryle published a handful of 'partly sympathetic' papers on Husserl's phenomenology.[14] The young Rudolf Carnap read Husserl carefully and in his first major work, *The Logical Structure of the World*, Carnap made several, mostly favourable, references to Husserl's *Ideas I*.[15] Other prominent members of the Vienna Circle, including Moritz Schlick, also read and discussed Husserl's work, though in an increasingly critical fashion.

Husserl's erstwhile protégé (and successor at Freiburg University), Martin Heidegger, made a very different impact, however. As Peter Simons suggests, 'Probably no individual was more responsible for the schism in philosophy than Heidegger'.[16] In 1929, Gilbert Ryle published a review of Heidegger's *Being and Time*. The opening lines of the review state that the book 'marks a big advance in the application of the "Phenomenological Method" – though I may say at once that I suspect that this advance is an advance towards disaster'.[17] As Ryle intimates later in the review, the disaster in question seems to be 'windy mysticism'[18] (whatever exactly he means by this). Ryle's review also contains praise of Heidegger's work,[19] but a mere two years later, Ryle's verdict is uncompromising: 'those metaphysical philosophers are the greatest sinners who, as if they were saying

[14] Ryle 1971: 8–9.   [15] Carnap 1967: 9, 101, 263.
[16] Simons 2001: 302.   [17] Ryle 2009a: 205.
[18] Ibid.: 222.   [19] See Braver 2011: 236–9.

something of importance, make ... "Being" the subject of their propositions ... For at best what they say is systematically misleading, ... and at
worst it is meaningless'.[20] Recalling his time as a student under Ryle at
Oxford in the 1940s, Dummett remarks: 'Heidegger was perceived only as
a figure of fun, too absurd to be taken seriously.'[21]

A few years after Ryle's review of *Being and Time* appeared, Carnap published a devastating critique of Heidegger's inaugural address at Freiburg,
'What Is Metaphysics?' Carnap's criticisms focussed on Heidegger's recur-
ring pronouncements about 'the nothing' – in particular on the tortuous
statement that '[t]he nothing itself nihilates'.[22] Carnap's response was
not that such sentences are false or pointless, but that they are devoid of
meaning altogether. The question of their truth and falsehood thus cannot arise.[23] Carnap did grant that Heidegger's pseudo-statements might
serve to express an 'attitude towards life'; but then, so Carnap prophet-
ically added, Heidegger should have openly adopted 'the form of art, of
poetry',[24] and not that of theoretical philosophy.

We cannot enter into Heidegger's reasons for expressing himself the way
he did, nor is it our business here to assess the extent to which Carnap's critique was justified. The point is merely to indicate how Heidegger was received
by up-and-coming analytical philosophers around 1930, and the impact that
reception had.[25] And it seems clear that most of the clichés about continental
philosophy are already in play: it is mysticism or even plain nonsense; it may
have literary qualities, but it should not be mistaken for serious philosophy.

In the very same essay that drew fire from Carnap, Heidegger anticipates
some of the characteristic continental responses to analytic philosophy. He
starts out by asserting that philosophy is incompatible with 'the point of
view of common sense'.[26] At various points throughout the essay he then

[20] Ryle 2009b : 48.   [21] Dummett 1978: 437.
[22] Heidegger 1993: 103.   [23] Carnap 1959: 61, 72.
[24] Ibid.: 78, 80.
[25] Half a century later, in a survey of twentieth-century philosophy, Ayer still sees
fit to brusquely dismiss Heidegger on the charge of displaying 'what can fairly be
described as charlatanism' (1984: 228). Heidegger's membership in the Nazi Party
(from 1933 until 1945) no doubt confirmed Anglo-American suspicions that his particular brand of mysticism was unworthy of serious discussion.
[26] Heidegger 1993: 93. Elsewhere, Heidegger declares that 'philosophy is nothing but a
struggle against common sense' (*die Philosophie ist nichts als ein Kampf gegen den gesun-
den Menschenverstand!*) (1995: 36).

proceeds to contrast his own metaphysical undertaking with the strictures of 'logic' (consistently placed in scare quotes). 'Universal "logic" … lays low' the questions of metaphysics, branding them as 'inherently absurd', Heidegger says. But for precisely this reason, we must question 'the reigning and never-challenged doctrine of "logic"'. We must not allow the 'objections of the intellect' to 'call a halt' to metaphysical inquiry. Instead, 'The idea of "logic" itself [must disintegrate] in the turbulence of a more original questioning.'[27]

Naturally, Heidegger's response to 'logic' and his plea for metaphysics will not be accepted by all continental philosophers. Nevertheless, it might not be too far-fetched to see in Heidegger's reaction to the doctrine of 'logic' an anticipation of the recurrent continental complaint that the 'misplaced rigour' of analytic philosophy arrests it at the starting gate, bogging it down by superficial disputes and technicalities which prevent it from penetrating to deeper and more 'original' or important philosophical issues. Analytic philosophy, on this sort of view, is philosophically shallow as well as pedestrian, and it is useless to anyone outside a usually very narrow circle of experts.

It seems, then, that core analytical clichés about continentalists, as well as some common continental reactions to analytic philosophy, were already formulated eighty years ago. For this reason alone one might expect these ideas to be hard to eradicate. And of course, if there is truth in them, they aren't ideas that we ought to eradicate. So let us now look at some of the more popular ways of explaining the differences between continental and analytic philosophy to see whether there is truth behind the clichés.

Topics

Essentialism about the analytic–continental divide, as we understand it here, is the view that it is possible to provide a set of individually necessary and collectively sufficient conditions for admission into the analytic (or continental) ranks. Very few people defend such essentialism in print.[28]

---

27 Heidegger 1993: 97, 99, 105.
28 Of the authors we discuss in this chapter, we suspect only Quinton and Smart have essentialist leanings. Still, it is useful to treat the various suggestions for characteristic features of the two traditions *as if they were* intended to support essentialist views, as this will allow us to gauge the precise extent to which they fail to do so.

In the course of this and the following three sections, it will emerge that essentialism faces serious difficulties. Hardly any feature held to be characteristic of one of the two camps is universally shared by all who belong to the camp in question. And most features, as we shall see, *are* shared by philosophers from the other side of the divide.

One way in which analytic philosophy and continental philosophy have been held to differ fundamentally is in terms of the *topics* addressed. In this vein, Neil Levy suggests that one thing distinguishing continental from analytic philosophy is the former's 'emphasis on art and literature'.[29] Levy offers a list of book titles, including Sartre's *What Is Literature?*, Foucault's *This Is Not a Pipe* and Derrida's *The Truth in Painting* to back up his claim. Although, as Levy acknowledges, all authors on his list are French, he also calls attention to Heidegger's 'On the Origin of the Work of Art' and to his preoccupation with Hölderlin and other poets. However, the supposed 'emphasis on art and literature' does not seem a plausible candidate for a necessary feature of continental philosophy. Surely, it would be misleading at best to ascribe such an emphasis to Levinas, Habermas or Husserl, for example. All, to be sure, have something to say about art - Levinas mainly in a critical vein,[30] suspicious that aesthetic experience is ultimately an evasion of the moral responsibilities inherent in social life - yet this is hardly central to their philosophical projects. Habermas, indeed, criticises Rorty and Derrida for blurring the distinction between philosophy and literature.[31] Nor, of course, is a *lack* of interest in art and literature defining of analytic philosophy. Wittgenstein, for example, 'attached extreme importance' to the 'aesthetic dimension of life'[32]; and, though perhaps his analytic credentials are debatable, so does Stanley Cavell. Other analytic philosophers who have laid 'emphasis on art and literature' include Nelson Goodman, Richard Wollheim and Roger Scruton.

More plausibly, several writers have drawn attention to the central role of history, including the history of philosophy, in continental philosophy. As Simon Critchley puts it, 'the texts of the Continental tradition' are 'marked by a strong consciousness of history'.[33] Particularly important in this context, Critchley thinks, is the central insight of continental thinkers into the way philosophical problems are shaped by their historical

---

[29] Levy 2003: 291.   [30] Levinas 1998: 1-13.
[31] Habermas 1990: 185-210.   [32] Hagberg 2007.
[33] Critchley 2001: 57; cf. Biletzki 2001: 292.

context. This insight 'perhaps explains why seemingly peripheral problems of translation, language, reading, text-reception, interpretation, and
the hermeneutic access to history are of such central importance in the
Continental tradition'.[34] Similarly, Chase and Reynolds suggest that continental philosophy is characterised by a '"temporal turn" that not only
affirms our historicity but argues for its philosophical primacy'.[35]

These suggestions may well indicate a topic that, in one way or another,
characterises the bulk of continental thought. Yet one might wonder about
the extent to which 'our historicity', or indeed *any* of the many problems
Critchley lists as central to the continental tradition – with the possible
exception of 'language' – are key themes of such an indisputably continental thinker as Emmanuel Levinas. And again, Husserl presents an even
clearer counterexample. To be sure, as Critchley notes,[36] history and historicity became important topics for the later Husserl, culminating in his last
great work, *The Crisis of European Sciences and Transcendental Phenomenology*.
But the early Husserl did not deal with these themes in any detail. They
hardly surface at all in the work that founded the phenomenological tradition: *Logical Investigations*. And when the early Husserl did broach topics in
this vicinity, he did so mainly to criticise Dilthey's 'historicism' for com-
promising the objective validity of science and philosophy.[37]

Nor is 'history' a plausible candidate for a theme that does *not* surface in
analytic philosophy. An old story tells of an analytic philosopher in a pres-
tigious American department having a note on his door reading 'JUST SAY
NO TO THE HISTORY OF PHILOSOPHY'.[38] And notoriously, at least some of
the Oxford ordinary language philosophers of the post-war period urged
that one should 'read something written by Plato "as though it had come
out in *Mind* last month"'.[39] But such sentiments should not be seen as representative of analytic philosophy as such. They were not representative of
all analytic philosophy in the 1950s and 1960s – think, for example, of the
work of Wilfrid Sellars, or of Bernard Williams' essays from the 1960s –
and they are certainly not representative now.[40] Here one might recall

---

[34] Critchley 2001: 59–60.   [35] Chase and Reynolds 2011: 254.
[36] Critchley 2001: 69.   [37] Husserl 1965: 122–47.
[38] Williams 2006: 204. The culprit seems to have been Gilbert Harman (Glock 2008: 92).
[39] Williams 2006: 181.
[40] As for saying 'no' to the history of philosophy, Williams urges that 'one must take
extremely seriously Santayana's warning, that those who are ignorant of the history

Alasdair MacIntyre's examination of the historical presuppositions of Western morality in *After Virtue*, or Rorty's classic *Philosophy and the Mirror of Nature*, which offers a radical critique of the entire tradition of modern epistemology. As Robert Brandom writes, analytic philosophy may have been 'viscerally hostile both to historical philosophical enterprises and to systematic ones' in its youth, defining itself 'in part by its recoil from the excesses of philosophical programs tracing their roots back to Hegel'. Yet, first, as Brandom adds, 'This self-understanding was never unanimous.' And second, it has become clearer with time 'that commitment to the fundamental analytic *credo* – *faith* in reasoned argument, *hope* for reasoned agreement, and *clarity* of reasoned expression (and the greatest of these is clarity) – is not incompatible with a philosophical understanding of philo-sophical understanding as admitting, indeed, perhaps even as requiring, both historical and systematic forms'.[41] Thus, Barry Stroud can declare that he thinks 'philosophy is inseparable from the history of philosophy'.[42]

David Cooper has proposed a related, though more general topic as central to continental thought, namely 'the background conditions of enquiry', whether these be 'historical, social, psychological, or whatever'.[43] This proposal certainly allows one to include Husserl's work, concerned throughout with unveiling the conditions for sense experience and cogni-tion, and arguably Levinas's as well. But surely, much analytic philosophy is concerned with the conditions of inquiry too. As Glock notes, 'Different types of background conditions for knowledge have played a role in Wittgenstein's uncertainty, Quine's naturalized epistemology and Searle's theory of social reality. Even sociological background conditions have been popular themes in analytic philosophy since Kuhn and Feyerabend.[44] One might also add that Strawson's descriptive metaphysics, Dummett's theory of meaning and Davidson's thoughts on radical interpretation are concerned, in various ways, with the conditions of inquiry. Indeed, if 'an

of philosophy are doomed to recapitulate it (not just reinventing the wheel, but rein-venting the square wheel)' (2006: 204). In response to the suggestion that one should read Plato's works as if they had just been published in *Mind*, he remarks that this is 'an idea which, if it means anything at all, means something that destroys the main philosophical point of reading Plato at all', the point, namely, 'of making the familiar look strange, and conversely' (2006: 181).

[41] Brandom 2002: 1–2.   [42] Stroud 2001: 43.
[43] Cooper 1994: 5.   [44] Glock 2008: 147.

interest in the background conditions of enquiry' is interpreted loosely enough to include all continental philosophers, from Bergson through Husserl to Irigaray, then it is probably interpreted loosely enough to serve as a rough characterisation of large parts of philosophy as such – whether continental or analytic.

Turning to analytic philosophy, Levy suggests that it is characteristic of analytic philosophers that they only address 'precisely delineated puzzles', for which reason 'the analytic philosopher cannot address herself to the meaning of life, or discovering the good life'.[45] Again, though, a counterexample is not difficult to come by: think, for example, of Thomas Nagel's early essays, dealing amongst other things with dreaming, sexual perversion, death and the absurd, and all published in paradigmatically analytic journals (most of them included in Nagel's *Mortal Questions* – arguably a classic of recent analytic philosophy).[46] Nor is it clear that the 'meaning of life' is a topic that all continental philosophers have lavished attention on – again, one might think of Husserl and Habermas here – although the significance of death was of course treated in detail by Jaspers and Heidegger and the absurdity of human existence was an important topic for the French existentialists.

In his aptly titled paper 'Phenomenology vs. *The Concept of Mind*', Ryle maintained that it was characteristic of the analytic movement that it had an interest in logic, whereas there was no interest in logic on the European continent.[47] Again, though, counterexamples to the first conjunct ought to have been readily accessible for Ryle: his Oxford colleague John L. Austin – despite translating Frege's *Foundations of Arithmetic* – showed more interest in the subtleties of English usage than in logic; nor were logical studies a main concern of the later Wittgenstein. As for the second part of Ryle's conjunction, he seems to overlook Husserl's lifelong interest in logic, as evidenced by the three decades separating *Logical Investigations* (1900/1901) and *Formal and Transcendental Logic* (1929).

An overriding concern with concepts and language has also been regarded as characteristic of analytic philosophy – indeed, it is still quite common for German-speaking continental philosophers to speak of 'language-analytic' philosophy (*sprachanalytische Philosophie*), rather than simply 'analytic' philosophy. But this overlooks the fact that not all

[45] Levy 2003: 293.   [46] Nagel 1979.   [47] Ryle 2009a: 189.

founding fathers of analytic philosophy overly concerned themselves with language, and it also ignores significant developments in analytic philosophy after Quine, in particular the almost complete disappearance of linguistic philosophy from the analytic scene. Just to illustrate the first point, Russell was certainly not an unambiguous advocate of the 'linguistic turn'. As against the view that 'it is not the world we are to try to understand but only sentences' – which Russell associated with the later Wittgenstein and Oxford ordinary language philosophy – he objected that it reduced philosophy to, 'at best, a slight help to lexicographers'.[48] The suggestion also overlooks the fact that concepts and language are important topics for continental thinkers such as Heidegger, Gadamer, Ricoeur and Derrida. Derrida, for example, gives language centre stage already in his groundbreaking book *Speech and Phenomena* – a work described as 'a first-class piece of analytical work in the philosophy of language'.[49] As for concepts, Deleuze and Guattari maintain that philosophy is nothing but 'the art of forming, inventing, and fabricating concepts'[50]; and Derrida portrays himself as being 'on the side of conceptual philosophy'. Apparently embracing the very suggestion we are currently criticising, this leads him to deny that he belongs unambiguously on the 'continental side' and, somewhat provocatively, perhaps, to assert that he could be described as an analytic philosopher.[51]

Doctrines

If analytic and continental philosophy cannot be sharply distinguished in terms of the topics addressed, then perhaps we should look instead at the positions taken on the shared topics. Dummett famously proposes that 'What distinguishes analytical philosophy, in its diverse manifestations, from other schools is the belief, first, that a philosophical account of thought can be attained through a philosophical account of language, and, secondly, that a comprehensive account can only be so attained.'[52] In a similar vein, he suggests that 'we may characterise analytical philosophy as that which follows Frege in accepting that the philosophy of

[48] Both quotes Russell 1959: 217.   [49] Garver 1973: ix.
[50] Deleuze and Guattari 1994: 2.
[51] Derrida, in Derrida et al. 2000: 381–2.
[52] Dummett 1993: 4.

language is the foundation for all of philosophy'.[53] It is quite possible that many analytic philosophers hold this particular combination of views. But it is equally clear that not all analytic philosophers do – indeed Dummett himself admits that the work of Gareth Evans must be expelled from the analytic family, since it reverses the priority, 'in the order of explanation, of language over thought'.[54] Nor is Evans alone in this regard. Another important analytic philosopher, John Searle, regards the philosophy of language as 'a branch of the philosophy of mind' and consequently maintains that '[l]anguage is derived from Intentionality and not conversely'.[55] We suspect many current analytic philosophers of mind – perhaps a majority – would agree with Searle on this point.

It also seems that some continental philosophers share Dummett's beliefs about language and thought. Gadamer, for example, declares that *'language is the universal medium in which understanding occurs'* and, famously, *'Being that can be understood is language'*. He elaborates these ideas as follows: 'man's relation to the world is absolutely and fundamentally verbal [*sprachlich*, i.e. linguistic] in nature, and hence intelligible. Thus hermeneutics is … a *universal aspect of philosophy'*.[56] Gadamer here seems to defend ideas very similar to those Dummett singled out as characteristic of analytic philosophy. On Gadamer's view, too, it seems, any philosophical account of thought – indeed of all ways for human beings to relate to the world – must be attained through an account of language, for which reason the philosophical account of language becomes not just a particular branch of philosophy, but a 'universal' philosophical task.

Cooper suggests that what unites continental philosophers – Husserl being the one 'exception to prove the rule' – is the view that the very notions of self and subject, and not merely 'certain conceptions of these', have to be rejected.[57] Cooper no doubt pinpoints an important trend in French 'post-structuralist' thought – visible in Derrida, Lacan, Deleuze and Foucault, among others.[58] Yet the claim that this supposed 'fall of the self' is a doctrine characteristic of continental philosophy as such seems implausible. Not simply because Husserl is once again the 'odd man out', but because it is questionable whether any of the major

[53] Dummett 1978: 441.   [54] Dummett 1993: 4.
[55] Searle 1983: vii, 5.   [56] Gadamer 1989: 474, 475–6.
[57] Cooper 1994: 7, 6.   [58] See Gilbert and Lennon 2005: chs. 4 and 7.

phenomenologists would defend the doctrine. Contra Cooper, Heidegger himself is clear that 'Dasein' is in fact another term for what the tradition calls the 'subject', and that his reason for avoiding the latter term is that he intends to perform 'a thorough revision of the hitherto reigning concept of the subject'.[59] In other words, it is precisely a widespread conception of the subject or the self that Heidegger wants to challenge – not the notion of the self or the subject as such. Similar points apply to Scheler, Merleau-Ponty, Levinas and even Sartre. Perhaps, as Cooper implies, Heidegger and others have criticised Husserl's conception of subjectivity for being 'Cartesian', for having 'intentional experiences merely within its own sphere'[60]; yet ironically, another later phenomenologist – Michel Henry – faults Husserl for conceiving of subjectivity as *insufficiently* immanent.[61]

Chase and Reynolds make the more plausible suggestion that a characteristic feature of the continental tradition is a 'suspicion of strong scientific naturalism'.[62] Although they themselves mention a possible exception (Quentin Meillassoux), there is certainly something to their suggestion as far as the major figures of continental philosophy are concerned. Yet it surely cannot be maintained that such suspicion is anathema to analytic philosophy as such. The analytic movement, for example, also encompasses the 'neutral monist' positions of Russell and Ayer, according to which the physical world was a mere construction out of sense data, ideas that live on in the idealist and phenomenalist theories of perception advanced by people like John Foster and Howard Robinson.[63] Having said that, naturalism is certainly the majority view within analytic philosophy. Yet, as we mentioned in Chapter 3, not all naturalists are of the 'strong scientific' kind. McDowell, for example, is clear to distinguish his own brand of naturalism from what he terms 'bald naturalism'. For McDowell, naturalism is a family of positions that have in common the rejection of 'supernaturalism' or the idea of 'mysterious gift[s] from outside nature'.[64] But if the rejection of supernaturalism in this sense amounts to being a naturalist, then surely Merleau-Ponty, for example, is a naturalist. The point of phenomenological analysis, he maintains, 'is not to oppose to the

[59] Heidegger 1996: 115. See also Carr 1999.
[60] Cooper 1994: 7.   [61] See Zahavi 2007.
[62] Chase and Reynolds 2011: 159.
[63] See Robinson 1994.   [64] McDowell 1996: 88.

facts objective science coordinates a group of facts that "escape" it'.[65] So, just as was the case with Cooper's suggestion concerning the conditions of inquiry, the apparent success of Chase and Reynolds's suggestion in terms of capturing something possibly characteristic of *all* continental philosophers is coupled with a rather obvious inability to pinpoint something *unique* to that tradition.

Though other doctrinal differences have been proposed, we shall leave the matter here and conclude that this seems the least promising route for an essentialist to take. As Scott Soames writes, 'Invariably, the harshest and most effective opponents of any analytic philosophers have always been other analytic philosophers'.[66] As for the continental tradition, Neil Levy compares it with Kuhnean 'pre-paradigm science', in which the aim is not to build on the arguments of one's predecessors, but to overthrow them altogether.[67] Surely, this makes universal agreement on any philosophical doctrine virtually impossible.

Methods

More promising, perhaps, is the idea that the fundamental differences between the two philosophical traditions are *methodological* ones. It is this idea, rather than any supposed topical or doctrinal differences, which lends credibility to the views we outlined in the introduction to this chapter, according to which analytic and continental philosophy represent two wholly different, and possibly incommensurable, visions of philosophy.

A simple proposal immediately suggests itself: analytic philosophy is characterised by the method of *analysis*. There are, however, two quite obvious problems with this proposal. First, analytic philosophers have understood 'analysis' in a variety of very different ways – as a decompositional method to reach the ultimate constituents of reality in Russell, as the assembling of linguistic reminders in the later Wittgenstein and ordinary language philosophy and so on – such that the idea of analysis 'is too elastic, capable of too many divergent, indeed conflicting, interpretations to be a useful litmus test by itself'.[68] It is certainly elastic enough to include early continental thinkers such as Brentano and Husserl ('intentional

---

[65] Merleau-Ponty 1964a: 22.   [66] Soames 2003: xii–xiii.
[67] Levy 2003.   [68] Hacker 1998: 6.

analysis' being a favourite term of the latter).[69] Second, as we saw in the last chapter, experimental philosophy is an influential movement in recent analytic philosophy, which seems critically directed at just about all twentieth-century conceptions of the method of analysis. Philosophy, experimental philosophers believe, should simply employ standard empirical methods. So regardless of how wide a net we cast, it seems it will not cover all of analytic philosophy.

It is not easy to point to plausible candidates for a methodological commitment common to all continental philosophers. Chase and Reynolds, however, surely come close when they suggest that 'some form of transcendental reasoning is close to ubiquitous' in the continental tradition.[70] But this should not be taken to mean that 'transcendental arguments' (as analytic philosophers understand these) are ubiquitous in continental philosophy. Rather, as mentioned in Chapter 2, for continental philosophers the transcendental is more like the fundamental domain of philosophising. Philosophy, on this view, is not an empirical science on a par with chemistry and biology, or even psychology, history or sociology. Rather, philosophy is a 'second-order' discipline – a reflection on the conditions of (first-order) inquiry. This obviously takes us back to Cooper's suggestion, against which we pointed out that the concern with the conditions of inquiry is not unique to continental philosophy. Indeed, the idea of philosophy as a 'second-order' discipline was popular in analytic philosophy at least until Quine's groundbreaking 'Two Dogmas of Empiricism'. And the idea still has its advocates within the analytic movement. According to Bennett and Hacker, for example, 'conceptual questions ... are the proper province of philosophy', and such questions 'antecede matters of truth and falsehood. They are questions concerning our *forms of representation*, not questions concerning the truth and falsehood of empirical statements. These forms are presupposed by true (*and* false) scientific statements'.[71]

What may conceivably characterise all analytic philosophers, however, is their positive attitude towards a small-scale, piecemeal approach to philosophical problems. As Soames puts it, there is 'a widespread assumption within the [analytic] tradition that it is often possible to make philosophical progress by intensively investigating a small, circumscribed

---

[69] See Beaney 2007.   [70] Chase and Reynolds 2011: 89.
[71] Bennett and Hacker 2003: 1–2.

range of philosophical issues while holding broader, systematic questions in abeyance'.[72] Formulated in this careful way, the assumption may not just be widespread, but actually universally accepted amongst analytic philosophers – even by those who aren't paradigmatic practitioners of small-scale investigation, such as, perhaps, Wittgenstein (early and late), McDowell and Brandom. Moreover, there is probably something to the suggestion that continental philosophers generally favour grander, more sweeping gestures.

But again, the sentiments of at least some phenomenologists are in line with analytic philosophers on this point. As Gadamer relates, Husserl

> regarded himself a master and teacher of patient, descriptive, detailed work, and all rash combinations and clever constructions were an abomination to him. In his teaching, whenever he encountered the grand assertions and arguments that are typical of beginning philosophers, he used to say, 'Not always the big bills, gentlemen; small change, small change!'[73]

The works Husserl published during his lifetime may bear little trace of this attitude, but that is at least partly explained by the fact that the published books were almost invariably attempts to provide synoptic overviews of the multitude of detailed investigations Husserl had recorded in his research manuscripts. Thus, the positive attitude to small-scale philosophical work may characterise all analytic philosophers to some extent, but it seems equally characteristic of some (in the logical sense of 'at least one') key continental philosophers.

Another and perhaps more promising proposal is that 'the continental tradition generally exhibits a thoroughgoing wariness of any close link between philosophical method and either common sense ... or science'.[74] Earlier, we quoted Heidegger saying that philosophy was a struggle against common sense. And for once, it may seem as if the recurrent continental 'odd man out' – Husserl – may be comfortably included within the continental ranks. For his epoché was 'a method that would suspend the assumptions of the "natural attitude", including even the common-sense conviction that we have perception of an "external world"'.[75] However, as Chase and Reynolds themselves concede, it would be wrong to conclude

---

[72] Soames 2003: xv.   [73] Gadamer 1976: 132–3.
[74] Chase and Reynolds 2011: 55.   [75] Ibid.

from this that Husserlian phenomenology is straightforwardly opposed to common sense. In fact, one could go a step further and say that not only was phenomenology in general, and the method of epoché in particular, not opposed to the commonsense conviction that we perceive an 'external world', they were in fact precisely intended to explicate that and other convictions and to reveal their sources in experience. As Husserl puts it in *Cartesian Meditations*, 'phenomenological explication does nothing but explicate the sense [the] world has for us all, prior to any philosophizing ... – a sense which philosophy can uncover but never alter'.[76]

Furthermore, it is not the case that all analytic philosophers are comfortable with close links between philosophical method and common sense. In 'The Cult of Common Usage', Russell is unequivocally dismissive of the idea. He writes:

> It used to be thought that there could not be people at the antipodes, because they would fall off, or, if they avoided that, they would grow dizzy from standing on their heads. It used to be thought absurd to say that the earth rotates, because everybody can see that it doesn't. When it was first suggested that the sun may be as large as Peloponnesus, common sense was outraged. I do not know at what date common sense became all-wise.[77]

But that leaves the suggestion that analytic – unlike continental – philosophers understand their methods as closely linked with scientific method. This claim is often connected with the more general idea that analytic philosophy emulates science while continental philosophy emulates art or literature. According to Neil Levy, continental philosophy 'models itself on modernist art, just as [analytic philosophy] models itself on modern science'.[78] And Searle maintains that 'one crucial difference' between the two traditions is that 'analytic philosophers tend to be very much concerned with science and to see philosophy as aiming for exactly the same sort of objective truth that one gets in the sciences. In my experience, Continental philosophers – with some notable exceptions – tend to see philosophy as less like the sciences and more like a branch of literature'.[79]

Searle is right, though, that there are notable exceptions to his characterisation of continental philosophy. Towards the end of his life, Husserl observed with regret that 'A powerful and constantly growing current of

[76] Husserl 1995: 151; emphasis removed.   [77] Russell 1956: 156.
[78] Levy 2003: 301.   [79] Searle 1999: 2071.

philosophy which renounces scientific discipline … is inundating European humanity.' Among those disputing the idea of philosophy 'as serious, rigorous, indeed apodictically rigorous, science', Husserl noted, were some who 'regard the philosophies as art works of great artistic spirits and consider philosophy "as such" to have the unity of an art'.[80] And while Husserl thus embraced the scientific ideal and rejected the notion of modelling philosophy on art, the later Wittgenstein was arguably more inclined to model his philosophy on art than on science. As already mentioned in Chapter 3, Wittgenstein explicitly distinguished between the methods and aims of his philosophical inquiries and the methods and aims of empirical science. Moreover, he declared, echoing something Heidegger might have said: 'I think I summed up my position vis-à-vis philosophy when I said: philosophy should really be written only as one would write *poetry*'.[81]

Phenomenologist Richard Cobb-Stevens claims that the analytic tradition has a 'preference for calculative rationality and remains suspicious of pre-modern categories such as formal causality and eidetic intuition'.[82] Leaving the question of formal causality, which not all continental philosophers would be keen to embrace, to one side, one might wonder to what extent Cobb-Stevens is right here. Thomas Nagel, for one, has this to say about his methodological commitments: 'I believe one should trust problems over solutions, intuitions over arguments, and pluralistic discord over systematic harmony … Given a knockdown argument for an intuitively unacceptable conclusion, one should assume there is probably something wrong with the argument that one cannot detect.'[83] And, quite generally, how does the suggestion that analytic philosophy shuns the 'pre-modern' category of 'eidetic intuition' square with the fact that appeals to ('conceptual') intuition are exceedingly common in analytic philosophy and that the advocates of this practice often stress that it can be traced back to Plato's dialogues?[84] Again, therefore, the attempt to point to a methodological feature uniting the analytic movement seems to fail.

---

[80] Husserl 1970: 390, 389.

[81] Wittgenstein 1998: 28. Here we follow Marjorie Perloff's translation, though we have changed the emphasis so as to fit the original German: 'Philosophie dürfte man eigentlich nur *dichten*' (2011: 715). See Perloff on the difficulty of translating the German verb *dichten* (2011: 716, footnote 3).

[82] Cobb-Stevens 1990: 1.   [83] Nagel 1979: x.

[84] DePaul and Ramsey 1998: vii.

Style

Perhaps, then, what the continental–analytic divide really comes down to is a question of *style*. On Bernard Williams's view, whether an essay counts as analytical is 'a matter of style'. Williams continues:

> What distinguishes analytical philosophy from other contemporary philosophy … is a certain way of going on, which involves argument, distinctions, and, so far as it remembers to try to achieve it and succeeds, moderately plain speech. As an alternative to plain speech, it distinguishes sharply between obscurity and technicality. It always rejects the first, but the second it sometimes finds a necessity. This feature peculiarly outrages some of its enemies. Wanting philosophy to be at once profound and accessible, they resent technicality but are comforted by obscurity.[85]

Brandom, too, as we have seen, refers to the analytic credo as involving 'faith in reasoned argument' and 'clarity of reasoned expression' – clarity being the highest virtue. Yet, Friedrich Waismann, whose analytic credentials were at least good enough for his essay on the nature of philosophy to be included in a volume on logical positivism (edited by A. J. Ayer), rejected the ideal of clarity. Clarity, Waismann held, 'is liable to nip the living thought in the bud'. He suggests that if 'pioneers of science' such as Kepler and Newton had to ask themselves as at every step whether their statements make perfect sense, 'this would have been the surest means of sapping any creative power'. Waismann concludes: 'I've always suspected that clarity is the last refuge for those who have nothing to say'.[86]

Besides, valuing clarity is obviously not the same as achieving it. Not only may one forget to try to achieve it, there is also such a thing as trying and failing (as most of us are reminded from time to time). Hans-Johann Glock has provided some excellent examples of analytic philosophising that is anything but clear, including the following specimen from Christopher Peacocke's hand:

> *Square* is that concept C for a thinker to possess which is for him
>   (S1) to be willing to believe the thought Cm, where m is a perceptual demonstrative, when he is taking his experience at face value, and the

---

[85] Williams 1985: vi.   [86] Waismann 1959: 359–60.

object of the demonstrative m is presented in an apparently square region of his environment, and he experiences that region as having equal sides and as symmetrical about the bisectors of its sides (we can summarise this as the object's "having appearance Σ"); and

(S2) for an object thought about under some mode of presentation m: to be willing to accept the content Cm when and only when he accepts that the object presented by m has the same shape as perceptual experiences of the kind in (S1) represent objects as having.[87]

As Glock comments, 'The speech of many contemporary analytic philosophers is as plain as a baroque church and as clear as mud.' Another difficulty is that, no matter how one attempts to specify the style typical of analytic philosophy, the later Wittgenstein's style is bound not to meet the specifications. For the later Wittgenstein, clarity might have been an ideal, but as even a sympathetic commentator such as Glock concedes, 'he pursued this end in a fashion that is at times extremely obscure'.[88]

Glock also raises doubts about the role that technicalities are supposed to play in analytic philosophy. Many such technicalities, he suggests, 'serve no purpose other than that of adopting an intellectual posture'.[89] He gives the following example:

> McGinn's (1991) idea of 'cognitive closure' is simply that certain phenomena transcend the cognitive capacities of creatures like ourselves. But he explains it as follows: 'A type of mind M is cognitively closed with respect to a property P or a theory T if and only if the concept-forming procedures at M's disposal cannot extend to a grasp of P or an understanding of T.' Dennett comments: 'Don't be misled by the apparent rigour of this definition: the author A never puts it to any use U in any formal derivation D.'[90]

The next question to ask is whether the ideal of 'clarity of reasoned expression' really is unique to the analytic tradition. Despite one continentalist's contention that 'unclarity belongs to the essence of what it is that Continental philosophers do',[91] it is questionable whether it belongs to the

---

[87] Peacocke 1991: 532–3.
[88] Both quotes from Glock 2004: 432.
[89] Ibid.   [90] Glock 2008: 171–2.
[91] Babich 2003: 92.

essence of what *all* continental philosophers do. The early phenomenologists generally strived for clarity of expression. Even Heidegger, despite
being responsible for such gems as 'the nothing nihilates', could express
himself clearly when he wanted to, as his lecture courses from the 1920s,
such as *Prolegomena to the History of Time* or *Basic Problems of Phenomenology*,
document. And while the early works of Husserl and Sartre may not be
easy to read, they are hardly obscure (let alone obscurantist). It is notable,
for example, that while Dummett does express a preference for reading
Frege over Husserl,[92] he does not charge the latter with being obscure.
In fact, to the extent that Husserl is difficult to read, it is rather, as David
Smith (himself an analytic philosopher) suggests, because over the years
he developed 'a battery of technical terms to express his philosophy'.[93]

That is not to say, of course, that to read Husserl is just like reading
Frege or Russell, or that reading Sartre is no different from reading
Austin. There are marked stylistic differences, though one may question
whether the most important such differences always coincide with the
continental–analytic divide. Nor do we wish to imply that continental
philosophy is never, or only very rarely, obscure. Continental philosopher
Simon Critchley concedes that 'obscurantism' is one of the major dangers
contemporary continental philosophy faces, and he recommends a return
to phenomenology to circumvent the danger.[94] He also makes the point
that although Heidegger and Derrida (in his view) are great philosophers,
'there is absolutely no point writing like them in English. The results are,
at best, embarrassingly derivative and, at worst, unintelligible'.[95] That
some continental philosophers do write (and talk) like their idols, with
the unfortunate results that Critchley mentions, is indisputable. But that
does not show that the continental tradition as such is opposed to the ideal
of clarity. To the contrary, the fact that Critchley explicitly singles out the
danger of obscurantism and suggests means to address it shows that at
least some continentalists adhere to the ideal.

To conclude this section, then, Bernard Williams may well be on the
right track when he writes, in a late essay, that 'what I want to call in
question is the idea that there is a style which defines fairly clearly and
uniformly what counts as clarity and precision ... and that this style has

---

[92] Dummett 1993: 192.   [93] Smith 2003: vii.
[94] Critchley 2001: 111–22.   [95] Ibid.: 49.

been defined by the typical procedures of analytic philosophy'.[96] There are probably more ways than one to achieve clarity in philosophy, and analytic philosophy has hardly monopolised all of them. Nor is it clear that the procedures of analytic philosophy are invariably designed to aim for – let alone achieve – clarity.

Revisionism and scepticism

After this brief survey of attempts to specify the natures of analytic and continental philosophy, the prospects for any such attempt might seem dim. This might incline some to try another tack altogether. One way to go is what we shall call 'revisionism'. Revisionists maintain that one or another characterisation of analytic or continental philosophy captures something central about the tradition in question, and they deal with counterexamples simply by redrawing the boundary between the traditions. Dummett, for example, makes a move of this sort when he expels Gareth Evans from the analytical ranks simply because Evans does not fit Dummett's characterisation of analytic philosophy.

One might be tempted to opt for revisionism for a variety of reasons. But one thing that makes revisionism particularly appealing is that it seems that fairly minor revisions will suffice to make at least some of the proposals we have reviewed work. In particular, if Husserl and Brentano, say, change places with the later Wittgenstein, so that he would count as continental and they as analytic, then the analytic–continental divide will arguably follow the contours of at least some of the distinctions canvassed earlier (e.g. philosophy as science versus philosophy as art).

Dagfinn Føllesdal openly embraces a revisionist account of analytic philosophy. In his eyes, 'what distinguishes [analytic philosophy] is a particular *way of approaching* philosophical problems, in which arguments and justification play a decisive role'. As he admits, this means that it is perfectly possible to 'be an analytic philosopher *and also* a phenomenologist, existentialist, hermeneuticist, Thomist, etc.'.[97] Føllesdal believes this characterisation still places Heidegger and Derrida firmly outside the analytic camp, but he has no problem with the fact that it counts other continentalists, Husserl in particular, as analytic. He also maintains – quite

---

[96] Williams 2006: 203.   [97] Føllesdal 1996: 206.

plausibly – that his characterisation does not exclude anyone commonly regarded as a paradigmatically analytical philosopher.

A different proposal can be extracted from remarks made by Hao Wang. Wang suggests that one can understand 'analytic philosophy' in both a broad and a narrow sense. The advantage of opting for the narrow sense, which Wang also refers to as 'analytic empiricism', is that it is 'more sharply defined'. Since it is characteristic of 'analytic empiricism' that it is, as Wang says, 'science-centered', Wittgenstein must be excluded from analytic philosophy in this narrow sense. For, as Wang writes, 'Unlike Russell, Carnap, and Quine, Wittgenstein … is art centered rather than science centered and seems to have a different underlying motive for his study of philosophy'.[98] Although Wang does not actually endorse the identification of analytic philosophy with analytic empiricism, and although it is questionable whether Wittgenstein can be positively described as 'art centred', his analysis at least suggests the possibility of a revision that would exclude Wittgenstein from the analytic movement and thereby give a 'more sharply defined' conception of analytic philosophy. Yet, arguably, neither Moore nor the ordinary language philosophers were 'science centred' in any obvious way, so Wang's proposal does seem to involve a rather radical redrawing of the boundaries.

Attempts to redraw the boundaries of continental philosophy in such a way as to exclude classical figures normally regarded as continental are exceedingly rare. Probably one important reason for this is that the main candidate for expulsion – Husserl – has played such a central role within the development of continental philosophy that excluding him would rid the continental tradition of one of its most important founding fathers. The list of people influenced by, and who have written extensively on, Husserl's phenomenology would have to include Heidegger, Sartre, Merleau-Ponty, Levinas, Derrida and Ricoeur. Even Gadamer has written essays on Husserl, and Adorno devoted an entire book to criticising Husserl's phenomenology.

A more common reaction from continental philosophers to the difficulties involved in attempting to articulate the differences between the traditions is *scepticism* about the divide as such. Such scepticism may be motivated by a variety of considerations. Some phenomenologists may

---

[98] Wang 1985: xi, 22, 75.

regard the postmodernist and deconstructivist movements with little sympathy, and they may feel they have more in common with certain analytic philosophers of mind than with their fellow continentalists. Simon Glendinning repudiates the idea of a continental tradition for a different reason. In his view, the so-called continental tradition is a fiction that analytic philosophers have conjured up. It functions simply as a term of exclusion, collecting the sorts of philosophy analytic philosophers think are inherently suspect and unworthy of serious consideration. Continental philosophy 'is not only *What we do not do*, but *What ought not to be done* if one wants to think seriously within the central channels of the Western philosophical tradition'. The way certain analytic philosophers, like Quinton and Smart, for example, dismiss the whole continental tradition as consisting of utter 'bosh' suggests that, for them, 'continental philosopher' simply functions as the current name of the old arch-enemy of philosophy, to whom we shall return in Chapter 7: the Sophist. Although Glendinning does not reject the idea of a distinctive analytic tradition, he thinks the notion of an analytic–continental divide is philosophically bankrupt because in reality, 'There is no such thing as the tradition of Continental philosophy'.[99]

One might feel that some revisionist proposals – Føllesdal's perhaps in particular – home in on important differences within twentieth-century and contemporary philosophy that may give essentialist views a new lease of life. But if so, this is bad news for defenders of the usual clichés about the analytic–continental divide. For those clichés were supposed to be valid for the common extensions of the terms 'analytic' and 'continental'. And if one accepts Føllesdal's redrawing of the map, then there is no good reason not to admit Brentano and Husserl – and arguably Merleau-Ponty and Sartre – into the analytic ranks. The question we examined in the previous sections was whether there were any fundamental differences between the philosophical thinkers and works we all commonly take as analytic and those we all commonly take as continental. To embrace revisionism is to answer that question in the negative.

Turning to Glendinning's scepticism, one might wonder whether it does not overlook at least two things. Previously in this chapter, we remarked that attempts to redefine continental philosophy in such a way

---

[99] Glendinning 2006: 11, 13.

as to exclude Husserl were rare, perhaps in part due to his indisputable status as one of the continental tradition's founding fathers. It seems, then, that regardless of all the differences amongst continental philosophers (and regardless of the fact that Husserl might not himself have liked the tradition his phenomenology helped spawn), there is a tradition here in the sense of certain 'patterns of influence over time'.[100] This is the first point Glendinning seems to overlook. The second point is that 'continental philosophy', irrespective of the term's origins, is not just a pejorative term used by analytic philosophers to designate 'what is beyond the pale philosophically speaking'.[101] It is a label many continental philosophers are quite happy to embrace.[102] So it seems that, despite the many and profound differences between continental philosophers, there is a widespread sentiment of forming some sort of tradition.

If revisionism and scepticism are problematic responses, then it seems we need, in the words of Chase and Reynolds, to chart a course 'between essentialism and deflationism',[103] the latter being the position that there really is no difference between analytic and continental philosophy as we know them – a position explicitly articulated by sceptics and implied by revisionists.

Trails of influence and family resemblances

In addition to putting forward stylistic and methodological traits supposedly characteristic of analytic philosophy, Scott Soames suggests that analytic philosophy is a *historical tradition* in the following sense: 'The work done today in analytic philosophy grows out of the work done yesterday,

---

[100] Chase and Reynolds 2011: 8.   [101] Glendinning 2006: 11.

[102] As Stella Sandford remarks, 'the idea that the phrase "continental philosophy" is primarily a disparaging one fails to acknowledge those who use it otherwise: for example, those who set up courses in "Continental Philosophy" in British university philosophy programmes' (Sandford 2000: 43). Also, it is worth noting that a leading continental journal is called *Continental Philosophy Review*. Glendinning may be right that these are results of the familiar reactionary move of embracing a pejorative label in order to change its meaning. Yet the fact that many philosophers embrace the term 'continental philosophy' shows – *pace* Glendinning – that they think of themselves as forming a philosophical tradition.

[103] Chase and Reynolds 2011: 6.

which in turn can often be traced back to its roots in the analytic philosophers of the early part of the century. Analytic philosophy is a trail of influence'.[104] As suggested in the previous section, continental philosophy seems to be a historical tradition in more or less the same way. Neil Levy may be right to point out that continental philosophers, unlike analytic philosophers, attempt wholesale revolutions where the aim is 'not to build on their predecessors, but to replace them'.[105] Yet this hardly affects the central point: a piece of philosophy can 'grow out of' previous work in more than one way, and it just so happens that (if Levy is right[106]) the primary way for continental philosophies to grow out of previous philosophies is by overthrowing them, whether the target is Descartes, Kant, Hegel, Bergson or Husserl. It is by responding precisely to *Husserl* in this way – and not Frege, Russell or Moore, say – that Heidegger, Levinas and Derrida place their work in the same tradition as Husserl's philosophy.

Perhaps it is even possible to retain the idea that there are real philosophical differences between the two traditions, despite all we have said in the previous sections. Hans-Johann Glock argues extensively that it is futile to attempt to provide necessary and sufficient conditions for analytic philosophy. But that does not mean that he thinks the analytic tradition is merely a trail of influence. Rather, in Glock's view 'analytic philosophy is a tradition held together *both* by ties of mutual influence *and* by family resemblances'.[107] Wittgenstein's idea of 'family resemblances' is that one member of a family may have the characteristic nose and eyes, another the eyes and mouth (but not the nose) and a third the mouth and nose (but not the eyes) – so that there may be no single trait all members of the family possess. In just this way, Glock suggests that the analytic family may be tied together by various traits – some doctrinal, others methodological and yet others stylistic – that criss-cross the analytic family, but where no individual trait must be possessed by all members.

---

[104] Soames 2003: xiii.

[105] Levy 2003: 301.

[106] Not *all* continental philosophers attempt patricide in this way. Merleau-Ponty, for example, quite explicitly builds on, rather than attempts to replace, the work of Husserl and Heidegger. Nor does Levy's model seem to fit the Frankfurt school, whose main thinkers (e.g. Horkheimer, Adorno, Habermas) may have been out to overthrow large parts of previous philosophy, but hardly *each other*.

[107] Glock 2008: 205.

The advantage of understanding analytic philosophy in this way is that some of the features discussed in previous sections may be characteristic of analytic philosophy even if not all analytic philosophers share them. And the same, of course, might be true of continental philosophy. This is, indeed, the conclusion of Chase and Reynolds in their extensive study of the analytic–continental divide. The analytic tradition, they maintain, is characterised by 'varying but overlapping commitments to the linguistic turn, the rejection of metaphysics, the claim that philosophy is continuous with science, a reductive approach to analysis, the employment of formal logic, a focus on argument and a concern for clarity', as well as several other features. The continental family, on the other hand, has amongst its distinctive features 'recurrent commitments to transcendental reasoning in philosophy, a "temporal turn" that not only affirms our historicity but argues for its philosophical primacy, a wariness of the philosophical value of common sense, the resistance to mechanistic or homuncular explanations (say, in regard to science and philosophy of mind) and anti-theoretical approaches to ethico-political matters'.[108]

We shall not attempt to adjudicate here whether these particular lists of family resemblances are the right ones. What matters for our present purposes is that family resemblance accounts can handle the arguments against essentialism canvassed in previous sections. Even if essentialism is a blind alley, it might still be the case that there are philosophically substantial differences between the two traditions.

Is philosophy one subject?

Where does all of this leave us with regard to the suggestions with which we started out? Is it true that we face two 'incommensurable conceptions of philosophy'? Are continentalists and analytic philosophers working in two different subjects? We end this chapter by suggesting two reasons for thinking that this way of looking at the situation is problematic.

First, even if plausible 'family resemblance' characterisations of the two traditions can be formulated, the preceding discussion has shown that significant overlaps are unavoidable. If 'science oriented', as Glock suggests[109] is one of the characteristic features of analytic philosophy, it is

---

[108] Chase and Reynolds 2011: 7, 254.   [109] Glock 2008: 218.

clearly absent in Wittgenstein's philosophy, yet present in Husserl's phenomenology. Similarly, while many analytic philosophers have taken the 'linguistic turn', it is not clear that Russell and Moore did, nor is it obvious that the majority of contemporary analytic philosophers believe they can only approach their respective topics through an examination of language. On the other hand, it seems evident that continental philosophers such as Gadamer and Derrida *do* take the linguistic turn. The family resemblance account permits us to conceive of continental and analytic philosophy as traditions tied together by more than just trails of influence; but it conceives the borders of the traditions as fluid and porous rather than hard and impermeable. Therefore, it lends no support to the idea of a gulf so wide as to exclude meaningful engagement. Rather, it suggests in fact that there is good reason to resist the notion of some monolithic opposition between two philosophical 'camps'.

Second, and equally important, meaningful engagement is already happening. Increasingly, analytic philosophers of mind and metaphysics seem to take seriously the work of Husserl, Heidegger, Merleau-Ponty and other phenomenologists. In the philosophy of perception, for example, philosophers such as A. D. Smith and Sean D. Kelly are explicit about the ways in which their views and arguments are indebted to phenomenologists, and many others, such as Tim Crane, refer to Husserl and Heidegger alongside analytic forerunners such as Broad and Strawson. As Kelly has recently put it:

> What is notable today ... is the desire to appropriate phenomenology, to forage among its branches for the tastiest fruit; and along with this desire, the belief – or at least a resolute openness to the possibility – that the phenomenological fruit might offer philosophical nourishment.[110]

This is not just a one-way street. Phenomenologists, too, seem to engage increasingly with debates in analytic philosophy of mind.[111] To be sure, this rapprochement is happening between branches of the two traditions that are contiguous to begin with. But where would one expect such mutual engagement to happen first if not precisely in areas where it is clear from the beginning that there are significant points of overlap in

---

[110]   Kelly 2008. See also Crane 2006; Siewert 2011; Smith 2002; Smith and Thomasson 2005.

[111]   See e.g. Gallagher and Zahavi 2008.

terms of topics, doctrines and methods? It would be silly – and ultimately revisionist – to maintain that prospects for genuine analytic–continental engagement should not be judged based on whether one could stage a dialogue between, say, Husserl and Searle on intentionality, but rather on the extent to which something similar could be done with, say, Deleuze and Quine on language. Surely, *any* genuine rapprochement between paradigmatically analytic philosophers and paradigmatically continental philosophers is just that: a genuine rapprochement.

Conclusion

In this chapter, we have examined various attempts to make sense of the idea that there is some fundamental opposition between two philosophical 'camps', labelled 'analytic' and 'continental' philosophy, respectively. We have suggested reasons for handling this notion with care. If our analysis is on the right lines, the most one can say is that there seem to be two partly overlapping but relatively distinct trails of influence, each of which is also associated with a loose set of family resemblances. None of this, however, lends much support to the Dummettian idea of a gulf so wide as to make communication extremely difficult, let alone impossible.

6 Philosophy and the pursuit of truth

Introduction

What sort of results can we expect from the activity of discussion and criticism that typifies philosophy? Philosophy, as we have seen in previous chapters, cannot easily be thought of as the same sort of cumulative discipline as mathematics and the developed sciences. It has not laid down, as yet at least, a body of statements whose truth is widely accepted and upon which other truths can be built. This should lead us to wonder about the status of philosophical claims. On the face of it they look like statements to be assessed for their truth or falsity, to be believed or disbelieved on the basis of the arguments for and against them. But appearances can be deceptive, and perhaps even this natural assumption should be questioned.

Not all statements that look like truth claims need to be interpreted as such. For example, the emotive theory of ethics asserts that moral judgements are not literally true or false because they do not state moral facts but function instead to express and elicit emotions of moral approval or disapproval. A speaker at philosophy conference was once heard to declare that, although few theses in the subject had been firmly established, one that had been was, indeed, the emotive theory of ethics. Since this was, after all, a philosophy conference, the speaker's claim was immediately challenged by members of the audience, some denying the truth of the emotive theory outright, others denying that it was firmly established. No one at the time denied that the emotive theory itself was the sort of thing that could be literally true or false, a fact or not a fact, in the way that this theory denies that moral judgements are, and denies that they are because it can allow no room for moral facts in a world constituted by physical facts. Yet if it is assumed that there are philosophical facts corresponding to true philosophical claims, as the emotive theory was alleged to be, it is, as we have seen, controversial what sort of facts they are. Are they very general scientific facts, facts about the uses of language, facts about the nature of human experience or what? As soon as we suppose that philosophy has a certain sort of fact as its subject matter we encounter the problem of specifying what it is. And then we may wonder if philosophical claims are candidates for truth or falsity at all.

Not all philosophers have wanted to accept the supposition that they are. Wittgenstein began his *Tractatus* with the words, 'The world is all that is the case. The world is the totality of facts, not of things' and ended it 'Whereof we cannot speak, thereof we must be silent'.[1] Among the topics we cannot speak of, strictly speaking, are such general observations about the world as the very ones he starts with himself. For these do not state simply such facts as those the world comprises, but rather attempt to state seemingly much more general facts than any facts within the world (as it happens to exist) could be. They are characteristically philosophical remarks and, as such, Wittgenstein held at this time, are strictly speaking nonsense, since all that sensible language can do is to make statements that the facts of the world render true or false. Philosophical remarks, despite their appearance, say nothing by this criterion. What they do do, Wittgenstein allowed,[2] is show us something about the world, and once we have seen what they show they are to be discarded, like a ladder up which we have climbed, so that there remains no body of philosophy recording facts about its subject matter. Without a factual subject matter the point of philosophy is not to discover truths.

It is important to notice that in the *Tractatus* Wittgenstein held that all philosophical remarks were strictly speaking meaningless, not just the 'metaphysical' ones which the members of the Vienna Circle who followed him believed to be so. These slightly later philosophers struggled to find some place for philosophical claims to be meaningful in virtue of stating some species of fact or, failing that, making recommendations as to how we should construct fact stating discourse. The latter idea shows a glimmer of realisation that there are other ways of being meaningful than stating facts, a thought that the later Wittgenstein developed at length and which motivated the emotive theory of ethics, for example. But what

---

[1] Wittgenstein 1961: 1.1. and 7.

[2] At least according to the standard interpretation, which has, however, been challenged in the last couple of decades (see Crary and Read 2000).

sort of role might philosophical remarks have other than a fact stating one, and what reason might there be for denying them the role of making claims to be assessed for their truth or falsity?

This is the question we address in the present chapter. Philosophers certainly seem to make claims to be assessed for their truth or falsity like any other claims. They typically consider arguments for and against them and present them as the results of such inquiries. But what is their status? For, Wittgenstein's early assertion of their nonsensicality notwithstanding, we do, for the most part, seem to understand them. So, if it were not as reporting some species of fact discoverable by philosophical methods, how could they convey anything intelligible to us? If they are fact stating there is no problem. But if we are reluctant to admit some category of philosophical facts then we need an account of what the role of the subject's claims might be, just as we need an account of what we are understanding when, having picked up a book we assumed to be a factual history, we discover after a little reading that it is a work of fiction, and none the worse for that.

In this chapter we focus on the work of Richard Rorty, the major philosopher within the Anglo-American tradition to question the assumption that philosophical claims are to be assessed as straightforwardly true or false, and to offer alternative suggestions as to how we should understand them. Within this tradition Rorty's views have largely served as a provocation rather than a decisive influence. But many of his ideas may chime with those of continental philosophers, with whom Rorty has increasingly found common ground. Thus, as we may recall from the previous chapter, one of the complaints made by analytic philosophers against continental philosophy is that it does not proceed by argument and justification. Yet, while argument and justification appear to presuppose the potential truth of the claims argued for and justified, to proceed otherwise than by argument and justification, as some continental philosophers seem to do, presupposes no pattern of truth claims to be defended in this way. The statements they make may have a different status; and, if Rorty is right, the statements analytic philosophers make do not necessarily have the status as truth claims that they take them to have either.

Metaphors and the contingency of language

To ask what philosophers have actually been doing, whatever they have taken themselves to have been doing, makes the very large assumption that common features exist here – an assumption about which we have expressed some scepticism. But we can perhaps ask what those we recognise as philosophers now are doing, including those from the past whom we recruit for our present purposes. One suggestion, which derives from the later Wittgenstein, is that philosophers have been presenting 'pictures' of the way the world is, and pictures like this are not candidates for truth and falsity in the same way factual discourse is. 'It is', writes Rorty, 'pictures rather than propositions, metaphors rather than statements, which determine most of our philosophical convictions. The picture which holds traditional philosophy captive is that of the mind as a great mirror, containing various representations – some accurate, some not – and capable of being studied by non-empirical methods'.[3] And Rorty suggests this picture has led philosophers at least since Descartes to suppose that 'Philosophy's central task is to be a general theory of representation, a theory which will divide culture up into the areas which represent reality well, those which represent it less well, and those which do not represent it at all (despite their pretence of doing so)'.[4] But Rorty thinks that philosophy itself, despite its pretensions, does not function to represent reality. And this is partly because it supposedly operates metaphorically.

We need to notice here that Rorty relies on a particular view of metaphor. One could hold that metaphors are in principle paraphraseable into literal statements. But if we understand them thus then to say that philosophers have been presenting metaphorical descriptions of the world does not contrast them with true or false representations. Rorty, however, takes a view of metaphor borrowed from Donald Davidson in which 'a metaphor is a voice from outside logical space, rather than an empirical filling up of that space'.[5] It does not contribute something true or false, but gets us to see things in a particular striking way. Metaphorical statements do not have cognitive content in the sense of being believed or disbelieved. Rather we accept them as apt or reject them as inapt.

The image of the mind as a mirror is, says Rorty, 'a picture which literate men found presupposed in every page they read',[6] at least since Descartes. It is, then, a hidden metaphor involved in the way philosophical issues have been addressed, by, for example, the way that ideas in the mind have been thought of as copies of things outside, which can be

[3] Rorty 1979: 12.   [4] Ibid.: 3.
[5] Rorty 1991b: 13.   [6] Rorty 1979: 42–3.

directly inspected from within. Rorty, like Wittgenstein, thinks such hidden metaphors hold us captive and need to be exposed to liberate us. But we need to ask in more general terms what reason Rorty has for denying that philosophy functions to represent reality propositionally.

One difficulty in answering this question is that Rorty advances some very general philosophical claims from which his specific conclusions about philosophy are intended to follow. While this procedure is quite general and unobjectionable, in philosophy we should attempt to limit the scope of the premises from which one draws one's conclusions as much as possible so as to secure the widest obtainable assent to them. We shall try, then, to identify the theses from which Rorty draws his metaphilosophical conclusions in descending order of generality. The first thesis to mention is Rorty's pragmatist theory of truth. Truth is not to be thought of, he claims, as correspondence to fact but rather as what is 'good to steer by',[7] as his hero John Dewey puts it. As such it is not the goal of our inquiry, something beyond whatever justification we may seek for our beliefs, since such a justification is all that we can in practice achieve. It follows from this that the traditional conception of philosophy as seeking after truth as correspondence to fact has to be abandoned. But what makes this line of thought less compelling is that it applies equally to science as to philosophy. Yet we may be much less happy to question whether science aims at the discovery of facts rather than simply being 'in the business of controlling and predicting things',[8] as Rorty claims. In any case, whatever account we give of science we will, unless we take the view that philosophy makes a contribution to it, be inclined to stress the differences between them. And this, as we have seen, may lead us to notice that while talk of facts is quite natural in science it has little purchase in philosophy, suggesting that the lines of business they are in are different.

It is worth pointing out, however, that Rorty's version of pragmatism is not the only possible one. All pragmatists deny the correspondence theory of truth with its conception of facts as parcelled up independently of human conceptualisation and awaiting representation by us. But arguably they do not need to abandon, as Rorty does, any notion of truth over and above what we are currently prepared to endorse as useful. The pragmatist Charles Saunders Peirce viewed truth instead as what would be agreed

---

[7] See Rorty 1996: 7-8.   [8] Rorty 1995: 32.

on at the ideal limit of inquiry; that is, as what 'would forever meet the challenges of reasons, argument and evidence'.[9] This gives us a notion of what beliefs should aim at other than representing reality, and, on the face of it, one well suited to fit the activity of philosophy.

A second thesis, less controversial than his account of truth, is Rorty's claim that there is no justification of beliefs outside of particular social practices of accepting and rejecting claims. There is nothing which 'compels the mind to believe as soon as it is unveiled',[10] as rationalists thought necessary truths do or empiricists the raw data of experience. Here Rorty appeals to Quine's attack on the analytic–synthetic distinction and to Wilfrid Sellars's exposure of the 'myth of the given' – the view that experience can justify beliefs independently of such social practices as a particular language to describe it in. Yet here we may wonder whether Rorty has established the strong conclusion he draws from the social character of justification, namely that philosophers cannot establish universal timeless truths. After all, this does seem to be what science does. Rorty, however, would question this assumption about science, pointing to the incidence of scientific revolutions which render previous science outdated. 'It is not clear', he says, 'what philosophical standpoint could show that revolutionary change in science had come to an end'.[11] Yet for all that, science is progressive in a way philosophy is not, as Rorty clearly accepts in view of his frequent strictures on attempting to practise philosophy on the model of a science. Why should the way in which all justification is socially mediated have the consequences for philosophy that it does? Is it just because science is a younger and more orderly discipline than philosophy?

A more promising suggestion arises from a third thesis of Rorty's, closely related to the second, his claim of 'the contingency of language'. This is the view that the languages, or vocabularies as Rorty sometimes calls them, which provide the criteria of justification for individual claims are subject to change which cannot itself be rationally justifiable, since that would require, per impossibile, criteria outside of any language. Our language changes, then, not because we have reasons for changing it, but, Rorty says in pragmatist vein, by analogy with 'the invention of new tools to take the place of old tools'. Rorty sees at least some philosophy – what he

---

[9] Misak 2000: 49.   [10] Rorty 1979: 163.   [11] Ibid.: 285.

calls 'interesting philosophy'[12] – as itself 'a contest between an entrenched vocabulary which has become a nuisance and a half-formed new vocabulary which vaguely promises great things'.[13] And from this we can see why he thinks that we should not expect philosophy to lay down timelessly valid results. It could do so only if its vocabulary did not and had no need to change. But evidently it has changed and so presumably needed to change as old vocabularies became less useful tools for picturing the world than new ones.

We may feel dissatisfied with this line of thought, suspecting that Rorty has somehow begged the question of whether philosophy could ever deliver results which represent the way the world is once and for all just by painting an alternative picture of the subject. Yet Rorty could, given his contingency thesis, readily accept this, observing that he can do nothing either from within or from without the representationalist framework to dislodge it. What would be required from within would be an argument to the conclusion that there are no timeless philosophical truths, which if true is, in that framework, timelessly true so that it contradicts itself. From within a new framework new criteria of acceptance could be invoked that would be rejected from within the old one. The representationalist is likely to be unimpressed by the claim that he depends on a historically specific picture whose time has passed without an argument that the picture produces inaccurate representations, which the anti-representationalist clearly will not provide. All Rorty can do, it seems, is offer a new picture which, if we are dissatisfied with the old mirror of nature one, may attract us.

However it might not attract us as much as Rorty would wish if we found his account of linguistic change uncompelling. For arguably language changes, not in the revolutionary way Rorty supposes, but simply in the course of its use. As Robert Brandom writes, '*applying* conceptual norms and *transforming* them are two sides of the same coin' because nothing determines what new applications can be made. Thus Brandom concludes in opposition to Rorty, 'To use a vocabulary is to change it. This is what distinguishes vocabularies from other tools'.[14] Consider as a possible example the way our ordinary psychological attributions have changed under the influence of the Freudian conception of the unconscious. Different criteria

---

[12] Rorty 1989: 12.   [13] Ibid.: 9.
[14] Brandom 2000b: 177.

for desire and so on have come to be accepted. But such changes have been gradual and unremarked so that no clean break between the old and the new vocabulary can be discerned.

One consequence of this would be to undermine Rorty's sharp distinction between the argumentation that takes place within a vocabulary and the redescription a new vocabulary promises. However, Rorty does have some reason for insisting on the more discontinuous story of philosophy he tells. Indeed we have already observed it in his claim that 'it is pictures rather than propositions, metaphors rather than statements, which determine most of our philosophical convictions'.[15] If this is so then the relevant changes in the subject are like changes in the tools we use, for the introduction of a new metaphor does do something that could not have been done before, getting us to see things in a light we would not otherwise have been able to see them in. John Wisdom gives the example of a woman trying on a hat and not knowing quite what is wrong with it until her friend says, 'My dear, it's the Taj Mahal'.[16] Similarly, Rorty believes, metaphors like that of the mind as a mirror changed the way philosophers thought of the world when they were introduced, and, indeed, changed the way they thought of their task as philosophers. Much would seem to depend, then, on whether Rorty is right in the historical story he tells which depends on such alleged changes, and this is highly controversial. Rorty himself, however, is more concerned to offer a striking narrative than a dry history; this again is a literary device designed to get us to see things in a new light.

Historicism

Meanwhile we need to draw out further consequences of Rorty's contingency of language thesis. From the claim that, because always subject to change, no vocabulary can be regarded as closer to reality than any other, Rorty infers that what philosophy is really offering is, as Hegel puts it, 'its time held in thought'.[17] Without a universal and timeless application as representations of reality, philosophical remarks have a point only in the time in which they are uttered (which may, arguably, include the recycling of much older philosophical thoughts). We must, of course, not

---

[15] Rorty 1979: 12.   [16] Wisdom 1953: 248.   [17] Rorty 1999: 11.

misunderstand this to mean that instead of a timeless subject matter philosophy has an historically limited one, for Rorty's anti-representationalism rules this out as well. Nor is it just that philosophical claims are relevant only to a particular time and place – claims about the Christian god, say, only being relevant to a society in which there is general belief. For although these claims can be understood without such beliefs, since someone can imagine what it is like to have them, still he can make no application of them to the world he lives in. And this is very different from their merely having no relevance to his present or predictable concerns. For without the possibility of concerns about sin, salvation and so on which presuppose belief, the claims about God have no point for him.

Rorty's historicist claim is, then, that in thinking of the point of philosophical claims we should consider their relation to the concerns of the time in which they are made. Absent these concerns they may have no point, so that continuing to engage with them may become a purely scholastic exercise. And this is just how Rorty regards the current state of analytic philosophy. One of the projects of analytic philosophy Rorty criticises is the 'quest for a theory of reference', which he diagnoses as 'a confusion between the hopeless "semantic" quest for a general theory of what people are "really talking about", and the equally hopeless "epistemological" quest for a way of refuting the skeptic and underwriting our claim to be talking about nonfictions'.[18] The quest began with the founders of analytic philosophy, Frege, Moore and Russell. But why, we may ask, were they so concerned with the problem of what it was for a referring expression to refer? Rorty is surely right to detect the influence of scepticism here, and the scepticism in question is, one might suggest, of a specifically late nineteenth- and early twentieth-century kind – a kind arising from the threat to religious belief posed by the rise of science and, in consequence, to people's wider sense of their hold upon reality. To counter this threat, philosophers, like Russell in his logical atomist period, aimed to show how the possibility of thought itself depended on our being directly related to elements of reality, and the whole programme of analysis was in large part motivated by the drive to discover what elements these were.

One might claim, then, that without some such drive the project of analysis would not have had the point it had. For analysis understood itself as

18 Rorty 1979: 293.

solving problems anyone, not just philosophers, might recognise, and in doing so it followed a tradition dating back at least to Descartes. This tradition, and analysis with it, sees these problems as sempiternal. But if we accept Rorty's historicist approach to the subject we shall see such problems not as somehow endlessly recurrent, but dependent upon specific sociohistorical conditions. How they are to be addressed is itself a function of the way these problems are experienced, which will depend on historical circumstances. Thus it is that some problems are experienced as troubling in a way that calls for a definitive solution. The question whether science is compatible with free will, as we saw earlier, concerned the Victorians in just this way, for scientific determinism threatened to rule out the freedom their religious beliefs required. But not all problems have this character. Some can be dealt with otherwise than by being solved, for example by finding a way to live with them. So, as we shall see, Rorty's rejection of analysis envisages that philosophers might adopt a different way of addressing problems in the future.

It is perfectly possible to take issue with Rorty's historicism by arguing that philosophy does confront perennial problems. Consider, for example, scepticism, which Stanley Cavell sees as 'the central secular place in which the human wish to deny the condition of human existence is expressed'. It arises from our necessary ability to reject our criteria for the application of words and to seek to speak 'outside language games', thereby repudiating the 'attunement with one another' these require. Scepticism is thus not 'merely a function of having set the sights of knowledge too high',[19] but the self-defeating desire of speakers to assert themselves which gives rise to that, and which thus involves the persistent possibility of an unhappy relation to the world. Rorty, by contrast, sees the scepticism philosophers have confronted since Descartes' introduction of a 'veil-of-ideas epistemology' as a new development stemming from 'a crisis of confidence in established institutions'[20] in the seventeenth century. But it is not clear how we are to choose between these stories.

Rorty's historicist conception of philosophy has consequences for what is to count as the justification of a particular philosophical thesis, which is, he maintains, to be understood only in terms of the specific cultural context in which it is advanced. He provocatively terms this view

[19] Cavell 1988: 5, 48, 147, 139.   [20] Rorty 1979: 113, 139.

'ethnocentrism'. Now if philosophical justification is context dependent in this way, then a powerfully influential view of what philosophy should aim at must be defective, namely that it should seek the foundations of knowledge. For the whole idea of this enterprise is to find a justification that transcends any specific context in which particular beliefs need to be justified. All we can do, Rorty thinks, is to give grounds for specific knowledge claims if these are challenged. Which may be challenged and what counts as a response will depend on the particular cultural context in which one finds oneself. Similarly Rorty attacks philosophers who 'speak as though political institutions were no better than their philosophical foundations', finding these foundations in accounts of human nature. In the absence of such universally valid justifications, all we can do to argue for particular institutions is, for example, to produce the grounds which within our own culture favour liberal democracy over other systems. 'When the two come into conflict', Rorty writes, 'democracy takes precedence over philosophy'. So we do not need a philosophical account to 'offer liberal social theory a *basis*',[21] though if one wants a suitable picture it can be provided. But because an attachment to democracy comes first in one's culture this is a superfluous add-on which cannot challenge it.

This may seem to lead us straight into relativism, for it may seem as if there is nothing to choose between, for instance, different sorts of political institution if each is justified within its own cultural context. This, Rorty replies, is a confusion, for the absence of some overarching standard of justification does not imply that we cannot criticise other institutions than our own. We do so in the only way we can, from within our own cultural context. And this is possible even if our reasons are not available to those within the different cultural context in which that other institution is regarded as justified. 'There is no truth in relativism, writes Rorty, 'but this much truth in ethnocentrism: we cannot justify our beliefs (in physics, ethics, or any other area) to everybody, but only those whose beliefs overlap ours to some appropriate extent'.[22]

Not everyone will be satisfied with this position, which seems to rule out thinking in terms of progress towards better beliefs or institutions. Rorty replies that we should switch from 'progress towards a *focus imaginarius* to improvement on the historical past. This amounts to switching from

---

[21] Rorty 1991a: 201, 178, 192.   [22] Ibid.: 30.

pride in being closer to Reality to pride in being further from cavemen'.[23] 'But how might we know that what seems better *is* better?' asks Hilary Putnam, continuing rhetorically that 'it could happen that a neofascist tendency wins out, and people cope better in the sense that *it comes to seem to them that they are coping better by dealing savagely with those terrible Jews, foreigners, and communists*'.[24] To counter this sort of response it is important for Rorty to resist any tendency to regard cultures as closed and to emphasise the possibilities of innovation and change within them. Then he can hold that we could in principle try to persuade the neofascists that they labour under an illusion without implying the existence of some neutral framework of justification. And if the neofascists are persuaded then progress will have been made by the only standards *we* have of progress. But it remains an open question whether this will satisfy the anti-relativist.

We can conclude our overview of Rorty's arguments against the traditional view of philosophy as representational, in the sense that its results are propositions to be somehow compared with reality or some segment of it – philosophy's subject matter – and are thereby true or false. More specific views of philosophy, as foundational or transcendental (in the sense of setting out the conditions of possibility of thought, etc.), as dealing with meanings rather than empirical truths or whatever, are all to be rejected for this reason. Rorty's arguments, as we have seen, are broadly of two kinds. One sort is ad hominem, turning the findings of analytic philosophers like Quine against analytic practice itself and the tradition that leads up to it. The other sort exemplifies Rorty's declaration that 'conforming to my own precepts, I am not going to offer arguments against the vocabulary I want to replace. Instead, I am going to try to make the vocabulary I favour look attractive'.[25] Thus we are meant to see his metaphilosophical descriptions as more compelling than the ones philosophers have standardly employed to characterise their own intended practice. Whether we will may largely depend on the degree of our own dissatisfaction with that practice, on whether we continue to find it a useful thing to be doing, and if this is the case Rorty will regard himself as, to this extent at least, justified. He will consider himself justified because he thinks that in any case purely pragmatic concerns will guide our choice, and that is grist for his mill.

[23] Rorty 1997: 175.   [24] Putnam 1997: 23–4.   [25] Rorty 1989: 9.

Philosophy as poetry

This brings us to the question of what Rorty recommends that our philosophical practice ought to be. We may best approach this by looking first at how he sees the history of the subject. Rorty sets philosophy within a history of people's search for what he calls 'redemptive truth' – 'a set of beliefs which would end, once and for all, the process of reflection on what to do with ourselves'. It is, he says, a need that first religion and later philosophy, as 'a set of beliefs which represent things in the way they really are', have sought to satisfy. But, he claims, 'since Hegel's time, the intellectuals have been losing faith in philosophy, in the idea that redemption can come in the form of true beliefs'. Instead, they have turned to literary culture, which replaces the 'bad questions' of philosophy with 'the sensible question, "Does anybody have any new ideas about what we human beings might make of ourselves?"' And this is progress, Rorty claims, because it is 'a process of gradually increasing self-reliance'.[26] Philosophy, as traditionally practised, is a 'transitional genre',[27] and what is needed is recognition of it as now part of literary culture in which 'a genius does something new and interesting and persuasive, and his or her admirers begin to form a school or movement'.[28] Its pretensions to being like a science should therefore be abandoned.

Within philosophy Rorty discerns two major traditions. One leads to analytic philosophy via Berkeley, Hume, Mill and Frege, ignoring Hegel, Nietzsche and Heidegger. The other, what we have earlier described as continental philosophy, models itself on these last authors, among others. But Rorty prefers to call the latter 'conversational philosophy'[29] in which trying something different replaces trying to get something right, and this is a somewhat different category from the continental.[30] This sort of philosophy is what Rorty earlier characterised as 'edifying' by contrast with

---

[26] Rorty 2000a: 2, 4, 5, 10.   [27] Rorty 2004.
[28] Rorty 1982: 218.   [29] Rorty 2007: 120.
[30] It is not obvious that many continental philosophers would like their work included under Rorty's heading of 'conversational philosophy'. As pointed out in an earlier chapter, Derrida arguably is 'trying to get something right' (see Plant 2012). Note also how Deleuze and Guattari poke fun at 'the Western democratic, popular conception of philosophy as providing pleasant or aggressive dinner conversations at Mr. Rorty's' (1994: 144).

mainstream 'systematic' philosophy. Dewey, Wittgenstein and Heidegger 'make it as difficult as possible to take their thought as expressing views on traditional philosophical problems, or as making constructive proposals for philosophy as a cooperative and progressive discipline'. Thus while the mainstream philosopher aims for something permanent, as science does, edifying philosophers 'destroy for the sake of their own generation'. They are, then, aiming at 'continuing a conversation rather than discovering truth'; and this, Rorty avers, is 'a sufficient aim of philosophy' because it sees 'human beings as generators of new descriptions rather than as beings one hopes to be able to describe accurately'.[31] For in Rorty's view 'the only thing that can displace an intellectual world is another intellectual world – a new alternative, rather than an argument against an old alternative'.[32]

How is one to respond to these recommendations regarding the future of philosophy, which, in Rorty's case, have led increasingly to an interest in figures who are literally continental, like Foucault and Derrida? One difficulty is that philosophers who adopt the 'Hegelian outlook ... tend to see philosophy as making progress by imaginative leaps, performed by individuals of genius, rather than by teamwork'.[33] But the complaint often levelled against Derrida, Foucault and so on concerns 'the pure and simple refusal of philosophical dialogue with which they regularly oppose potential contentions'.[34] If there is even a grain of truth in such claims, then it is hard to see what 'conversation' might consist of in these circumstances. It is not enough for Rorty to comment that 'the effect of taking science as the model which philosophy should imitate has produced, among the analytic philosophers, a civilised and tolerant community'.[35] Since he rejects this model he needs to show how an alternative one, practising philosophy in the way he recommends, can support the kind of community in which conversation is possible. How, if it is not to involve 'arguments against an old alternative' is conversation to take place in a manner that does not consist only of bald assertions and counter-assertions? Not, of course, that this is the way Rorty himself conducts discussion, engaging, in fact, in what often look remarkably like arguments against the views he rejects, contrary to his own precepts.

[31] Rorty 1979: 366, 368, 369, 378.
[32] Rorty 1991b: 121.   [33] Rorty 2003: 25–6.
[34] Bouveresse 2000: 143–4.   [35] Rorty 2000b: 147.

Rorty often sees the sort of philosophy he favours as breaking with Plato's condemnation of poets as against philosophers. Wittgenstein and Heidegger, he says, tried 'to work out honourable terms on which philosophy might surrender to poetry'. His reasons are clear; for it is poets pre-eminently who invent new metaphors that change the way we talk, thereby 'changing what we want to do and what we think we are'. And Rorty applies this description to philosophers like Hegel and Donald Davidson too. Very early on he envisaged this as one possible future for philosophy 'after the dissolution of the traditional problems', namely that philosophy should 'cease to be an argumentative discipline, and grow closer to poetry',[36] citing Heidegger's later essays as an example. Elsewhere he regards Heidegger as 'defending the poets against the philosophers'[37] when he writes that 'the business of philosophy is to preserve the *force of the most elemental words* in which Dasein expresses itself'.[38] Rorty sees this as stressing the importance of the actual words we use, in contrast to the traditional philosophical view of the pre-eminence of the ideas the words express, for which metaphors and so on are supposedly dispensable. Yet the elementary words, Rorty comments, 'are not revealers of anything except us … They reveal us because they *made* us'.[39]

At this point, Rorty's antagonism to any pretensions to universality in philosophy, not just to pretensions to universal truth, reveals itself. For Rorty comments that though Heidegger is stressing the importance of words rather than propositions he 'thought he knew some words which had, or should have had, resonance for *everybody* in modern Europe', whereas 'the elementariness of elementary words … is a private and idiosyncratic matter',[40] as authors like Proust realised. But this seems to make conversation even more difficult. For now we seem to have not a conflict of vocabularies, each of which claims the allegiance of all of us, but a mere difference of taste as to which vocabulary suits us individually. Yet is this not just where poets and philosophers do differ in the sort of reception they expect? Poets do not compete with other poets for exclusive appreciation, so that we can, as Rorty clearly does, appreciate both the oracular Yeats and the self-deprecating Philip Larkin, finding room for both in the language we may use in thinking about what we are. Admittedly, literary

[36] Rorty 1989: 26, 20, 34.
[37] Rorty 1991b: 34.   [38] Heidegger 1962: 262.
[39] Rorty 1989: 116.   [40] Ibid.: 118–19.

critics may get us to see some poets as better than others in this regard, and Rorty's references to literary culture sometimes seem to imply that he sees criticism as a model for future philosophy, but still there is a plethora of legitimate possibilities for our private appreciation here. Philosophers, by contrast, do compete for our allegiance, as Rorty's own partialities and advocacies clearly demonstrate. Arguably they do so because of a certain sort of universality they claim. Nothing in Rorty's anti-representationalism seems to rule this out.

Yet Plato's own condemnation of the poets, though founded on several different charges, is in large measure directed at the diversity of possible views of the world which they present, in particular the variety of models for human behaviour they offer. It is not just that this is morally confusing, but that it conceals the fact, as Plato believes, that there is a single story to be told. 'The god would least of all have many shapes', he writes, in criticism of poets who depict gods in a multiplicity of shapes and characters. So if philosophy with its single vision replaces poetry then the city will 'naturally become one, but not many'[41] – a conclusion to which we return shortly. Rorty's advocacy of poetry contra Plato is, then, much more than support for a certain style of philosophising after the demise of 'systematic philosophy'. For turning to poetry for one's ideals is, he suggests, 'a return to polytheism'.[42] And Rorty endorses Nietzsche's realisation that 'Plato's "true world" was just a fable' and 'only poets … can truly appreciate contingency. The rest of us are doomed to remain philosophers, to insist that there is really only … one true description of the human situation.'[43] So Rorty recommends the poets' diverse approaches over the traditional philosopher's unified one – recommends it, one might suggest, rather than asserting that there is no single view of the world to be had, since to assert this would itself be to take up a philosophical position to be argued for in opposition to the Platonic one. And this would be to try, contrary to Rorty's precepts, to get something right rather than to say something different.

Here we may wonder if Rorty's opposition between getting something right and saying something different is not a false dichotomy, because saying something different may be, in certain circumstances, getting something right, even if it is just the right thing to say in these circumstances,

---

[41] Plato 1892: *Republic* 381b, 423d.
[42] Rorty 1998: 22.   [43] Rorty 1989: 27, 28.

not right *sub specie aeternitatis*. This does not mean, as we noted earlier, that philosophers are still saying something about human nature, say, but only what we are like now. It may be that they are introducing a new way of talking, but a way of talking that makes a claim to rightness of a kind that the poet's or the novelist's does not. And this, one might suggest, is because its claim is contestable through philosophical conversation, no parallel for which exists in relation to poems and novels. That no vocabulary is likely to be universally accepted or accepted by people for very long does nothing to show that putting it forward in the way philosophers do is only misguidedly to claim a kind of rightness for it that poets and novelists do not claim. And for there to be a notion of rightness here as a regulatory principle conversation must count as something more than members of a school founded by a genius tracing out the implications of his or her thought, though, as we shall see, it would involve this. It must also involve ways of assessing different geniuses' texts; which is, of course, what Rorty himself does, though without giving an account of how this is actually possible.

The line of criticism we suggest here is related to that put forward by Jürgen Habermas, who accuses Rorty, like Derrida, of 'levelling the genre distinction' – the distinction, that is, between philosophy and literature and hence between logic and rhetoric. Rorty prioritises what Habermas terms 'linguistic world-disclosure' over problem solving, taking the 'anomalies' which trigger the latter 'to represent only symptoms of waning vitality or aging processes' as against 'the result of *deficient* solutions to problems and *invalid* answers'. But, claims Habermas, in philosophy 'the tools of rhetoric are subordinated to the discipline of a *distinct* form of argumentation'.[44] Rorty responds that this simply begs the question against Heidegger and Derrida, and by implication himself, since he regards 'the question of universal validity as irrelevant to their practices'[45] – irrelevant because these practices are directed towards private processes of self-formation rather than towards solving the problems of society publicly.

The possibility of criticism

Rorty's reasons for rejecting the view of philosophy suggested by contrasting it with poetry seem in part to be political ones. In opposition to Plato's

---

[44] Habermas 2006: 29, 32.   [45] Rorty 2006: 50.

vision of a unified city Rorty's liberalism leads him to stress the importance of individuals choosing their own visions of life, or, in his terms,
their own final vocabularies. But because they should be impressed by
the contingency of language they ought to be what Rorty calls 'ironists' –
entertaining irremediable doubts about their own final vocabulary in
the face of others, and not thinking it 'closer to reality than others'. For
ironists 'since there is nothing beyond vocabularies which serves as a criterion of choice between them, criticism is a matter of looking on this picture and on that, not of comparing both pictures with the original', writes
Rorty, calling the process 'dialectic' as against 'argument'.[46] The political
benefits of irony are apparent, for ironists will not want to frustrate others
in their different visions of life, and the liberal programme of possible
private diversity will be secured. But this simply assumes that specifically
philosophical vocabularies are among those that articulate private visions.
And from the lack of an original to compare pictures with it does not follow that 'looking on this picture and on that' is not regulated by any criterion of choice.

   None of this implies that Rorty finds no room for interpersonal agreement. Rorty, like other liberals, draws a sharp distinction between the
private and the public realm. But in the public realm 'the desire for objectivity is … the desire for as much intersubjective agreement as possible, the
desire to extend the reference of "us" as far as we can'. And Rorty finds in
science a model for this 'solidarity' as he calls it. In ethics Rorty believes
there is moral progress 'in the direction of greater human solidarity', and
that this consists not in the 'recognition of a core self' but in the 'ability
to think of people wildly different from ourselves as included in the range
of us',[47] in particular in virtue of their common vulnerability to suffering.
But the sort of agreement there is in science would be out of place and
tend to intolerance in ethics, so that it is not through theory, but rather
through genres like the novel that Rorty sees the extension of solidarity
progressing. There seems little room here, then, for any philosophical support for solidarity. In an ideal liberal society public culture would have
no need of answers to questions like 'Why are you a liberal?' as against
'requests for concrete alternatives and programs' to those already in place
and argumentative exchange about them. Thus 'philosophy has become

---

[46] Rorty 1989: 73, 80, 78.   [47] Rorty 1991a: 23, 39, 214.

more important for the pursuit of private perfection rather than for any social task', Rorty suggests, and it counts as philosophy only because 'it counts philosophers … among its causes and topics',[48] not because it offers a kind of theory.

Rorty sees the work of philosophy after the demise of systematic philosophy as 'transformative' in this way. There are, on the one hand, as we have seen, individual geniuses who effect such transformations by giving an account of 'how things, in the largest sense of the term, hang together, in the largest sense of the term', as Rorty writes, quoting Sellars.[49] They do so by providing new pictures, fresh vocabularies. But not all of us can do this, so what is there for the rest of us to do? One might have expected Rorty to stress with Heidegger the role of preserving such vocabularies, for 'the preservers of a work belong to its createdness with an essentiality equal to that of its creators'.[50] And some have seen the task of criticism in relation to poetry and novels in this light. Rorty, as we saw, regards the formation of schools around geniuses as natural, but he does not relate this to the preservation or, indeed, to the development of the vocabulary they introduce. He sees, instead, the role of ordinary philosophers in the post-systematic era, like that of others in the humanities, as the production of narratives – 'stories about past transformations … connecting many successive transformations in social and individual self-images'.[51] These, Rorty believes, enable further transformations to take place even if they do not effect transformations themselves. This broadly historical role is, then, what Rorty envisages for all but the very best philosophers.

Yet it is far from clear what the criteria for acceptable philosophical narratives are. We have seen something of Rorty's own narrative and, as Christopher Norris dryly remarks, although 'Rorty can readily concede that his is just one story among many, to be picked up, developed or abandoned according to its present and future utility', still for all that, 'it raises a specific set of cultural values – those of bourgeois liberalism – to the status of a wholesale teleology and universal ethics'. This, as Norris goes on, runs counter to the deconstructive project of those like Derrida whom Rorty admires. For they aim to 'undermine the kinds of consoling

---

[48] Rorty 1989: 87, 94.
[49] Rorty 1982: xiv. Cf. Sellars 1991: 1.
[50] Heidegger 1971: 71.   [51] Rorty 1989: xvi.

self-image given back by a dominant cultural tradition'. Norris calls Alasdair
MacIntyre in aid to argue 'that tensions should exist between philosophy
and ideology is … an inherent necessity of rational thought'.[52] Many will
agree with this judgement of the important role of philosophical criticism
and wonder how it can continue to be fulfilled.

Arguably, however, a role for philosophical criticism can be found even
if we jettison the traditional picture of philosophical propositions as true
in virtue of correspondence to a mind-independent reality and adopt
an historicist outlook. Then we may accept that philosophy is what the
Italian philosopher Gianni Vattimo calls 'weak thought' – 'a philosophy
that abandons claims to global and metaphysical visions' in favour of a
'plurality of interpretations' – a position Rorty appears to endorse. Vattimo
applauds Nietzsche's aphorism, 'There are no facts, only interpretations',
adding that this too is an interpretation.[53] All that can be done on this
account is to try to make an interpretation convincing to other members
of one's community at a particular time. Whether or not one agrees with
this anti-representationalist position, at least it must be admitted that this
is at least part of what one is doing in advocating a philosophical view. But
this does not rule out criticism in philosophy any more than in, say, music,
where different interpretations of a piano sonata, say, are allowed, while
some are judged too sentimental, too lacking in feeling or whatever.

Similarly what Vattimo thinks of as the interpretations of our situation
delivered by philosophical works are open to criticism along a variety of
dimensions. One, like the criticism of a sonata rendition, concerns the
work as whole. The picture it paints may, as some have said of Rorty's
own, seem overly optimistic, or, perhaps like Derrida's, too frivolous.
The reaction on which such criticism depends – 'Things aren't really like
that!' – does not, *pace* Rorty, presuppose an unacceptable hypostatisa-
tion of reality. But it does, as in the sonata case, solicit agreement from
others, moving away from a purely private and subjective reaction. And if
we think of philosophical accounts, as Rorty wishes us to, as metaphors,
then it is worth reflecting that this is the way we treat metaphors as well –
as, for example, overblown, crass, feeble, one-sided and so on. There are

[52] Norris 1985: 159, 166.
[53] Zabala 2007: 18. This is of course also Nietzsche's view. As he writes in *Beyond Good and Evil*, 'Granted that this too is only interpretation – and you will be eager enough to raise this objection? – Well, so much the better' (1990: 53).

standards here, albeit imprecise and unspoken ones, and where there are standards there is the possibility of criticism.

Assuming that this applies to philosophical metaphors as to any others, then Rorty's view that some just catch on and others do not fails to allow for the sort of criticism which appears, on the face of it, to be independent of any particular vocabulary which imagery may introduce. It may be that the ultimate test of a metaphor is its success but this does not imply that criticism is redundant. Indeed the fact that it is possible allows for a metaphor catching on while still falling foul of such criticism. Indeed this would go some way to answering the objection made against Rorty that quite rebarbative vocabularies, like those of fascism, may gain widespread currency. For example, its organic picture of nationality, derived from the German Romantic philosopher Herder's claim that 'the nation is a natural growth, like a family'[54] is open to many criticisms: first, that it hovers uneasily between the literal and the metaphorical; second, that its vagueness allows it to be accepted on slender grounds but later to be applied in intolerant ways; third, that the imagery of 'natural growth', with its suggestion of trees (including 'family trees'), is wildly inappropriate to actual nation formations. We do not just let metaphors, similes and so forth ride away without challenge, so what Rorty terms 'redescription' is not immune to a critique.

Yet in the case of philosophy we do not leave criticism of accounts there, with reflection upon their ruling metaphors. We regard a more detailed scrutiny to be required. And much of this criticism is internal in the sense that it seeks to expose lack of support, unclarity or contradiction in the account criticised. Now for this to be possible the account must be in some sense systematic. It must, that is to say, exhibit a certain degree of comprehensiveness and interconnectedness, for it is relations between its parts that exposes it to internal criticism. Now it is not clear that Rorty can deny this, even as he denies the utility of what he calls, with a narrower target in his sights, 'systematic philosophy'. 'Philosophers boast', wrote A. N. Whitehead about some, 'that they uphold no system. They are then prey to the delusive clarities of detached expressions which it is the very purpose of their science to surmount'.[55] For a philosophical view to offer clarity in a way other than by simply producing some striking images in the way a

---

[54] Herder, in Barnard 1969: 324.   [55] Whitehead 1933: 287.

poet might is for it to organise a range of elements of our experience. This is what the mirror of nature trope does and what Rorty's preferred image of 'our minds gradually growing larger and stronger and more interesting by the addition of new options'[56] is intended to do. This is more than its capacity 'to cause tingles'.[57]

Rorty implicitly acknowledges this when he treats 'The earth goes round the sun' as starting life as a metaphor, for this evidently plays an organising role in astronomy, getting us to see the planets differently, as a solar system. His claim is that in performing this systematising function the metaphor's figurative force is lost and this is no doubt true. But this is because it articulates a scientific theory in which questions like 'What is the earth's orbit?' arise and must be answered by observation and measurement, so that a lot of literal statements are seen to support it. Scientific models have this character, becoming, in their scientific application, literally true. Nothing similar happens to philosophical metaphors of the mind, say. For it is precisely as pictures that they continue to exert their grip on us. Rorty seems to confound the deadness of some metaphors, as in a river's 'mouth', with the banality of others, as in a department's 'dead wood'. Metaphors in philosophy become banal without completely dying.

Systematicity in philosophy

Rorty has, one might suggest, an overly narrow view of system which sees it as 'a way of making further redescription unnecessary by finding a way of reducing all *possible* descriptions to one'.[58] Rorty thinks of system in philosophy as aping that in science by setting out fundamental principles which explain specific results. But there is no need to regard a philosophical system in this way, nor to view a desire for system as having this sort of aim. Rather we can think of it as the avoidance of 'detached expressions' by the building of a bigger picture in which the different elements are connected. Indeed if we are to give an account of 'how things hang together' a system of this sort must be constructed. One of the principal motives for this is precisely to counter criticism of parts of the account by invoking connections between them. Systematicity like this arises from the exigencies of philosophical discussion as well as being a pre-condition

---

[56] Rorty 1991a: 14.   [57] Rorty 1989: 152.   [58] Rorty 1991a: 14.

of part of it – the sort that involves internal criticism conducted in one's opponent's own vocabulary with a view to exposing inadequacies in it.

As we have seen, Rorty thinks 'edifying philosophers' who 'destroy for the sake of their own generation' do not go on to effect 'the institutionalization of their own vocabulary' and to offer arguments for their positions. Instead they 'offer satires, parodies, aphorisms' because they do not 'want to put their subject on the secure path of a science'.[59] But this surely betrays the assimilation of all systematisation in philosophy to a scientistic version of it and ignores the possibility of internal criticism. Internal criticism in fact often leads to external criticism of one's opponent's picture as less able to account for the same phenomena. Rorty's image of the mind growing larger and stronger is intended to be preferable to Thomas Nagel's of us climbing out of our own minds in accounting for moral change. But even if it is only a picture or metaphor a philosophical position has to be defended against criticism – why is larger necessarily stronger? – and this would seem to require systematisation and institutionalisation within 'normal' professionalised philosophy, *pace* Rorty. The alternative appears to be not just the end of anything we would want to call philosophy but its replacement by oracular pronouncements that even 'literary culture' would baulk at.

Furthermore the sort of systematicity that philosophy typically involves permits the kind of co-operation that Rorty thinks edifying philosophers reject. For while they may introduce a new vocabulary, in addition to the fact that objections to its application will have to be countered, it will need to be applied to a variety of cases not originally considered. What members of the schools formed around geniuses commonly do is just this kind of systematising and developing work. One has only to think of Wittgensteinian and Heideggerian treatments of new areas. Moreover the fact that their approaches can be extended in this way is rightly regarded as enhancing their plausibility, for even on Rorty's own pragmatist principles this demonstrates an augmentation of their utility.

One might claim, then, that systematisation in this (not necessarily representationalist) sense is a necessary consequence of the activity of criticism and defence of philosophical views where this involves, as usually it does, reliance upon generalisations in support of particular theses. None of this

[59] Rorty 1979: 369.

implies any broad metaphysical ambitions, only a desire for consistency and order in one's thought. It is a result of the fact, as Habermas claims it to be, that 'philosophical conversation cannot but gravitate towards argumentation and justificatory dispute. There is no alternative'.[60] Rorty would jib at such systematisation on at least two grounds. The first is that one contrast with 'edifying' philosophers still holds, namely that they 'destroy for the sake of their own generation'[61] rather than build systems. But we have suggested that the two activities may be mutually dependent rather than in opposition. A second ground springs from Rorty's Nietzschean preference for a plurality of views of the world rather than the single one systematisation seems to presuppose. But the fact that different people are attracted to different views offers an argument that one view will not suffice only on the assumption that their role in self-formation is their primary purpose. If this is so then indeed there cannot be any criterion for judging whether a philosophical view gets us to see the world aright (even if rightness is not conceived as accurate representation). Then philosophical views become simply optional. Yet though it may not be clear what a criterion of philosophical correctness might be, at least we can say it would involve standing up to the test of criticism. For the activity of philosophical discussion presupposes that the views criticised may be incorrect, even if no ultimately correct answer will become available.

Conclusion

One might conclude that Rorty's recommendations for philosophy are not mandatory even if one goes along with both his anti-representationalism and his historicism and with his stress on the role of metaphor and, more generally, the importance of the actual words used to articulate a philosophical position. But this will then lead us back to again ask what is the status of philosophical remarks. It may be suggested that we have a choice between at least three views. The first is the traditional representationalist one. The second is the Rortyean account which sees them as, despite their representational pretensions, in fact little different from other literary productions, a situation that, once recognised, should lead us to adjust our practice accordingly. Then we would have no special need to study

---

[60] Habermas 1986: 309.   [61] Rorty 1979: 369.

philosophical as against other literary works. The third and middle way is to rescue as much as we can of the way philosophy has traditionally been practised as criterial of the subject, without regarding it as a representational discipline.

On this third kind of account philosophical claims will be objective in a fairly strong sense. First, their acceptability or otherwise will not depend on the reactions of particular individuals as they would seem to be on Rorty's account of their use as private consumables. Second, their acceptability will not solely depend on the common reactions of a community of readers, as arguably an artwork's claim to capture some truth about the world does. For such truths, as we may think of them, may be discerned in quite contrary visions. Philosophical views, by contrast, are oppositional, always presenting a story in competition with others as literature does not, so that we do not harvest truths from its contrary visions and leave the matter there. This is not to say that philosophical views are intelligible quite independently of their audience's reactions, for they may be accessible only to those who have the reactions in virtue of which they present initially plausible pictures. And this possibility would contrast the third kind of account we are considering with representationalism.

The oppositional character of philosophy just noted is evidently related to the kind of critical activity it involves, in which attacks on one claim typically foreshadow counter-claims which themselves have to be defended. This brings us, then, to a further feature of the kind of objectivity philosophy arguably possesses, namely that there are agreed procedures for testing its claims, at least to the extent that any procedure practised may itself be subject to criticism along agreed lines of permissible objection, and so on. This feature seemingly applies also to representationalist accounts, in which case it is up to the representationalist to explain how following such procedures of argument and debate might yield accurate representations of the world. In this respect the possible third way is more modest. The criterion of correctness it yields is simply that of standing up to criticism of the relevant sort. But it makes no assumption that there will or could be systematic philosophical views which will stand up to criticism in this way, either ultimately or for a particular time and place. In this respect it assumes no species of philosophical fact to which such views correspond or fail to correspond. For only representationalism would seem to give us a warrant for thinking there could be such invulnerable views. Otherwise we are left with a picture of philosophy as it certainly has so far always been, one of views ever changing in the face of criticism and innovation.

This, we suggest, should be regarded as an encouraging rather than a depressing picture. Only representationalist assumptions should lead to the latter attitude, for then the apparent fact that we fail even to get any closer to an accurate representation of the relevant reality might well cause despondency and a questioning of the methods philosophers employ. Otherwise the fecundity of the philosophical imagination and the resourcefulness of philosophical criticism are surely causes for celebration. If we ask what the point of philosophy is on this picture then one answer is that the its point, like that of other activities such as painting or music, is internal to the subject and will be grasped only by those who have a feel for it – a capacity to appreciate the ebb and flow of philosophical argument, usually through some measure of participation in it. On this account the practice of philosophy just is the activity of such debate. But is the activity really worthwhile, or as worthless as pushpin seems to others, however absorbing to its devotees? This is the question we tackle in the final chapter.

7 What is good philosophy?

Introduction: a question of standards

Whatever philosophy is or ought to be, it is the sort of subject in which there are standards in terms of which good and bad examples can be distinguished. There may be disagreement over exactly what these standards are, but no practitioner of philosophy believes that anything goes, that any philosophical opinion is as good as any other. Even a Polish logician who declared, 'In philosophy notoriously there are no standards' meant only that his own particularly demanding standards were not commonly followed. But other philosophers were as likely to reject his standards as to fail to comply with them. In this situation agreement on what is good and bad philosophy often exists only among a particular group of philosophers working together in the same way.

A striking illustration of this concerns the controversy over the French post-structuralist philosopher Jacques Derrida. In 1992 Derrida's name was put forward for the award of an honorary degree from Cambridge University. Very unusually a number of Cambridge academics objected to the award so that a vote had to be held. In the event the proposal was carried and Derrida was awarded the degree. Meanwhile, however, a letter appeared in *The Times*, signed by Barry Smith and eighteen other philosophers, objecting to the honour on the grounds that 'M. Derrida's work does not meet accepted standards of clarity and rigour'. The letter accuses Derrida of employing 'a written style that defies comprehension'. 'Where coherent assertions are being made at all', the letter continues, 'these are either false or trivial', Derrida's reputation being based on 'little more than semi-intelligible attacks on the values of reason, truth and scholarship'. His influence, the letter asserts, has been 'almost entirely in fields outside philosophy', for example in departments of English literature. But that someone's work is 'taken to be of merit primarily by those working in other disciplines' itself casts doubt on its quality as philosophy.[1] It is not our intention to adjudicate upon the merits of Derrida's work, though we accept the presumption that it is for philosophers to arbitrate upon that. Indeed we shall go on to stress that such judgements are part and parcel of philosophical practice. The subject could not proceed without them. Here, however, we want to place the Derrida controversy within a tradition of debate about philosophical standards – a tradition that starts with Socrates' attack on the Sophists in the fifth century BC. It is, we argue, a debate that is necessary to define and redefine the boundaries of the subject.

The Sophists, such as Gorgias, Protagoras, Hippias and Prodicus, were philosophers in the sense that they expressed views on recognisably philosophical topics. These views were broadly sceptical – Protagoras, as the story goes, faced expulsion from Athens for claiming there was no way of knowing whether the gods existed. He also famously declared that man is the measure of all things, which was taken to mean that no standard of truth exists over and above human opinions – an attack on the value of truth perhaps not dissimilar from that of which Smith and his co-signatories accuse Derrida. Yet it is not Sophists' views but their approach to advocating them which is the principal target of Socrates' attack on the Sophists, and it is in virtue of this approach that he wishes to deny them the title of philosophers, just as Smith and co. come close to denying it to Derrida, though 'he describes himself as a philosopher, and his writings do indeed bear some of the marks of writing in that discipline'.[2]

How the Sophists did in fact operate is a matter of debate, but they were teachers, and in particular teachers of rhetoric – the art of speaking, which was of especial importance in the democratic assemblies and courts of ancient Athens. Yet in Plato's dialogues Socrates characterises the Sophists' use of rhetoric in a way that enables him to represent them, in the words of one commentator, as 'the other of the philosopher, whom philosophy never ceases to expel from its domain'.[3] Socrates accomplishes this by regarding rhetoric as the art of persuasion, so that a Sophist's primary purpose is to persuade people to accept some proposition, not

[1] Smith 1992.   [2] Ibid.   [3] Cassin 2000: 106.

to discover its truth, like the philosopher. Thus in Plato's eponymous dialogue the Sophist is described as 'belonging to the conscious or dissembling section of the art of causing self-contradiction, is an imitator of appearance, and has divided off from the class of phantastic which is a branch of image-making into that further division of creative art, the juggling of words, a creation human, and not divine'.[4]

One might almost have thought Smith had these words in mind when composing the *Times* letter, in which Derrida is accused of 'tricks and gimmicks similar to those of the dadaists' as well as of falsehoods and incoherencies analogous to the Sophists' phantasms and contradictions. Thus the letter can concede Derrida's verbal originality, but 'such originality does not lend credence to the idea that he is a suitable candidate for an honorary degree',[5] as, presumably, a philosopher. Again there is a parallel with the Sophists' 'creative art', for, as Hippias tells Socrates, he always tries 'to say something new'.[6] Furthermore, Derrida's appeal to non-philosophers resembles the Sophists' capacity to 'persuade the multitude', as Gorgias claims to be able to persuade them 'on any subject',[7] including subjects like medicine about which neither he nor they have any knowledge. Indeed, 'it seems that the rhetorician is most effective in persuading people that are ignorant of the subject under debate'.[8] All told, both Derrida and the Sophists are represented as failing to measure up to the standards required of philosophers because they quite deliberately reject them in the pursuit of other objectives than those that count as philosophical ones.

Philosophers and Sophists

There are several ways in which Sophists, as Plato's Socrates sees them, appear to differ from philosophers. One important but rather narrowly focussed one concerns their influence upon those they teach. This can be bad as well as good, since rhetoric itself, unlike philosophy, is not directed at inculcating virtue. While we touch on this aspect of Socrates' views in the final chapter, we shall not discuss it further here. Nor do

---

[4] Plato 1892: *Sophist* 267.   [5] Smith 1992.
[6] Xenophon, quoted in Poulakos 1983: 44.
[7] Plato 1892: *Gorgias* 458.   [8] Santas 2001: 24.

we undertake a scholarly assessment of which features of the Sophists' approach weighed most heavily with Socrates in marking off philosophers from them. Instead we shall set out a number of supposed characteristics of the Sophists which appear to contribute to the picture Socrates wishes to draw. These characteristics contrast with a set of corresponding standards to which philosophers, we suggest, should conform, and which we discuss in turn in the rest of the chapter.

The first characteristic of Sophists we should notice is that they are professional wordsmiths, masters of a 'creative art, the juggling of words'. The charge against them, then, is that they aim for rhetorical effect. This is not just because they sought to persuade, for, as Socrates would have known despite his stress on this purpose, they also aimed to give pleasure, just like the poets he also anathematises as we notice in the next chapter. Neither persuasion nor pleasure giving, however, provide constraints upon the sort of style the Sophists adopt of the sort that are imposed upon philosophers. For by contrast with practitioners of 'the art of image-making' who produce fanciful images, philosophers seek an accurate representation of what they are discussing. The Sophist 'runs away into the darkness of not-being'[9] and as a result there is nothing to restrain him from obscurity of expression if it serves his purpose. What imposes a requirement of clarity upon philosophers is the need to get a 'likeness' of their subject, so that it is no longer concealed – *aletheia*, the Greek word for truth, literally meaning unconcealment. The Socratic view, then, seems to be that everything stylistically inessential to this end should be avoided. Thus one thing that marks Sophists off from philosophers is a recognisable stylistic difference.

The next characteristic to observe is the opportunistic nature of the Sophists' methods of persuasion. They adopt whatever strategy is best calculated to convince an audience. Socrates equally wishes to convince, but he adopts different means, specifically what the Greeks called dialectic – the question and answer technique exemplified in Plato's dialogues. By means of this technique Socrates gets his interlocutor to see something for himself, not just to agree to it because impressed by someone's advocacy. But to see it for himself he must be conducted through a series of logical steps towards it – the process that leads to 'dialectic' acquiring its later meaning.

---

[9] Plato 1892: *Sophist* 254.

It is in the context of such a process that we can speak of rigour or thoroughness in argument, or of the lack of it. Plato contrasts dialectic as used by philosophers with the Sophists' employment of eristic, in which persuasion may be accomplished by specious argument. So the requirement of rigour in philosophy is directly related to its aim of getting someone to see the right answer, and it is to this end that its methods are geared. 'Ordinary men', as Alexander Sesonske observes, 'can … apprehend logical relations between statements and terms. Otherwise the Socratic mission could not have even gotten under way. Hence ordinary men are capable of distinguishing strong and weak in argument'.[10] What the Sophists claimed to be able to do, however, was to make the weak argument defeat the stronger. The methods philosophy employs, by contrast, must be fitted to expose such inversions and to exhibit arguments in a way that does not disguise their weaknesses or exaggerate their strength.

The third contrast Socrates draws between philosophers and Sophists is implied by what we have observed about the first two. It is that the philosopher is a seeker after truth while the Sophist is unconcerned by the merits or otherwise of the case he is advocating. He is a 'dissembler', which is a defect not only intellectual but seemingly also moral. So we can regard the philosopher as displaying, instead, the virtue of integrity. However, it needs to be remembered that the Sophists provided a training designed to equip citizens to speak in the courts and councils of Athens, where the norms applied were scarcely those of philosophical discussion. Here someone may be arraigned or defended, some cause championed or censured, so that partiality or partisanship seem quite in place. It is where such stances are adopted in the context of trying to uncover the truth, as Socrates takes philosophers to do, that they are inappropriate. Or, to put the Socratic point differently, to the extent to which they are admissible, to that extent the activity in which they are employed does not count as philosophy. For to try to get at the right answer to Socratic questions like 'what is justice or virtue?' involves recognising that to have an interest in getting a particular answer or to experience a predilection for one rather than another are obstacles to success in one's attempt. Trying to get the right answer requires adherence to certain standards concerning one's frame of mind and not just one's methods – standards which are the measure of a certain kind of virtue.

[10] Sesonske 1968: 219.

Fourth, and related, we may notice another aspect of Socrates' attitude which allows him to contrast himself with the Sophists. It is what we may call his intellectual modesty, expressed in repeated confessions of ignorance, which inhibit him from unguarded assertions, and in his willingness to be refuted in order to avoid erroneous opinions. Sophists, on the other hand, have intellectual pretensions far exceeding their grasp. As Socrates puts it, 'the rhetorician need not know the truth about things: he has only to discover some way of persuading the ignorant that he has more knowledge than those who know'. And is it not 'a great blessing', asks Gorgias, 'not to have learned the other arts ... and yet to be in no way inferior to the professors of them?'[11] The intellectual modesty Socrates enjoins upon philosophers is, of course, a concomitant of their desire to get things right, whereas the intellectual arrogance of the Sophists reflects their desire to impress. But we can connect intellectual modesty with a kind of self-awareness that contrasts with the Sophists' self-assurance. This sort of self-awareness, one might suggest, gives rise to the philosopher's modesty. For it is not a modesty arising from the desire not to be shown to be wrong, which might be as self-serving as the Sophists' desire to be thought right. Rather it stems from a realisation of the difficulty of getting things right and a consequent willingness to expose one's possible opinions to scrutiny. This requirement of reflectiveness imposes standards distinctive of philosophy, such that nothing should be taken for granted or lie beyond the possibility of criticism and retraction.

Finally in this list of features distinguishing philosophers from Sophists, we come to a characteristic of a philosopher's conclusions which may seem surprising in view of his putative modesty. It is that his conclusions should display commitment, in that the assent of others to them is sincerely sought. Philosophers should, in a word, be serious. The Sophists' theses lack this feature. Sophists cannot be serious. One of their amusements was to marshal arguments – so-called *antilogiai* – in favour both of a thesis and of its contrary. And when they did argue in favour of just one position it was often unclear how this was to be taken, as when Gorgias in his *On Not-Being* argues that nothing exists, which seems to have been a parody rather than aimed at securing assent to its conclusion. Socrates sometimes treats the Sophists' more bizarre claims with wry disdain, asking, in the

---

[11] Plato 1892: *Gorgias* 459.

Euthydemus, why they bother to engage in teaching if, as they assert, there is no such thing as ignorance or falsehood. They themselves, he suggests, cannot be taking their own assertion seriously.

There is, then, a standard of seriousness to which claims should conform in order to count as philosophical. For philosophy is not a game, as the Sophists sometimes treated their pursuits.[12] And for it not to be it is not enough that it is done with the desire to get things right, for this could motivate performance in games like puzzles. There must be the desire to get things right because it matters – because it is the sort of thing one should take seriously. It is no accident that one of the things that exasperates Smith and co. about Derrida are the 'elaborate jokes and puns ("logical phallusies" and the like)' he employs,[13] for these seem to his critics to cast doubt upon his seriousness. Yet seriousness, as is often said, is not solemnity, and Socrates, unlike Smith, is playful, not portentous. What tone one adopts, what literary devices one uses, are matters of style, not reliable guides to one's intellectual seriousness or otherwise. It is to style in philosophy that we now turn.

Philosophical style

There is no single style proper to philosophy, although at different times and places certain styles tend to predominate. This is partly because style and substance are not entirely separable. Berel Lang distinguishes a neutralist model of the relation between form and content in which they are independent of each other from the more plausible interactionist one in which content is partly determined by the form in which it is presented.[14] Thus a writer on stylistics in the early 1970s observes, 'Recent British philosophy has very often been written in a gentlemanly conversational or casual style', and he goes on to ask, 'does this already commit the writers to a standpoint about the seriousness of life and action very different from that in the philosophy of Marx or Aquinas?'[15] If the answer to questions of this sort is 'yes', we can regard criticism of the style a philosopher adopts as a substantive philosophical criticism and not just a stylistic one. For the

---

[12] A complaint which, as we shall see in Chapter 8, Russell levels at the later Wittgenstein for reducing philosophy to 'an idle tea-table amusement' (1959: 217).

[13] Smith 1992.   [14] Lang 1990.   [15] Turner 1973: 190.

criticism that a Marxist, say, might have made of these British philosophers is that they had the wrong standpoint; the style they adopted was inappropriate to the seriousness with which pressing problems of life and action should be treated, and, indeed, with which they had to be treated by those unable to enjoy the gentlemanly existence of Oxford philosophers.

Criticism of philosophical style, then, is criticism internal to the activity of philosophy, and it is part of the to and fro of debate about philosophical claims. The criticism that someone's position is not clearly expressed, for example, is not usually that his position might be satisfactory, but that his literary expression is poor. It is that his position is itself obscure because his words do not express any readily arguable thesis. They may be ambiguous, vague, ill-defined, over-blown and so on. Then the charge of unclarity is, or ought to be, an invitation to rectify such defects, so that some position can be engaged with in argument with a view to determining its merits. For the merits of a position can only be determined under a certain formulation of it. What counts as an adequate formulation depends on the sort of debate within which the position is argued for or criticised. And similarly for the general style in which such formulations are made. Styles are suitable or unsuitable for the sorts of debate in which the theses they characterise figure, though this is not to suggest that there are Chinese walls between different sorts of debate, constructed in terms of the diverse styles in which they are conducted. As we saw when comparing analytic and continental philosophy, apparent stylistic boundaries can usually be crossed with more or less difficulty.

There is a temptation to suppose that some styles of philosophical writing are inherently clearer than others, and the others sometimes just woolly. By this it is usually meant that some are more precise. But the degree of precision required is relative to both the subject matter and the state of the debate. Some areas of philosophy, such as branches of logic, may aspire to the condition of mathematics, in which terms are defined precisely so that formal proofs can be constructed. But in general 'Define your terms!' is, as Peter Geach is alleged to have rudely described it, 'a gambit for idle tosspots'. His point is that a definition of the sort demanded here will be a stipulative one, which indicates how it is intended that a term shall be used for a particular purpose – whether, for example, what counts as the 'population' of a town shall include students, whose homes are elsewhere. What is usually needed in philosophy, however, is not this, but rather an understanding of how a term is actually used. In the case of logic one can define notions like material implication by specifying truth conditions for propositions involving it. But while material implication can stand in for 'if ... then' in chains of reasoning, this notion arguably fails to capture the sense of the informal connective.[16] For example, a false proposition materially implies any proposition whatever, while we would scarcely wish to assert, 'If 2 + 2 = 5 then 2 + 2 = 4' or the like. Precision is gained only at the risk of losing touch with the real life of language, and this is an ever present danger of trying to model philosophical style on the seductive example of mathematics. This, indeed, is an old insight. As already emphasised by Aristotle, 'the same degree of precision is not to be expected in all discussions'. An account should hence aim to achieve 'such clarity as the subject matter allows',[17] not impose upon the latter a degree of precision that doesn't befit it.

Some philosophical subjects seem quite unsuited to such an attempt. Notwithstanding Spinoza's axiomatic presentation of ethics, this area, like many others, resists the sort of exactitude of expression some philosophers hanker after. It does so because the terms of ethics lack it themselves, having senses heavily dependent upon the contexts in which they are used. This is not to say that that philosophical discussion of ethics cannot be technical. Technicalities commonly enter philosophical debates as these develop over time. We noticed how a charge of obscurity needed to be answered by a clearer expression of a position. This may involve the introduction of technical terms for which a stipulative definition is in order just because they are not terms of common speech. The distinction drawn between a claim right and a liberty right, for example, introduces technical terms of this sort in order to carry discussion of rights further and in a more orderly way. Philosophy heavy with such technical terms exemplifies a certain style, one which flows naturally from the narrowing of focus often brought about by the movement of debate. But there is nothing inherently preferable in such a style, too ready an adoption of which can lead philosophers to overlook questionable assumptions made at the outset of their debate.

Philosophy written in the sort of style we have been describing is typically dry and often dull. But dullness is not, so far, a philosophical criticism,

---

[16] For a different way of handling the problem see Grice 1989.
[17] Aristotle 1976: 1094b.

for dullness of expression may hide an interesting thesis. We need, however, to distinguish the use of figurative language, irony and other literary
devices merely to jazz up a philosophical position from cases where these
are essential to it. As a possible example of the former one might take
Gilbert Ryle's characterisation of the dualist's conception of the person as
'the ghost in the machine'.[18] The point of the image is not least to mock
those who take the conception seriously. But a philosopher who adhered to
dualism for religious reasons would reject Ryle's characterisation for this
very reason, claiming that it is a travesty of his thesis, which demands to
be engaged with in less emotive terms. And Ryle can, of course, make his
point without reliance on the objectionable image. There is, nonetheless,
no standard of what the right tone to adopt here is, independent of the
philosophical position one takes up.

However, metaphors, as we have observed in the previous chapter,
often seem essential to the expression of a philosophical view, despite
repeated demands for literalness of expression in philosophy. Quine
attacks Kant's account of analyticity in terms of the containment of the
predicate in the subject as merely metaphorical. And yet, as Ole Martin
Skilleås points out, Quine's own account of sentences thought of as
analytic in terms of their centrality in our web of belief appears to be
similarly metaphorical.[19] Derrida attacks hostility to metaphor on the
grounds that it is itself due to a metaphysical belief – a belief in the existence of a set of concepts appropriate for describing the way the world
is, which an ideal philosophy could lay bare in a vocabulary expressing them.[20] Metaphors would not figure in such a vocabulary since their
meanings are dependent upon those of terms which may not be part of
the preferred vocabulary. There is some plausibility in this argument,
hyperbolically formulated as it is in Derrida's writings. But whether or
not it succeeds it illustrates the general point that there is no standard of
what a philosophical vocabulary should be like independent of a particular philosophical position – a position which would need to be argued for
and not just taken for granted.

Style is, of course, more than just the use of language. It also includes the
literary form in which a philosophical work is cast, such as the dialogues
in which Plato exhibits Socrates' use of the dialectical method. Different

[18] Ryle 1949: 15–16.   [19] Skilleås 2001: 119–23.   [20] Derrida 1982.

philosophers have adopted different forms and again there is no reason to favour one over another, or, at least, none without the justification provided by a specific philosophical view. There is, for instance, no prima facie reason to prefer a form which follows a chain of reasoning through to its conclusion. Such a form does, however, exemplify a type of narrative structure characteristic of philosophy. One way of construing Socrates' criticism of the Sophists is as complaining that their works do not display this structure – namely, the narrative of a quest. In the tale of Jason and the Argonauts, say, the object of their quest is the Golden Fleece. So, with philosophers, the object of their quest is the truth about reality, or some more modest version thereof, which can only be reached through many trials and tribulations viz. the production of arguments and the demolition of counter-arguments. Much philosophical writing exhibits this narrative structure, and it presupposes a view about the aim of philosophy itself, a view that Socrates, for example, held but the Sophists perhaps did not. Much, though perhaps not all. For other philosophers see the subject in different terms and adopt a correspondingly different narrative form. We can see the later Wittgenstein, for instance, as telling a story about the slaying of a monster. In his case the monster is the evil philosophical influences which threaten to ensnare us and destroy our peace of mind, as we see in the final chapter.

There is an interesting difference between the more purely literary narratives on which philosophical forms of quest or monster slaying are modelled and their philosophical instantiations. It is that in the former the trials that the questing hero faces are incidents in the text alone, and any monster to be slain lurks only there. But philosophical works address a reader who will herself test the hero's ingenuity and determination. She may even be the monster he aims to destroy and who will defend herself against his darts. The philosophical writer imagines his readership and to some extent determines it by his choice of style. He tries to anticipate the obstacles she puts in his way and parry her thrusts. Whether he succeeds in his quest or subjugation is in her hands as much as in his. It is a feature of philosophical form, then, that the reader is always a participant in the debate, not just an onlooker. One might suggest, then, that the philosopher should always write in a style that makes him, so to speak, approachable, unlike the Sophists.

Philosophical rigour

Good philosophy does well what philosophy should do, and, as we have seen, exactly what this is is contestable. Doing something well usually requires skill, and skill presupposes a way of doing things properly, which we can rather crudely call a method. Now while the overall methodology of philosophy is open to debate – whether it is, say, a purely a priori discipline or a partly empirical one – what is less controversial is that in the detailed practice of the subject there are methods which can be employed more or less rigorously. How rigorously depends upon the skill and application of the practitioners. 'Even if Frege's exceptional clarity and rigor required innate genius', writes Timothy Williamson, 'after his example they can now be effectively taught'.[21] Frege, suggests Williamson, had 'a little help from his mathematical training', and Williamson's preferred model of the sort of rigour which can be taught is that which is exhibited in mathematics, though he does not appear to explain why this should be so. He is apt to contrast the progress in mathematics which its rigour facilitates with the lack of advances in philosophy supposedly occasioned by its absence: 'the community of participants has not held itself responsible to high enough methodological standards', he writes; for example, 'crucial claims are vaguely stated'.[22] It has to be said, unfortunately, that Williamson's own claim here is not sufficiently explicit to be readily assessable.

Rigour is the strict application of some rule, and in mathematics there are agreed rules to be applied in the construction of proofs and so on. There are at least three ways in which the rules may not be strictly applied. They may not be applied at all, for example when they are broken and invalid moves are made. Or they may not be applied in a manner that shows they have been applied, and this in one of two ways. First, steps such as questionable assumptions on which the truth of the theorem to be proved would depend may be omitted. Second, a mathematician may omit steps linking lines in the proof because it is fairly obvious how these are to be filled in, and this is done solely for economy and readability. In philosophical argument it is seldom possible to aspire to rigour of the mathematical sort, and, correspondingly, lack of rigour may not be

---

[21] Williamson 2007: 286.   [22] Ibid.: 288.

ascribable to any of these categories. Of course philosophical arguments may be fallacious. But that is usually because some informal fallacy has been committed, not because some recognised rule of philosophical reasoning has been breached. Similarly, implicit assumptions may be made which, when exposed, would not be accepted without further argument. But this is not because there is a correct way to set out the argument in which such assumptions are made explicit, as in mathematics. Finally, it is not often the case that intermediate steps in a philosophical argument can all be laid out so that its validity is obvious. There simply seem to be no rules of the sort that exist in mathematics whereby this would be possible, since although there is a language of mathematics there is no comparably well-defined language for philosophy. Some philosophers such as Spinoza have sought to overcome this by defining key notions and adopting an axiomatic method for deducing the relationships between them. But the problem here is, as indicated earlier, that the philosophical interest is usually in the definitions themselves. Failing agreement on these, such as exists in mathematics, philosophy seems unable to aspire to providing the sort of formal systems in which strict rules of reasoning can be applied. Absence of rigour in philosophy consists, we might suggest, in failure to apply informal rules strictly. It does not consist in the absence of strict rules to be applied.

When philosophical work is criticised for lack of rigour the standards being invoked do not need to be thought of as analogous to mathematical ones because the corresponding rules are not, for the most part, analogous to the rules of mathematics. To suppose there cannot be rigour in philosophy unless they are, as Williamson seems to do, cannot be assumed. In philosophy claims are made and reasons are offered for accepting them. But this is not the same thing as providing a proof. This is partly because philosophers cannot anticipate every objection that might be made in the to and fro that characterises the subject – a mode of discussion quite alien to mathematics. Trying 'to remove in advance every conceivable misunderstanding or misinterpretation or objection, including those that would occur only to the malicious or the clinically literal-minded ... is often rather mournfully equated with the boasted clarity and rigour of analytic philosophy', writes Bernard Williams. And he goes on to suggest that this 'can serve as a mimicry of scrupulous scientific procedures'. There is, Williams allows, 'some work in philosophy which quite properly conducts itself as an extension of the natural sciences or mathematics, because that is what it is … But in many other areas, the assimilation is a mistake'.[23]

Instead we can think of rigour in a more Socratic way, as the conscientious use of methods designed to remove or avoid error, just as the dialectic was designed to do by testing people's beliefs. The rules to be applied strictly in this activity are seldom explicitly specifiable ones. They are recognised more in the breach than in the observance. Thus, as we said, an obvious way of failing in rigour is to commit fallacies in one's reasoning to a conclusion. Less obviously, one fails if one does not make it clear to the argument's addressee how she is meant to see the conclusion as derived from one's premises. She has, as we put it earlier, to see it for herself, not just to take it on trust. But this does not imply that there must be some detailed chain of reasoning to be unpacked, since all that needs to be supplied is what is needed to get the argument's addressee to appreciate the intended connection. This is not to say that the argument is therefore sound. But the soundness of arguments in philosophy can seldom be demonstrated by more detailed reasoning. Rather, rigour is manifest in making connections as clear as they are required to be by members of the philosophical community, whose demands may change over time. Yet who else could one envisage maintaining such standards? Standards of performance here, as elsewhere, are laid down by those engaging in the activity. If we set the bar too high, so that whole swathes of philosophy are regarded as lacking in rigour, then the term ceases to be of use in day-to-day philosophical criticism.

Remembering Socrates' attack on the Sophists, there are yet other ways in which philosophical argument may fail to be rigorous, namely those in which the tactics of persuasion adopted do not answer to some standard of rigour because they do not employ a form of reasoning which can be judged to conform or fail to conform to rules. As Sesonske puts it, 'the Sophist cultivates those techniques of distraction, digression, exploitation of ambiguity and emotional appeal that still remain the stock in trade of demagogues'.[24] No doubt such techniques are sometimes utilised in philosophy too. To expose them is to convict their user of failing to employ any philosophical method, not of employing one badly. Here it is tempting to contrast the use of reason, on the one hand, with resort to emotional

---

[23] Williams 2006: 197.   [24] Sesonske 1968: 220.

appeal and so forth on the other. Yet it is hard to give a positive sense to the term 'reason' in this contrast without falling into the overly narrow conception of it which we have suggested is inadequate. In the absence of further analysis there seems no alternative but to fall back on the fact that there is usually agreement on distinguishing a philosophical method of persuasion from emotive deviations from it.

Philosophical reasoning skills can to some extent be taught, not least through the cultivation of a sense of the fallacies and faults in argument to be avoided. But there are no recipes for the production of reasons. Some philosophers content themselves with following through the consequences of clearly stated theses, as in the sort of moral philosophy that applies ethical theories like utilitarianism to particular cases. But evidently this sort of activity by no means exhausts what counts as the production of reasons in philosophy, much of which is less easily distinguishable from the effects of rhetoric than the tempting contrast just mentioned might suggest. When Wittgenstein asks us to try to imagine a stone having sensations, he continues 'How could one so much as get the idea of ascribing a *sensation* to a *thing*? One might as well ascribe it to a number! – And now look at a wriggling fly and at once these difficulties vanish and pain seems able to get a foothold here, where everything was, so to speak, too smooth for it'.[25] Here 'too smooth' gives a reason for not ascribing pain to a stone. Yet what distinguishes this from a purely persuasive gambit in which we are led by the descriptions to feel differently about the stone and the fly?

This is too large a question to address adequately here. Yet arguably it is primarily that we can scrutinise Wittgenstein's statement of a reason further to see what being 'too smooth' really comes to, for as a philosophical statement it invites this scrutiny. To the objection that Wittgenstein's reason as to why we differ in our reactions to the stone and the fly is, to echo Williamson's complaint, 'vaguely stated', we may reply that this is here an advantage: the metaphor of smoothness may open up a new way of exploring the situations in which we would or would not wish to ascribe pain. The line of reasoning the metaphor suggests may or may not, as the phrase goes, prove fertile. By contrast some lines of reasoning, especially those of a routine, consequence-chasing character, may be sterile; they do

[25] Wittgenstein 1958: § 284.

not advance thinking in the subject, which is, after all, the aim of philosophical reasoning.

Philosophical virtues

To make any progress towards satisfying answers to philosophical questions requires, as Socrates saw, a desire to get things right – a desire which
overrides the desire to persuade others to accept one's own opinion or any
other ulterior motive. And this is an aspect of the desire to find an answer
to such questions. David Hume famously attributes the origin of his philosophy to an inclination to investigate its problems which he experiences
when 'tir'd with amusement and company'. 'These sentiments spring up
naturally in my present disposition', he writes, 'and shou'd I endeavour to
banish them, by attaching myself to any other business or diversion, I *feel*
I shou'd be a loser in point of pleasure'.[26] However, in the ordinary course
of life when he is not in this disposition he is reduced to an 'indolent
belief in the general maxims of the world'. Hume seems right to draw
this distinction. There does seem to be a difference between one's need
for practical knowledge in everyday life and the desire for a philosophical
understanding of life and how it should be lived. But not everyone shares
Hume's natural inclination for philosophy. Indeed, Socrates' practice of the
dialectic presupposes that not all do, since his method aims to induce the
desire for understanding as much as to satisfy it. And he aims to induce it
because he takes it to be a virtue to have this desire – this love of wisdom,
enshrined in the etymology of the word 'philosophy'.

There are two aspects to the virtue, or perhaps we should say two virtues combined in it. First, it is commendable to seek understanding rather
than to remain in ignorance. Curiosity is an intellectual virtue. Second, it
is good to try to get things right rather than to tolerate error. Intellectual
integrity which requires this sort of conscientiousness is also a virtue.
Thus someone may have some curiosity about philosophical questions but
lack any conscientious desire to get the answers right. Conversely, another
may regard these questions as puzzles to be solved correctly, but lack the
kind of curiosity involved in finding their subject matter compelling. Both
virtues seem necessary to do philosophy as it should be done.

[26] Hume 1978: 271.

So good philosophy is good, in part, because it displays the exercise of these virtues. We can follow this thought further if we develop an analogy between the right way to do philosophy and right action generally, as the latter is understood by some virtue ethicists. Rosalind Hursthouse, for example, maintains: 'An action is right iff it is what a virtuous agent would characteristically ... do in the circumstances'.[27] We might maintain, then, the right way to do philosophy is the way a practitioner with the intellectual virtues we have indicated would do it. This test should not be expected to deliver a unique solution to the problem of how to do philosophy. Rather, it directs our attention at the intellectual character of a philosopher, as Socrates repeatedly does, so that from the way she pursues an argument, inserts qualifications, considers alternatives and so on we learn what it is to do philosophy in the right way, whatever specific methodology we adopt.

Virtues no less than skills can be acquired, and they are typically acquired through the formation of habits. Just as conscientiousness in the general performance of duties is largely a habit, so too is the intellectual conscientiousness which is a component of philosophical integrity. It can be learned as an aspect of what doing philosophy properly requires. Even the relevant kind of curiosity is arguably a habit of mind, the habit of pursuing certain sorts of intellectual questions rather than, say, solving crossword puzzles. The habits that constitute the virtues the philosopher exercises in her subject shape her intellectual character, and to have this sort of character is, on this account, good in itself. To say this is to side with the so-called virtue-responsibilists against virtue-reliabilists.[28] Virtue-reliabilists argue that what makes something an intellectual virtue is that it is instrumentally valuable because it makes for reliability in reaching the truth. But while this view may be plausible for areas where it is evident when the truth has been attained, the perennial problem of attesting to the truth of philosophical conclusions makes it difficult to see how to apply it to this subject.[29] Virtue-responsibilists, however, hold that

---

[27] Hursthouse 1999.

[28] For virtue-reliabilism see e.g. Sosa 1980, and for virtue-responsibilism, see Code 1987.

[29] It might be argued that the virtues recognised by virtue-reliabilists in the areas where they can be seen to be conducive to delivering truth are general intellectual virtues, which can then be utilised to good effect by philosophers. (We are grateful to an anonymous reader for this suggestion.)

intellectual habits are virtues just because they contribute to an intrinsically valuable character, as we have suggested they do.

We have sketched out an account in which philosophical virtue is a trait of intellectual character, as we may call it. But is it also a trait of moral character, or, to put it differently, is it qua intellectual virtue also moral virtue? Does doing philosophy in the right spirit make one, other things being equal, a better person? This is a question to which we return when discussing the benefits of philosophy in the last chapter. Here, however, it perhaps needs to be said that Socrates' attack on the Sophists as morally deficient seems to link their alleged lack of a love of wisdom much too closely to moral defects of dishonesty and manipulativeness. It is not necessary to charge one's opponent with moral vices to criticise him for perverting the philosophical project. Someone fails to pursue the subject in the right spirit if he retails opinions he suspects of being false, engages in special pleading for a cause he has non-philosophical reasons to support and so on. Such things are specifically philosophical vices if they employ philosophical methods without concern for such goals as disinterestedness and soundness in argument at which philosophy aims. It should not be thought, though, that there is a distinction between the philosophical and the non-philosophical which is somehow fixed outside the subject. As we suggested earlier, there is a boundary-drawing process involved here which constitutes some approaches to the subject as illegitimate because actuated by inappropriate motives. Yet this process is itself carried forward through philosophical debate.

This does not imply that philosophy is a totally self-contained subject. We have already discussed its relation to other subjects, including the view that it is continuous with the sciences, in which case the intellectual virtues exercised in it would be the same as those in the sciences. If philosophy can legitimately have a normative function – a question addressed in our final chapter – then again there may be continuity between philosophical and moral reasoning, with the virtues exercised in the latter applying also to the former. We may cite Socrates' argument in the *Crito* that he should accept death as a possible example. Similarly, political discourse and philosophy may merge into one another, though there is often controversy over whether borderlines have been crossed. Yet whatever stance one takes regarding the relationships involved here, we can still identify, it may be suggested, the end proper to the philosophical aspect of such reasonings. And this is the end of getting things right, whatever other, more pragmatic considerations may bear on the final outcome.

Reflectiveness

The intellectual modesty which distinguishes Socrates from the Sophists is, of course, itself an intellectual virtue – a concomitant of his desire to get things right, which we have identified as a virtue required of a philosopher. One needs to be modest, since the more ambitious, unqualified or unsupported one's claim the less likely it is to escape destructive criticism. For our present purposes, however, we wish to separate out this kind of intellectual modesty from other intellectual virtues and to link it to the distinctively philosophical quality of reflectiveness – the willingness to expose any of one's philosophical moves to scrutiny and the possibility of retraction. It is distinctively philosophical because it is perhaps in philosophy alone that any claim or transition is open to question: none is secure. It is the requirement of reflectiveness consequent upon this feature which gives rise to the intellectual modesty which characterises most good philosophy, leaving aside the intellectual arrogance supposedly allowed to genius.

Socrates famously denies that he possesses wisdom. He compares himself adversely to skilled craftsmen, who are wise in relation to their art. It may not be entirely fanciful to detect a contrast here between a craft like carpentry, in which there are clear and agreed rules for the successful production of wooden objects, and philosophy, where, in the absence of such rules, any move towards a conclusion is open to challenge. In this situation it would be presumptuous to say that one knew how to arrive at the right answer to a philosophical question, and for this reason one could not claim the sort of wisdom carpenters can boast. The vulnerability of one's conclusions to scrutiny and revision is just what requires reflectiveness on the part of the philosopher. On this account, a philosopher's intellectual modesty is not merely a general intellectual virtue. It is a characteristic forced upon her by the nature of the subject. If philosophy had secure foundations and definitive procedures then this specific sort of modesty would not be needed. Or, to put it the other way round, that it is needed shows that such secure bases are absent. The arrogance of philosophical geniuses is often due to their having thought that they had finally found a firm footing, as Wittgenstein did when he wrote the *Tractatus*. But so far this always seems to have been an illusion.

Philosophical reflectiveness displays itself in self-consciousness about what methods to adopt. The dialectic employed by Socrates exemplifies this concern and contrasts with the methodological promiscuity he attributes to the Sophists. This self-consciousness about method is itself a major driver of philosophical change. Conceptual analysis, for instance, has to a large extent been due to reflection upon the way philosophers have handled concepts in their own arguments. The beginnings of this sort of analysis can be traced back to methodologically innocent questioning as to what a philosopher means by his claims, of the kind employed by G. E. Moore. Thus when G. F. Stout asserts, 'Every character which characterizes either a concrete thing or concrete individual is particular and not universal', Moore remarks, 'I confess that I find it extremely difficult to be sure what Professor Stout does mean by those words'. He goes on to ask what Stout means by 'is particular' and how he uses the word 'character'.[30] Moore then undertakes a trawl through the various possible meanings, leading us to realise that if Stout had himself reflected upon what he meant he might not have made his bold assertion in the first place. Moore's technique exhibits a certain species of reflectiveness which Stout's signally fails to display. Stout is not an isolated figure here. Moore was aiming this sort of critique at a whole tradition of philosophising which had grown insufficiently modest in its claims.

Full-blown conceptual analysis emerged in a similar atmosphere of mistrust about bold claims. J. L. Austin's critique of A. J. Ayer's account of perception is a paradigm of this, and underlying the detailed exposure of conceptual misuse is the implicit criticism that Ayer is inattentive to what he is saying in producing the arguments that he does.[31] He is not reflective enough. Here, however, the particular type of reflectiveness required, with its close attention to ordinary usage, was arguably unavailable to Ayer – even assuming his method would have benefitted from it – prior to the initiation of these techniques by Austin, Ryle and others. Another example of a new sort of critique, made possible by methodological developments, is Heidegger's criticism of Descartes' way of describing the world of his experience in terms of spatially extended objects – a way passed

---

[30] Moore 1959: 17.   [31] Austin 1962.

down automatically through generations of subsequent philosophers.[32] Heidegger applies the relatively novel phenomenological method to show that we normally see the world not like this but in terms of things relevant to our activities. Had the method been available to Descartes he would have been able to reflect upon his description and to see its deficiencies. But without it Descartes could not have foreseen a problem here.

Developments of this sort are unpredictable. This is one of the reasons for remaining modest about philosophical claims. However reflective one is about them within the limits of what can currently be expected of someone by way of reflection, it is always possible that these limits will be expanded. While no one can be blamed for failing to foresee the unforeseeable, someone can be blamed for overconfidence in a situation where this is a demonstrably risky attitude. Paradoxically perhaps, over-confidence is an attitude most likely to be adopted precisely when new developments of the kind described have opened up fresh opportunities for criticism. This situation is bound to be exhilarating. But such developments may prove abortive, either succumbing themselves to novel methodological critiques or simply turning out to be dead ends in the onward movement of philosophy.

It may seem that the sort of reflectiveness we have enjoined upon philosophers is really a form of scepticism. In that case Socratic modesty might appear to collapse into corrosive Sophistic doubt about the possibility of getting any worthwhile results at all from philosophical reasoning. Indeed, it has sometimes been hard to keep the Socratic questioning of any claim far enough apart from outright scepticism. As evidence of this it might be mentioned that, within about a century after Plato founded it upon Socratic principles, the Academy came to be dominated by sceptics. It is true that both sceptics and those who adopt the reflective, questioning approach are opposed to the dogmatic assertion of philosophical claims. But it does not follow that they are therefore indistinguishable. Socrates certainly thought he had managed decisively to refute many false views, especially those advanced by Sophists. And we are also entitled to put forward positive claims so long as we do so tentatively and with the necessary qualifications.

The difficulty with scepticism about philosophy, as with its other forms, is that it expects too much of philosophical results. It assumes that unless

---

[32] Heidegger 1962: 91–148.

a claim can be made with complete assurance it cannot be worth making at all. Yet this is a jump that should be challenged. Many of our ordinary judgements are rightly tentative, for example those about people's characters – characters which are often obscure and unstable. Yet character judgements have their place in explaining and assessing people's actions despite their provisional nature. Similarly in philosophy, the provisional status proper to its claims reveals, as we have seen, its lack of unquestionable foundations. Much more argument would be needed to show that its results were therefore worthless. For philosophical results are surely to be judged on the basis of the standards philosophers do actually use for assessing the rigour of the arguments, the strength of the evidence supporting them and so forth. They are not to be judged on the basis of the quite unattainable standards sceptics demand here, as they do in other areas where they threaten to overturn our ordinary cognitive practices.

Seriousness

The last of the features of good philosophy which arise from the contrast with Sophism is what we termed its seriousness. We suggested that the earnestness with which philosophers seek to persuade others to accept their views is due to the fact that they take the issues they have views about to matter, even when these do not seem obviously important issues like the existence of moral duties or of free will. When they do not obviously matter, however, we expect these issues to have some connection, remote though it may be, with those that do. We therefore cannot accept a frivolous response, as the Sophists' *antilogiai* seem to have been. We expect some definite stand on philosophical questions, or, failing that, a reasoned scepticism about the possibility of answers.

The stand we are invited to take must be one we can seriously entertain, even if it takes a lot of argument to get us to do so. It cannot be, so to speak, a mere flight of fancy – something simply weird or intriguing like the supposition that human affairs are influenced by intergalactic visits from telepathic, mind-controlling aliens.[33] Provocative positions are,

---

[33] Though of course such far-fetched scenarios may play other roles in philosophical arguments, for example as possibilities that help establish conclusions about essential properties. Witness, for example, the 'Twin Earth' debates generated by Putnam 1975.

however, the stock in trade of philosophy, designed to disturb unexamined assumptions and to open up alternatives. Paul Churchland, for example, argues that there are no such psychological states as beliefs and desires because the whole of our 'folk theory' in which these concepts figure is false.[34] This so-called eliminativism seems hard to stomach – we should not say 'believe' – but it is nonetheless intended to be taken seriously, though it may have 'seemed to most philosophers to be preposterous'.[35] It is not simply the expression of an idiosyncratic notion about the world as is the supposition about aliens. The proponent of the aliens idea could at best hope that others might come round to it, impressed, perhaps, by the force of his own crazy conviction. The eliminativist philosopher, by contrast, coolly gives reasons for taking things to be as he does, and these are reasons of which people can see the force. He argues, for instance, that people used to believe in witchcraft as an explanatory factor but that the rise of science has led them to reject it. Something similar, he predicts, will happen to folk psychology. It is then up to us to consider this analogy.

Even a seemingly bizarre view like eliminativism must be anchored to our ordinary experiences of the world through the arguments adduced for it. We can call this the requirement of realism for serious philosophy. It is the demand that serious philosophical claims be grounded in reasons most of us can appreciate – in facts we all accept or, if we do not, then this is due to personal eccentricities. Serious philosophy cannot appeal to experiences vouchsafed only to some minority of initiates, to beliefs held only by a clique and so on. This is because, since its issues matter, it must strive for maximum assent, and this will not be forthcoming on the basis of limited appeals. The requirement of realism has sometimes been taken to impose conditions stronger than that we must always appeal to some consensus. It would be a fallacy, however, to argue from the fact that in any argument we must appeal to premises on which there is agreement to the conclusion that there must be a common set of premises on which there is agreement that can be appealed to in any argument whatever. The latter position, which holds that there is a fixed set of such premises, is espoused by some philosophers of common sense. Thomas Reid, for example, seeks to identify 'first principles, which are really the dictates of common sense'. 'To judge of first principles', he writes, 'requires no more than a sound

[34] Churchland 2008.   [35] Cockburn 2001: 59.

mind free from prejudice, and a distinct conception of the question. The learned and the unlearned, the philosopher and the day labourer, are upon a level, and will pass the same judgment, when they are not misled by some bias, or taught to renounce their understanding from some mistaken religious principle'. Reid goes on to observe that 'opinions which contradict first principles … are not only false but absurd',[36] as eliminativism strikes many as being. Yet this is not an argument against it. For while some principles must be kept fixed for any discussion to start, others normally unquestioned can be put up for debate.

None of this is an argument against the philosophy of common sense. It is simply to say that the requirement of realism does not imply it. There is, nonetheless, an affinity between this suggested requirement and commonsense philosophy's presumption that if the outcome of a philosophical debate is to be anchored in reality then we must be able to identify propositions on which there is consensus. Much more is needed than that a group of philosophers should accept these propositions. At any one time and place there is likely to be a purely academic consensus on them. Until Quine and Wittgenstein unsettled it, for example, there was probably an Anglo-American philosophical consensus on the existence of such entities as meanings. We do need the inclusion of Reid's day labourer in the consensus required to ground a philosophical argument. Without a layman's input at some point it is hard to see that philosophical conclusions will matter to more than a merely academic audience. But then without any connection to the concerns of a wider public they would lack the sort of seriousness we have suggested they should possess.

Yet to establish the necessary sort of consensus does not, perhaps, require any special sort of investigation. Arguably the philosopher only needs to doff her academic hat and pull on her day labourer's cap to see what she would agree to in that guise. She does not need to see what fundamental beliefs our opinions and our actions presuppose, as a commonsense philosopher seeking 'first principles' might do. Still less need she worry about what evolutionarily advantageous beliefs she might have inherited from her Pleistocene predecessors, and which, it has been argued, are therefore likely to be true ('while there was no selective pressure … for philosophical ability in the ancestral environment').[37] Unlike the foundations

---

[36] Reid 1969: 607, 604–5, 606.   [37] Boulter 2007: 44.

such investigations aim to uncover, the propositions for which a consensus is obtained for starting a debate may change over time. The realism requirement may be no bar to this, if the reality to which these consensual propositions anchor the arguments grounded on them is reality as it is perceived to be. This perceived reality may change over time, as, for example, the unquestioned religious beliefs of the Middle Ages were shed and scientific ones became mandatory. There are thus some discussions of past philosophy with which we can easily engage and others with which we cannot. The latter satisfied, one might say, the realism requirement as it was then construed, but they no longer do. However, many philosophers would dispute the idea that reality as it is perceived should anchor philosophical discussions and argue rather that reality as it actually is should anchor such discussions, for example as it is revealed by the natural sciences. We take up this matter for discussion elsewhere.

We have suggested that philosophy should be serious in the sense that its results are taken to matter. But this is easily misunderstood. It is often said that worthwhile philosophy should be 'relevant', in the way that moral philosophy might be relevant if it changes people's views about how they ought to behave. This is an idea we look at in the final chapter, but it is not the point we are making here. To say that philosophy matters, in the sense we intend, does not imply that it must be able to change our behaviour. For example, Stanley Cavell considers how we are to respond to scepticism about the existence of material things. He concludes that 'I cannot "live" material object skepticism'. This is because 'there is an alternative to its conclusions that I am bound, as a normal human being, to take'.[38] But this does not imply that it is not important to engage with the sceptic's arguments. To do this matters, Cavell argues, because the sceptic subtly undermines our sense that we can know what reality is like. Scepticism is 'the central secular place in which the human wish to deny the condition of human existence is expressed',[39] and, tempted by this denial, we need to recover our grasp on what he calls the ordinariness of the world. So too it is with much philosophy, we might say, even if it does not affect the way we act in our everyday lives. If we have a sense of its seriousness we cannot avoid responding to it as saying things about the world that matter.

---

[38] Cavell 1979: 448.   [39] Cavell 1988: 5.

Conclusion

In this chapter we proposed that certain standards are used as bound-ary markers between philosophy proper and what may be passed off as philosophy, so that serious violations of these standards disqualify some discourses as philosophy at all. The standards we have itemised are sug-gested by Socrates' critique of the Sophists – a kind of critique which finds contemporary parallels in attempts to demarcate the subject. They are, then, standards broad adherence to which is constitutive of what it is to do philosophy. But they also serve as measures of quality in the subject, less serious failures to live up to them being grounds for adverse criticism and exemplary performance reasons for approval. There are, of course, other such measures. Originality and profundity come to mind as features of very good philosophy. But these do not have the constitutive status of the standards we have discussed, and, furthermore, perfectly good, if not very good, philosophy can be done without them.

8 What good is philosophy?

Introduction

At the end of his *Problems of Philosophy* Bertrand Russell inquires 'what is the value of philosophy and why it ought to be studied'.[1] Surprisingly few philosophers ask these questions, though philosophers frequently find themselves being asked them. In this chapter we suggest possible answers and debate their various merits. For once again these are philosophical questions and, like all philosophical questions, they are open to debate, not least because what it is for some activity to have value and thus to be worthwhile is a quintessentially philosophical question. Obviously it is beyond the scope of this book to provide an answer to that big question. Anyway, to do so would unduly restrict the interest of any account of philosophy's value based upon it, since such an account would then be acceptable only to those who shared the answer given to the big question, which, one can confidently predict, most philosophers would not. In this chapter, then, we try to clarify what we are looking for when we seek a value for philosophy, and we float various conceptions of it, noting their relation to general accounts of value where appropriate.

Yet, since the answers we give to Russell's questions will also depend upon the account we give of the nature of philosophy it may seem as if we need to once more rehearse the possibilities and draw out the supposed value the subject has on each of them. If, for example we take philosophy to be a contribution to science then it will have the value that scientific knowledge has for those who possess it and of the utility of that knowledge for others. Alternatively, however, we might first ask what sort of value the subject could possess and allow our answers to influence our view about

[1] Russell 1998: 89.

its nature. That is to say, we decide what we want from philosophy and let that shape our conception of it. And we decide what we want on the basis of a philosophical consideration of what sort of values we might realise in studying philosophy.

It is certainly not novel to adopt this strategy and make a judgement upon a conception of philosophy on the basis of the value it supposedly has under this conception. Russell himself famously rejected the later Wittgenstein's view of how philosophy ought to be practised because, he said, it would then be 'an idle tea-table amusement' rather than 'serious thinking'. Russell rejects here not just one way of doing philosophy but a conception of it in which 'it is not the world we are trying to understand but only sentences' – a conception which, he thinks, is not carrying on the tradition of 'Philosophers from Thales onwards'. 'If this is all that philosophy has to offer', he continues, 'I cannot think that it is a worthy subject of study'. In fact Russell understands Wittgenstein very imperfectly in these remarks. But they illustrate a certain sort of challenge to a conception of philosophy, namely that it would then lack the value which under another conception it possesses. Understanding the world is 'a grave and important task', while understanding sentences is 'at best, a slight help to lexicographers'. Thus traditional philosophers at least had worthy aspirations, even though they were 'unduly optimistic as regards their own successes'.[2]

Now Russell's assumption that it is worthwhile to try to 'understand the world' in the way philosophers have done has itself been questioned. More famous than Russell's strictures on Wittgenstein is Karl Marx's general objection: 'Philosophers have only interpreted the world. The point, however, is to change it'.[3] Here Marx criticises all previous conceptions of philosophy on the grounds that under them the subject fails to do what is most needed. To answer his objection one must either deny that changing the world for the better is a reasonable demand to make of philosophy or specify a conception under which the demand is being addressed.

At this point it is worth comparing some features of Russell's triviality objection with Marx's uselessness one. Two distinctions should be noted. The first is between what is worthwhile for its own sake, as Russell regards understanding the world to be, and what is worthwhile instrumentally, that is, worthwhile because good consequences like changing the world are

---

[2] Russell 1959: 217, 230.   [3] Marx 1969: 286.

brought about. The second distinction is between two groups of people for whom philosophy might be of value: its students, as on Russell's account, or those beyond them for whom the world should be changed for the better on Marx's. Whether something has greater value because it has value for a greater number of people is itself, of course, a philosophical question, though not one we pursue here. One might just recall, however, that the value of a work of literature is not generally judged on the strength of its readership. Similar considerations may apply to philosophy.

Challenges to philosophy

Let us consider, then, the various challenges to its value philosophy faces. First, what we called the triviality objection has several different forms, all questioning the importance of the subject through comparison, explicit or implicit, with that of others. One form is analogous to Russell's strictures about the later Wittgenstein, namely that its subject matter is of very limited importance. Another initially more plausible view is that its actual results concerning its subject matter are of little significance, because obviously true, obviously false or quite uncertain. That is to say, philosophy yields either no new knowledge or no knowledge at all. And the comparison here is with the sciences or other fact-gathering subjects whose importance is due to their contribution to our understanding of various aspects of the world.

This is not the place to reopen the question discussed in Chapter 6 of whether philosophy does indeed aim at knowledge or whether it might yield results that contribute to understanding in a different way. Yet it is worth asking what criterion of importance is employed here. Some branches of knowledge seem more important than others, as Russell's disparaging reference to lexicography implies. But why? In some circumstances we need to know one sort of thing rather than another for practical reasons. This is to value certain pieces of knowledge instrumentally rather than for their own sake. What could the latter value consist in? Is it that certain bits of knowledge are more fecund than others in the sense that they may generate more knowledge beyond themselves than other bits do, as knowledge of atomic particles, say, may be more productive than knowledge of the life history of butterflies? But butterflies may be more interesting than microscopic bits of matter, so might not knowledge of butterflies be more important, at least for most people? One might multiply competing criteria of importance here, and wonder whether there are any universal criteria. Perhaps it is a feature specific to our culture that the physical sciences take pride of place, and in another the history of the tribe.

In any case the claim that philosophy is a subject of little importance will need to be defended, and defended against philosophers who think otherwise. The criteria of importance involved will need to be specified and defended against rival criteria. Then the critic of philosophy will be drawn into acknowledging that the subject has at least some importance since the activity he is now engaging in is itself philosophical activity. If he claims to be using philosophical discussion simply to show its uselessness and as not to be engaged in it further then we can at least ask why it is of such limited application, and it is hard to see what else he can do but start philosophising again, contrary to his avowed intention. If he can be persuaded that this activity of clarification and criticism is of quite general application then he might even be convinced that it is of considerable importance, contrary to his initial claim. The only alternative open to him seems to be to abandon the task of rationally justifying his judgement, while justifying it proves more difficult and exasperating than he took it to be.

This sort of ad hominem defence against triviality objections is in some ways weak and in other ways strong. It is weak in that it can secure for philosophy only so much value as the objector is forced to concede. In this respect it is analogous to a principle that Daniel Dennett suggests for determining whether a problem within philosophy is trivial or worthwhile, namely asking the question, 'Can anybody outside of academic philosophy be made to *care* whether you're right?'[4] Yet the defence is strong if it can be mounted against a range of objections by questioning the grounds on which they are made and luring the objector into a philosophical debate whose value he cannot entirely deny.

However we must now introduce an important distinction. The triviality objection, as we presented it, was about the products of philosophy – the nature of its results in respect of their subject matter and cognitive status. But the defence offered against it has been of philosophy as a practice. We need to distinguish, then between the value of philosophy as far

---

[4] Dennett 2006: 40.

as its products are concerned and its value as a practice of argument and criticism. Is the defence offered against the triviality objection, then, an *ignoratio elenchi*? Surely not, for philosophy is certainly a practice, whatever its products, so that it is quite reasonable to insist that it should not be judged on the value of its products alone.

Bearing this distinction in mind we can turn briefly to some initial comments on the uselessness objection. Evidently a similar response is available to that made against the triviality objection, namely by asking the objector what test of usefulness he has in mind and how he defends it. If he can be brought to concede that this discussion is a useful one then since it is a philosophical one, the philosopher will observe, he is forced to concede that the practice of philosophy has some use. He may not think it of much use, in which case we can tease out of him some criterion – a utilitarian one, say – by which he makes this comparative judgement. Then, assuming he agrees that utilitarianism is a philosophical product and that it has some effect, presumably by its own lights a beneficent one, he must grant that philosophy can affect the world for the better. In the next section we shall see what sorts of effects the products of philosophy might have and what kind of value might be found in them.

The products of philosophy

If we are to think of the products of philosophy as having value then that seems to be because they either add something worth having or remove something we are better off without. If they replace something we have then they can do both. But leaving aside for the moment the subtractive function, as we shall call it, what could the additive one provide? Traditionally it is, of course, wisdom, of which philosophy is, etymologically, the love. How wisdom is thought of, however, varies hugely. Wisdom is evidently an attribute of value and here the attraction of scientific knowledge as a model is obvious in virtue of its certainty and utility. But, as Robert Nozick observes, 'wisdom is not just knowing fundamental truths, if these are unconnected with the guidance of life or with a perspective on its meaning'.[5] Nozick thinks that wisdom consists in the knowledge or understanding you need to live well. Others, following Aristotle,

---

[5] Nozick 1989: 269.

distinguish such practical wisdom from theoretical wisdom. If a philosopher needed only the latter then he could mess up his life without losing his academic reputation. As we shall see, different philosophers have varied in the importance they attach to locating the value of philosophy in its answers to practical questions as well as to theoretical ones.

Yet there is another tradition which avoids equating the love of wisdom with the accumulation of knowledge or understanding, theoretical or practical, and so avoids locating the value of philosophy in them. Thus Russell maintains that we cannot 'include as part of the value of philosophy any definite set of answers' to the 'fundamental questions' with which it deals. 'The value of philosophy', he continues, 'is, in fact, to be sought largely in its very uncertainty'.[6] Here he is following out the Socratic idea that the lover of wisdom never achieves his goal. Instructing Socrates on the nature of love in Plato's *Symposium*, the goddess Diotima observes that 'neither do the ignorant seek after wisdom', 'nor does any man who is wise', because he already possesses it, so that 'a lover of wisdom is in a mean between the wise and the ignorant',[7] always searching for what he ultimately never finds. On this account the products of philosophy always fall short of what is desired and so are not valued for themselves but as positions to be tested and possibly found wanting. Thus Socrates disavows knowledge of the nature of justice, for example, because, though he can show that other accounts fail, better dialecticians might do the same for his own. The value his own account has is at best provisional and comparative. But without some account there is nothing to carry on the dialectic (literally, in Greek, the conversation), and it is this dialectic which is the expression of a love of wisdom, of wanting to get things right insofar as one can, a virtue we discuss later. The value of such products of philosophy is, then, dependent on the value of the practice, and not freestanding.

Russell, however, attempts to specify an independent value for the products of philosophy, albeit an instrumental one. The uncertainty of its results makes the subject valuable, he believes, because it is 'able to suggest many possibilities which enlarge our thoughts and free us from the tyranny of custom'. Thereby 'it removes the somewhat arrogant dogmatism of those who have never travelled into the region of liberating doubt'. These are psychological benefits conferred by philosophy precisely because

---

[6] Russell 1998: 91.   [7] Plato 1892: *Symposium* 204.

certain possibilities cannot be ruled out, at least at a particular stage in the subject's development, and thus have to be adjusted to. Yet it is to a feature of philosophy's subject matter rather than to its cognitive status to that Russell turns for 'its chief value ... the greatness of the objects which it contemplates'.[8] For, he continues, 'the free intellect will value more the abstract and universal knowledge into which the accidents of private history do not enter, than the knowledge brought by the senses'.[9] Thus he thinks of philosophy as aiming at a comprehensiveness and impersonality which liberates us from our own narrow and troubling concerns. There is a debatable ethical attitude presupposed here which this is not the place to discuss. Nor will the idiosyncratic mystical way in which Russell goes on to develop his theme detain us.

What needs to be noticed about Russell's defence of philosophy, however, is that the consumption of its products is taken to confer moral as well as psychological benefits. In an echo of Aristotle's account of pleasure, Russell holds that 'the enlargement of the Self', as he characterises these benefits, 'is best attained when it is not directly sought. It is obtained when the desire for knowledge is alone operative, by a study which does not in advance wish that its objects should have this or that character, but adapts the Self to the characters it finds in its objects'.[10] This renunciation of what Russell terms 'self-assertion' is a moral improvement achieved only if the products of philosophy are consumed in the appropriate way, so that it is the cultivation of this attitude to which philosophy owes its value, as much as to its products. For both Russell and Socrates the value of philosophy is a value for the individuals who study it rather than, as Russell puts it in a comparison with science, 'because of the effect on mankind in general'.[11] For both philosophers, then, philosophy is an 'improving' study, as science is not.

We suggested earlier that for Socrates the value of philosophy's products is dependent upon that of its practice, the latter being what expresses a love of wisdom. Yet it is worth remarking that many of the notions of which he seeks an account are moral notions and a correct account of them is intended to effect a moral improvement in the person who accepts it. But what in general is the value of such accounts? Socrates' answer

---

[8] All quotes Russell 1998: 91.
[9] Ibid.: 93.   [10] Ibid.: 92.   [11] Ibid.: 89.

would seem to be that their value lies in preventing us from making or acting on claims which reveal a misunderstanding of the concept being investigated. So in the *Gorgias* Socrates aims to persuade Polus that he would in fact rather suffer injustice himself than do it to others despite Polus's disclaimers to the contrary. Socrates does so by unpacking what it is to be just in a way to which Polus can assent because he does actually have an understanding of the concept – an understanding of which he has been reflectively unaware.[12] The point of an account or partial account of a concept like justice for Socrates is, then, subtractive rather than additive. Its value lies in combating false and possibly pernicious beliefs. And the accounts are as piecemeal as are these beliefs, given for particular purposes and thus having a value relative to the achievement of these purposes.

Uses of analysis

We may note here that Socrates uses his accounts of concepts to counter the false beliefs of people who do not necessarily hold them as philosophers. The extra-philosophical application of philosophical analyses is not necessarily subtractive, however. Again we may have analyses as piecemeal as the problems to whose resolution they aim to contribute. But what they are often intended to do is not to remove false beliefs but to answer unanswered questions or to raise and answer new ones. Consider, for instance, the differing accounts of the concept of law offered by H. L. A. Hart and Ronald Dworkin. Hart sees the law as sometimes indeterminate with judges in effect making new law through their decisions in hard cases. Dworkin believes that unless there was a right answer judges would not be deciding in accordance with the law. This difference has consequences. For example, if Hart is right then perhaps it would be reasonable for judges to be elected just as legislators are. But if Dworkin is correct then they must be impartial in their attempts to uncover the law on any issue and should therefore stand outside of electoral politics.[13]

Many cases of what has come to be called applied philosophy take a similar form, in which analyses of concepts throw light on substantive questions and whatever value they have derives from this. This is how

[12] Plato 1892: *Gorgias* 469–79.   [13] See Himma 2002.

to answer Richard Posner, who, in a version of the uselessness objection, declares, '*Something* ought to turn on an answer to the question "What is law?" if the question is to be worth asking by people who could use their time in other socially valuable ways'. Posner goes on to assert, 'Nothing does turn on it'[14] – a conclusion we have just seen reason to doubt. But the value claimed for piecemeal analysis of this sort is not just of the ground-clearing kind, as when someone asserts that 'we cannot study law until we know *what we mean* by "law"'.[15] The response to this is that for most purposes we do know what we mean and that it is only in respect of particular puzzling questions that such unreflective knowledge may not serve, as we have just seen in relation to the question, 'Is the law always determinate?'

Yet it should not be assumed that the only value of analysis lies in its service to other disciplines such as the law. Peter Winch effectively criticises this 'underlabourer conception' of philosophy, whose ambition is, in John Locke's words, 'removing some of the rubbish that lies in the way to knowledge'.[16] It is implausible to suppose that the problems of philosophy are all set for it by other subjects. Thus, Winch claims, 'The motive force for the philosophy of science', for example, 'comes from within philosophy rather than from within science',[17] since it is concerned with what scientific understanding, and understanding generally, is, not just with furthering scientific understanding. The principal value of its results will lie, on this account, on how much they further philosophical understanding. Their value in assisting the practitioners of other subjects to get clear about what they are doing, and thus to do it better, is incidental.

Philosophers like Russell and G. E. Moore deploy their analyses specifically against what they take to be false philosophical views. Russell's analysis of definite descriptions, for instance, has a subtractive role in showing that we do not need to attribute some mysterious sort of being to non-existent items like the tooth fairy in order to talk about them sensibly. But an additive value also accrues if it is thought that the way to understand the world, as philosophy supposedly aims to, is to provide a fairly systematic account of the way the concepts in terms of which we

[14] Posner 1996: vii.   [15] Bix 2003: 542.
[16] Locke 1997: 11 ('The Epistle to the Reader').
[17] Winch 1958: 20.

think of it interrelate. This additive function, so conceived, would, then, be systematic rather than piecemeal. It is what Peter Strawson has in mind when he says that analysis may be pursued for its own sake as 'pure research' rather than as '*ad hoc* therapy'.[18] He later took this to contribute to 'descriptive metaphysics' which delineates 'the actual structure of our thought about the world', and differs from 'what is called … conceptual analysis … only in scope and generality'.[19] On this picture the value of analyses is an independent value, consisting in whatever value such a descriptive metaphysics which consists of them possesses.

But does describing our conceptual scheme really do the same job as traditional metaphysics by providing an understanding of the world or, as Russell claimed against Wittgenstein, does it only describe some general features of our language? Arguably this is a false contrast, since, as Winch puts it, 'The world *is* for us what is presented through … concepts'.[20] Then descriptive metaphysics might have value in providing that kind of understanding. One objection to conceding this value stems from the Nietzschean claim that 'language imposes order on the world … as a kind of violence', to overlook which is to 'mistake an act of power for a revelation of truth'.[21] Then the value of systematic analysis could at best be only a dependent one – dependent upon its contribution to exploring the relationships of power within which we live. But it would take us well beyond our present remit to discuss this controversy.

Meanwhile it is worth comparing the role of analysis in descriptive metaphysics with the use that Frank Jackson finds for it in his 'defence of conceptual analysis'.[22] Jackson believes our ordinary concepts need to be analysed in order to solve what he calls 'the location problem' – the problem of showing how it is that matters described in terms of these concepts can be made true by matters described in terms of the concepts of physical science. For the view of the world with which Jackson starts, the physicalist view, is prior to anything that analysis might reveal. All that analysis achieves is demonstrating how much of our ordinary conceptual equipment can survive if it needs to divide the world up along the same lines as physicalist concepts do. Thus 'free action', for instance, cannot survive as

[18] Strawson 1956: 106.   [19] Strawson 1959: 9.
[20] Winch 1958: 15.   [21] Taylor 1995: 16.
[22] Jackson 1998.

it stands since this concept is incompatible with the determinism required at this level by physicalism. What we must do is either eliminate such concepts or, more conveniently, modify them in ways that allow their continued use. Jackson does not allow that analysis might show that the world is really indeterministic if this is how the analysis of our ordinary unmodified concept of free action requires it to be. Jackson's preferred view of the world is thus prior to his analysis. To use Strawson's contrast, Jackson is engaging in 'revisionary' rather than 'descriptive' metaphysics. The value of analysis within this programme is primarily subtractive rather than additive – revealing where, if our world view is correct, we should revise beliefs couched in terms of certain concepts such as our current concept of free will.

World views

In discussing the value of analysis we have slipped into talking about views of the world. Indeed the systematic character of much philosophy has led many to think of the subject's principal product as *Weltanschauungen* or world views. Even smaller-scale products such as accounts of the mind–body problem or free will may be regarded as contributions to a more comprehensive view of things. For the point of such accounts is often either to accommodate problematic cases within a wider world view, for example, the materialist one, or to argue that they cannot be accommodated there and thus that such a world view is untenable. The latter course is then often associated with advocacy of a different world view, for example dualism, since consistency in one's accounts of different issues may require a more comprehensive story covering them.

The value of a world view will, on what we saw Richard Rorty characterise as 'representationalism', depend upon how close to the truth it gets. But even representationalists expect their world views to affect people's attitudes in a way that ordinary scientific theories do not. This suggests the possibility of a rather different conception of their point, one in which they articulate the perspective of a participant in the world and are thus not fully intelligible independently of the reactions one has as a participant. We can get a sense of such a conception of world views by comparing them with what literary texts present us. 'Certain truths about human life,' writes Martha Nussbaum, 'can only be stated in the language and forms characteristic of the narrative artist'.[23] What she means is that some novels and stories get us to see things in the sort of way that elicits the response, 'How right!' So her talk of truth here is to be understood in terms of such an endorsement. 'Human life' does not pick out a subject matter in the way it would for anthropologists who collect facts about it. Rather, it directs our attention at those aspects of the novel that invite our endorsement. Similarly, it might be suggested, 'the world' does not function in philosophy to pick out a range of very general facts. It captures the indeterminate direction of our attention when we exclaim 'Yes, that is how things are!' when we are impressed by a philosophical world view. But this is the sort of endorsement that is possible for us only as participants rather than as disinterested spectators.

There are, as we noted in Chapter 6, important differences between works of philosophy and novels. In particular, the latter operate independently, not taking issue with one another as they would if each claimed the reader's exclusive endorsement. Different novels allow us to take up either pessimistic or optimistic attitudes to life, for instance, without being in competition with each other. A pessimistic philosopher like Schopenhauer, by contrast, disallows any optimistic view as fanciful. Yet there are also affinities between literature and at least some sorts of philosophy which present world views, for both can elicit what Vladimir Nabokov calls 'participative emotion'.[24] In the case of a novel I imagine myself in the situation it describes and I am moved in a way I might be in life, if the description is successful. In philosophy I can be similarly moved if I take a world view to convey the way things are. I have feelings which strike me as the sort of feelings I ought to have about the world.

As an example we might naturally take the unease that is felt if one falls under the spell of scepticism, for example the doubt that one's attempts at reference fail to latch on to anything, which we looked at earlier. Then seeing the world as presenting this threat is necessary for one to grasp the story that Russell tells about analyses needing to terminate in objects of direct acquaintance like sense-data. Whether one thinks this is the right story will depend partly on whether one thinks they can do the work of providing this foothold on the world, but it is the sceptical anxiety which gives us a drive to find the right story, the right view of the world.

---

[23] Nussbaum 1990: 5.   [24] Quoted in Rorty 1989: 146.

Types of world view

Philosophical world views are thus not presented as optional but as the right answers to our concerns. Nevertheless there is a distinction to be drawn between two ways in which what can be seen as world views may be presented for our acceptance. In the first, exemplified by Wilhelm Dilthey's classification of metaphysical systems in terms of the kind of world views they express, a view like naturalism is presented as a perspective on the world we ought to adopt: we are just part of the natural world, so we should accept this and adopt the attitude that goes with it. Yet not everybody does do this; it is not a perspective we necessarily already have. Heidegger's criticism of philosophy as producing world views in this sense rests partly on this fact. 'Philosophy', he writes, 'is not essentially the formation of a world-view; but perhaps on this account it has an elementary and fundamental relation to all world-view formation'. It cannot present a specific world view for our acceptance because it needs to show how any such world view is possible. Thus 'philosophy itself is a distinctive *primal* world-view'.[25] Such a 'primal' world view is presented to us in a second and different way from the first. It is presented as one we are invited to recognise as a perspective we already have on the world and as one we cannot change.

In addition to Heidegger one might, perhaps slightly heretically, cite the later Wittgenstein as offering the 'primal' kind of world view. Wittgenstein suggests that his own method of providing a 'perspicuous representation' of phenomena by bringing order to the way we speak of them indicates 'the way we look at things', and he continues parenthetically, 'Is this a "Weltanschauung?"'[26] If it is, then it is a world view freed from the confusions induced by philosophical accounts which misunderstand our ways of speaking, and it restores to us a world to which our relation was threatened by scepticism and mischaracterised by metaphysical systems. We already have what Wittgenstein calls a 'world-picture' which is operative in our ordinary unreflective dealings with the world. What is needed, Wittgenstein seems to suggest, is to bring this to reflective awareness.

The difference between the specific and primal conceptions of world views concerns their functions and consequent value. The primal type

---

[25] Both quotes Heidegger 1988: 8.   [26] Wittgenstein 1958: § 122.

adds nothing to our unreflective picture if correctly drawn, only subtracting extraneous elements. But, in addition to this subtractive function and
value, it potentially offers a form of self-knowledge, making us aware of
how life is for creatures like us. There is, however, an opinion, deriving
from German Romantic philosophers like Herder, that different peoples
in different circumstances have fundamentally different world views, so
that the kind of primal view sought by Heidegger and others is unobtain-
able. His complaint against the philosophical production of specific world
views, that they are 'always in fact determined historically',[27] while philosophy should concern itself with what makes any view possible, cannot,
in that case, be overcome. Herder himself thought that a people's language, value system and consequent world view conferred on them a distinct cultural identity, so that the value of articulating their world view
might lie in awakening an awareness of that identity and strengthening
it. Not only are the philosophical underpinnings and political implications of this position highly dubious, it is hard to see distinctively philosophical world views, perhaps by contrast with religious ones, fulfilling
that function.

The specific type of world view, by contrast with the primal type, aims
to add to our outlook on the world, getting us to see things of which we
previously had not had even a tacit awareness. Its value, then, will depend
upon whether we really need such world views. The answer to this is,
perhaps, that we already have such views and their attendant attitudes,
inchoate though they may be, and that it is better to make them explicit and expose them to criticism. But does one need to be convinced of
any particular world view, as philosophers seek to convince us? Russell's
remarks, mentioned earlier, on the benefits of keeping open a range of
possibilities are telling. Yet at the same time, unless one has a reason to
adopt a principled perspectivist position that none can be wholly right,
it seems that one must be prepared to be persuaded by the arguments.
No doubt this preparedness should itself be qualified by openness to the
possibility of still better arguments for another view, and this stance mit-
igates the risk of attachment to a dangerously wrong view spilling out
into over-confident action. The value of a world view, then, may be partly
dependent upon the manner in which it is held.

---

[27] Heidegger 1988: 8.

The alternative to accepting a specific world view is to withhold assent to any. This is not just to agree with Robert Nozick that there is at any given time a range of permissible views, but to resist the urge to assent to one view precisely because one doubts the value of any. There are several possible reasons for taking up this position. One might want to keep one's attitudinal options open, believing that there is nothing about the world, as against events in the world, that should bear on them. Or one might think that world views could only be rationalisations for attitudes adopted from other motives. This comes close to the challenge against the project of articulating world views that they are, whether explicit or implicit, inevitably ideological. The dominant world view is a reflection of the interests of the group dominant in society and competition among views mirrors competition among groups for dominance. On this Marxian account, the value of a world view for a particular audience might be quite negative. Its acceptance will disguise from them how the world of their experience really is and stand in the way of attitudes that might serve their own interests rather than those of others.

This is not the place to discuss the theory of ideology, but we should notice that the theory itself does not make the distortions of ideology undetectable. It can be part of a philosophical critique to unmask them. This is what feminist philosophers, for example, have done in recent years, adapting the Marxian theory to scrutinise philosophical views they regard as androcentric and thereby reflecting the interests of men as the dominant group in society. Among such criticisms is the claim that philosophical world views typically employ metaphors of vision which presuppose an active male subject and a passive female object. While this claim is open to debate it would have the consequence that talk of *views* of the world as the products of philosophy is itself questionable.

Philosophy and values

An aspect of world views we have so far not discussed is that they do or should contain an evaluative component, and this is certainly part of Dilthey's account, for example. Different philosophical systems may be taken to promote different ideals of life, Kantian ethics, say, advocating different ends from utilitarianism, each embedded in a wider world view. On this account world views involve an injunction to adopt a certain outlook rather than recognise one we already have, so that it is the more specific type that seems to have this evaluative aspect. Some philosophers have argued that philosophy is in this sort of way 'essentially a practical endeavour', to which its speculative or descriptive aspect is secondary. David Cooper grounds this view in the claim that philosophy is a response to 'human beings' sense of alienation from the rest of reality' and to their concern with whether 'what they thought, felt and did ... was properly *answerable* to anything beyond itself'. Thus 'philosophy is indeed oriented towards the Good', needing to find 'a measure of our lives'.[28] And he illustrates this by the different approaches of 'transcendentalists', who believe that without an absolute reality our lives would be answerable to nothing, and the 'humanists', who hold that the measure of our conduct is internal to human existence. Whether one accepts this view of philosophy will turn on the plausibility of Cooper's story of alienation and of the threat of anomie. However, it is not clear that we should look for independent phenomenological confirmation of his story, or whether it is the world views themselves that evoke these anxieties and seek to still them.

What, then, is the value of such 'practical' world views? Perhaps we do need some 'measure' of our lives, as Cooper claims. But does it need to be backed up with a general world picture such as has been variously provided by Stoics or by Heidegger, say? A negative answer might emphasise the harm philosophical productions can do in providing a rationale for unsavoury moral views. Philosophers like Nietzsche are often cited in this connection, since his distinction between the 'overman' and 'the herd' was employed with terrible consequences by the Nazis. It would, however, be a fruitless task to counter this in favour of a positive answer by claiming that the beneficial effects of other productions outweigh the baneful effects of some. The calculation would surely be impossible to compute. We need to look elsewhere for an argument that a philosophical world view is required to provide a 'measure'.

One might start by turning back to the idea of a world view as articulating a participant's perspective on the world. Now a participant will not only have beliefs about it but reactions and attitudes as well. Capturing a set of attitudes will inevitably have an ethical dimension. Cooper's transcendentalists, for example, who think of themselves as reacting to a world

[28] Cooper 2009: 4, 7, 8.

already replete with value, will have a different range of ethical systems available to them from humanists, who think of values as projected on to the world in virtue of human traits or volitions. These different possibilities are a direct result of their different world views – views which could not be fully articulated without bringing out whether our reactions are seen as responses to its evaluative features or as stemming from our own nature or will. On this account the evaluative component of world views is not a worthwhile extra but an integral aspect of their performing the perspective-providing function that they do.

In this case, while world views provide an underpinning to ethical systems, there is no reason to suppose they would be accepted independently of the systems to which their proponents already adhere. Conversion, as in religion, may sometimes be possible, but it is surely rare and, worryingly for philosophers, often rationally inexplicable. It is, for example, at best doubtful whether those who bought into the vogue for existentialism – an extreme form of humanism, on Cooper's classification – were convinced by the arguments of Sartre's *Being and Nothingness*, rather than just attracted to its novel world view. If this is so then we should not expect to attribute value to evaluative world views on the grounds that they provide people with a previously lacking ethical outlook. Their value will not be a directly ethical value, but instead the intellectual value of bringing greater systematicity to one's experience of the world, which necessarily embraces one's ethical outlook upon it. Yet, as suggested previously, this has its dangers, for the more systematised one's beliefs the harder it may be to change them, and such rigidity may be especially dangerous in ethics. It is, as noted, for this reason that Russell emphasised the availability of many possible systems as an antidote to dogma.

Moral improvement?

'But,' it may be replied, 'should not philosophy aim to change people's ethical outlook and change it for the better, as most religions aim to do?' If so, then the charge that moral theory 'has no prospect of improving human behaviour', made by Richard Posner,[29] for example, seems a serious one. This raises, of course, the question of what counts as a moral

---

[29] Quoted in Brennan 2008: 278.

improvement. Philosophers are divided on whether they wish to answer this question between those who offer a so-called normative theory and those who do not. Normative theories characteristically offer a small set of principles from which moral judgements about particular situations can be derived, such as Jeremy Bentham's principle of utility or Kant's categorical imperative. Then an improvement in behaviour should result from embracing the right principles, whatever these are, assuming that people can be motivated to act on them. But motivating people does not seem to be part of philosophy's job, unlike religion's, if getting them to see things in a certain light is insufficient to provide the required incentive. Nonetheless there may be a case for saying that a normative theory may sometimes convince someone to do the right thing, which she would otherwise not have done, though it is hard to see how a general case for this could be made out. But if this is so – if, to use an example touched on earlier, utilitarianism might get people to behave more altruistically than they would have done before they encountered this theory – then normative ethics will have ethical value, contrary to Posner's prognostication.

Other philosophers reject the demand to provide a normative ethics. One reason would be that they tell a more primal story than those that entail particular sorts of moral principle, or, more generally, that they seek only to show how a normative ethics is possible, not to formulate one. Another, sometimes connected, reason stems from a conception of the philosopher's task as restricted to the analysis of ethical concepts as against prescribing their application. As we saw when discussing Socrates' technique, this may still have moral benefits, not least in making us see more clearly what it is to act morally, even if we still do not see how to act. A third reason for refraining from normative ethics derives from the particularist doctrine of what allows us to identify a good or right action, namely that we compare it with paradigm cases to which the epithets apply. Then there may be no general principles to be inferred from them and hence none for a normative theory to articulate.[30] Arguably, settling upon the paradigms is not a philosopher's job either, though bringing them to light, and showing how particular judgements depend upon them in specific moral practices, may be. Perhaps this activity may have a value in removing moral confusion, but particularism itself will, its proponents

[30] See Dancy 2004.

claim, make people more sensitive to particular cases and thus less prone to moral rigidity and dogmatism.

Perhaps, however, we should not think of philosophical accounts as conveying such explicit ethical messages as we have been assuming. It may be better to conceive of them as having an ethical use rather than an ethical content expressed through the employment of ethical predicates in prescriptions or proscriptions. Thus Cora Diamond instances Wittgenstein's *Tractatus* as a work having such a use.[31] 'Ethics cannot be put into words', he writes,[32] so that the ethical point of his book is to get us to cultivate a certain sort of ethical sensibility rather than to rely upon articulated moral judgements. The problem here is that different sorts of sensibility are themselves open to ethical criticism. If, for instance, Wittgenstein's own sensibility could crudely be described as one of resignation then that could be criticised as morally pernicious if, say, it militates against efforts to change the world. And the criterion for such a criticism needs to be articulated and defended. Arguably we cannot rest content with the ineffability that Wittgenstein's dictum asserts.

Applied philosophy

In ethics, as elsewhere in philosophy, what philosophers consider it their job to do and what value they attribute to doing it depend upon doctrines they hold within philosophy. But these are also influenced by what topics they want to talk about and what sorts of thing they want to say about them. When these topics lie outside the subject's traditional repertoire the work that deals with them is often counted as 'applied philosophy', especially if it involves 'the application of philosophical reasoning to matters of practical concern'.[33] For, as we saw in Chapter 2, we can discern a range of topics with which the subject has traditionally dealt. This should not mislead us, however, into thinking that there is such a thing as 'pure philosophy' with a special subject matter untainted by non-philosophical associations, in the way in which pure mathematics has its own special subject matter of mathematical objects, like numbers and so on. The world philosophy describes is, notoriously, the world which contains the very

[31] Diamond 1996.   [32] Wittgenstein 1961: 6.421.
[33] Uniacke and Carter 2008.

table at which the philosopher sits writing, the creature about whose nature she asks is she herself. In this sense, all philosophy is 'applied', in that its findings are taken to be relevant to our own situation, in which we will undoubtedly have practical concerns. But the term 'applied philosophy' is used of philosophy which is relevant to our situation in a much more specific way. It is intended to be relevant to our situation in a world of global warming, of hugely unequal distribution of economic resources, of new medical technologies and so forth. It is when philosophers want to contribute to dealing with the problems which these raise that they think of the subject's value as lying, at least partly, in the benefits its application to these problems might bring.

To speak of 'applied philosophy' may give the impression that the rest of philosophy supplies theories which can be applied to the problems we face in the way in which theoretical physics, say, provides the theoretical resources for applied physicists. But this analogy is questionable for several reasons. First, as we shortly see, applied philosophy need not proceed by the application of theories at all. Sometimes it does, as when a theory like utilitarianism is applied to social or political problems. But utilitarianism was devised precisely for this purpose, rather than being discovered in the annals of philosophy and employed to serve it. A further disanalogy has been noted by Onora O'Neill in relation to normative principles. While empirical theories need to fit the facts, the aim of normative reasoning is 'to *enact* rather than to *apply* principles'.[34] Its aim is to change the facts of behaviour for the better, not to adjust our principles to fit these facts, as psychological principles would need to be adjusted.

Not that we should think of applied philosophy as being restricted to applied ethics. In regard to such problems as the permissibility of abortion or the proper treatment of animals, it is evident that the nature of human and animal life is as much at issue as more obviously normative questions. That said, it is applied ethics that comprises the greater part of this subject. Many practitioners prefer the term 'practical ethics' precisely to avoid the misleading suggestions of the 'applied' label. But they still tend to think of themselves as building theories: 'when we think carefully about practical issues we are compelled to theorize – although that does not mean we merely apply a theory. Such reflection reveals the connection

[34] O'Neill 2009: 225.

between particular cases'.[35] Here ethical theory is conceived more as stemming from reflection upon cases than as generated from metaphysical claims arising in another part of philosophy; and this is the usual approach in practical or applied ethics. However, the result of a theoretical approach is that the subject becomes increasingly professionalised as different theoretical frameworks are tested against problem cases in long running research programmes.

The danger here is that those outside the profession are decreasingly likely to read its productions and to benefit from them in the way they need to benefit if the productions are to have the sort of value claimed for applied philosophy. To combat this, a movement has arisen for what is called 'public philosophy'. One prominent exponent writes of his essays in this genre (many published outside of academic journals) that they

> constitute a venture in public philosophy, in two senses: they find in the political and legal controversies of our day an occasion for philosophy, and they represent an attempt to do philosophy in public – to bring moral and political philosophy to bear on contemporary public discourse.[36]

One of the problems with this endeavour is to assess the capacity in which philosophers should enter such controversies. Should it be with the sort of academic detachment we usually expect of philosophers, or with the commitments they will have as citizens? Another concerns what sort of expertise we can expect from philosophers in the public realm. We take up these questions in a slightly different context in the next section, the latter very directly.

Ethical experts?

Philosophers increasingly find themselves called upon to advise professionals such as doctors, businessmen and so forth faced with difficult moral decisions. The doctors and businessmen are experts in their fields, people with superior knowledge and special skills in their fields, but they turn to philosophers who are taken to have a corresponding expertise in ethics. But what would an ethical expert be, if she is thought of as someone offering knowledge and skill of benefit to decision makers?

---

[35] LaFollette 2003: 8.   [36] Sandel 2005: 5.

First, she should have the sort of knowledge of ethical ideas and skill in moral reasoning which would allow her to explain and justify an opinion on moral matters. And, so Peter Singer claims, 'someone familiar with moral concepts and with moral arguments and who has ample time to gather information and think about it, may reasonably be expected to reach a soundly based conclusion more often than someone who is unfamiliar with moral concepts and moral arguments and has little time'.[37] That is the basis of her claim to expertise. Thus, second, her advice should derive solely from her professional role as an ethicist and not from any other role she happens to occupy. For the idea behind the notion of ethical expertise is that there is a separate province of ethics, in which what Thomas Nagel calls our 'common ethical faculty'[38] can be drawn upon, but be drawn upon more reliably by the experts. Yet this is not to imply that ethical experts are necessarily the best moral judges, even if their judgements are more 'soundly based'. We can distinguish a substantive conception of their role, in which they do indeed offer an unconditional opinion on the right decision to take, from a formal conception in which only their clarifying and reasoning skills are involved. Then the opinion they deliver is conditional only, offered to decision makers who take responsibility for the ethical premises on which it is based. On the formal conception someone with faulty moral judgements could still be an ethical expert while on the substantive conception he or she could not.

Orthogonal to this distinction is the cut between ethical experts conceived as theoreticians, deploying general moral principles, and as what we may call analogists, who rely upon comparisons with already decided cases. Theoreticians are like engineers, though unlike the principles on which engineers rely theirs are notoriously contestable. It is hard to see, therefore, how they could form a satisfactory basis for advice to decision makers. On the substantive conception the general principles proffered may well seem less certain than the judgement they are taken to support, so that the ethical expert's backing for her judgement may add little weight to it. But things seem little better on the formal conception, for the decision makers are ill equipped to arbitrate between the different general principles on offer – utilitarianism, Kantianism and so on. This is the philosopher's field. The use of her advice, therefore, is likely to be that

[37] Singer 1972: 23.   [38] Nagel 1986: 148.

of giving intellectual backing to decisions taken for other reasons; and giving such advice is scarcely a respectable occupation for a philosopher. This is the case, then, that someone making a claim to ethical expertise by applying theory to professional practice needs to answer. It cannot simply be assumed, as it often is, that this species of applied ethics is uncontroversial.

By contrast with theoreticians, analogists – sometimes unpejoratively dubbed 'casuists' – use methods that parallel those of case lawyers. They find analogies between decided and as yet undecided cases. As in case law, the contestable character of many ethical judgements can be acknowledged, owing not to disagreement at the level of general principle but to disputes as to which cases present the closest analogies to the undecided one. Analogists are unlikely to fit the substantive conception of the ethical expert's role since it is to the professional they will turn for the paradigm judgements to which they will appeal. On the formal conception, then, their task will be to identify these paradigms in the professionals' practice and to draw out similarities and differences between the situation requiring decision and those on which such decisions have been made. And it may be thought that philosophers would be especially skilled in this and therefore able to offer expert advice. But is this in fact so?

The question is hard to answer in the abstract, so let us consider an example where applied ethicists have offered advice on a topical problem. In contemporary so-called asymmetric wars there has been considerable concern about what tactics against insurgents are legitimate. In traditional wars a distinction is drawn between legitimate killing in the field of battle and assassinating identified individual combatants, which is regarded as unethical. But should 'targeted killing' of terrorists who lurk among the civilian population be viewed as unethical too? The political philosopher Tamar Meisels argues that it should not. She writes that 'assassinating avowed terrorists in the course of an armed conflict as a preventive, rather than a punitive, measure is a legitimate act of self-defence, no less, and perhaps more, than is killing soldiers in combat'.[39] But Meisels's analogy between assassination and self-defence quite overlooks the place of chivalry as a value in military

---

[39] Meisels 2008: 161.

thinking – assassination traditionally being thought of as cowardly. And in such thinking even self-defence must be restricted by necessity – the principle that combatants should use only such force as is strictly required for achieving their military objectives.

Indeed Meisels assumes that she can easily discern analogies in this area without pausing to investigate the values usually taken to characterise military ethics: humanity, chivalry and necessity. But these are, it would seem, values specifically for fighters. Humanity, for instance, as exemplified in the conduct of fighters would scarcely qualify as such in anyone else's, since a fighter must kill or wound his enemy, but do so while still regarding them as human beings like himself. Civilians might find this attitude hard to imagine and therefore difficult to comprehend the value it encapsulates. So in order to understand what such values come to we will need to see how they are taken by soldiers to be realised in their paradigms of ethical and unethical conduct. It is, arguably, not enough to find analogies with these in terms of some general ethical values to which a 'common evaluative faculty' gives us access. But if the analogies have to be made in terms of specifically military ones it is reasonable to ask if philosophers are well equipped to perform this task, or whether it is soldiers who are best placed to do this themselves because they have internalised the values in a way others cannot hope to emulate. And if this sceptical story is generalisable then the prospects for ethical experts as moral advisors seem gloomy indeed. Philosophers may have to content themselves with a less ambitious conception of their role. They may have to rest content with offering opinions from within roles they do occupy, such as teacher, citizen and so on. It was, indeed, from within such roles that Socrates' own ethical opinions were delivered.

The foregoing discussion of the value of applied ethics has been very limited in scope, restricting itself to the making of moral judgements, conditional or unconditional, about situations where decisions need to be taken. These are, in our classification, piecemeal products of philosophy, as are the analyses of concepts used by professional and others or the unmasking of their hidden assumptions. All these latter may be useful, but they are incidental to the practice of philosophy as applied to topics outside its traditional problems, and it is to the value of philosophical practice generally that we next turn.

The practice of philosophy

It is possible to think of philosophy's value as lying both in its products and in its practice. It could even be thought to derive from a dialectical relationship between the two, the former getting us to see things in a certain light, the latter raising doubts about that, so that neither is sufficient on its own. Certainly if philosophy was nothing but a succession of world views, say, each involving no critique of its predecessor, then we would have inadequate rational grounds for accepting any view as against another, since no criticism of it would have been aired and answered. We would also have too little reason to doubt whether the one we do accept is the right one, since it is the possibility of criticism which is needed to restrain our confidence in our views. The latter point recalls Russell's location of philosophy's value in its uncertainty; the former identifies the value of philosophical world views in the kind of grounds we have for them, by contrast with those we acquire by 'the tyranny of custom'. In both cases it is their place within the practice of philosophy as a critical and argumentative discipline that allows these products to have any value they may have.

It is also possible, however, to regard the value of philosophy as lying solely in its practice, so that its products are of only derivative value in providing the material for that practice to work upon, though this does not imply that they are produced only for this purpose, many philosophers having much more ambitious aims. Philosophers who do not may attempt to eschew any positive productions, contenting themselves with results that have the subtractive value of ridding people of false beliefs. This approach is likely to stem from the view that people are particularly prone to error in certain areas, those in which philosophy deals. It is this view that seems to have motivated Socrates and after him a long line of philosophers from Descartes to Wittgenstein and the deconstructionists. Thus, when Wittgenstein asks, 'Why do I wish to call our present activity philosophy, when we also call Plato's activity philosophy?'[40] he suggests, among other things, that 'the new activity takes the place of the old because it removes mental discomforts the old was supposed to'. Instead of the systems of his predecessors, Wittgenstein offers to 'demonstrate a

---

[40] Wittgenstein 1979: 28.

method, by examples ... Problems are solved (difficulties eliminated), not a *single* problem'.[41] Socrates' own method does not seem that different in this respect, especially if we view it, with some commentators, as essentially subtractive – undermining false conceptions rather than arriving at a final correct one.

There is, though, a difference between Socrates and Wittgenstein worth noting. Wittgenstein seems to assume that the problems of philosophy are already puzzling to us, already trapping the fly in the fly bottle, to use his famous image. Socrates apparently assumes no such thing, and describes himself as a gadfly, troubling those who were previously untroubled. Thus his method of *elenchus* involves asking questions of those who claim to know what something, like justice, is, with a view to demonstrating their actual ignorance. So they do not start off puzzled. Rather Socrates induces puzzlement by bringing out inconsistencies between their claims about justice, on the one hand, and their tacit assumptions about it, on the other. Thus he shows Thrasymachus the Sophist that he really believes things which imply that justice is a virtue despite his claims that the reverse is true.[42] In this situation Thrasymachus cannot know what justice or virtue is, and he must pass through this phase of puzzlement before being able to concede a more acceptable account.

It is not, or at least not only, because the *elenchus* dislodges some people's immoral beliefs that Socrates' use of it demonstrates his care for their souls. Rather, Socrates aims to purge them of their unexamined convictions and to get them to subject their own beliefs to his questioning method. An improvement to their souls, which Socrates sees as a moral and not merely intellectual improvement, results from people adopting this inquiring stance. It is the virtue of wanting to get things right which we noted in discussing Socrates earlier. It may even be suggested that the 'moral perplexity' resulting from the adoption of this stance 'is not a transitional stage between the elimination of error and the steady progress towards moral truth; rather, as the precondition of *thinking*, this perplexity is the primary goal of Socratic purging'.[43] The presumption here is that someone who adopts this attitude to their beliefs, and perhaps not just to

[41] Wittgenstein 1958: § 133.
[42] Plato 1892: *Republic* 348–54.
[43] Villa 2001: 19.

their explicitly moral beliefs but to all those that reflect their attitude to the world and to others, is in this respect better than someone who does not. She is better, for example, than someone fiercely committed to her beliefs and loath to expose them to criticism. So if the value of philosophy is located in the sort of practice which exemplifies this kind of inquiring stance then this is a presumption that would need to be defended.

In addition, however, one would need to defend the further presumption that the practice of philosophy can be sufficiently justified against uselessness objections by the value it brings to the perhaps not numerous individuals on whom it has improving effects. For it may be claimed that 'Socratic conscience is, at bottom, a form of *self*-interest' – a prioritising of care for one's own soul over concern for others. Dana Villa responds to this objection, which has been raised by Hannah Arendt, by arguing that it depends upon a false dichotomy because it 'fails to take account of the indirect relationship Socrates is trying to establish between care for the self and care for the world'. Only 'by cultivating a certain distance between the self and the passions and energies of the demos … does moral reflection provide a deeper sense of injustice, one which transcends the customary and everyday and does not vacillate according to the moods of the public'.[44] There is not space here to pursue this debate. What it brings into focus, however, is the possibility of a conflict between whether it is individual or collective value that is to be sought from philosophy, as mentioned earlier.

Those who believe that collective value is forthcoming, and yet it is the practice of philosophy rather than its products which confers it, may point to the advantages of a philosophical education for a broad constituency of citizens in encouraging a critical outlook. And they might cite the beneficial effects of such an outlook in the clarity and rationality of public discourse. Yet any such collective value is dependent upon philosophical practice having been of value to certain individuals. So what benefits does it confer? We should not think here only of the general benefits of what is termed 'critical thinking', which prevents people falling foul of the dangers of imprecise expression, emotive language, logical fallacy and so on. For critical thinking is not a specifically philosophical discipline, even if the practice of philosophy sharpens one's critical thinking skills, which

[44] All quotes from Villa 2001: 52–3.

arguably it is especially equipped to do. Certainly in the heyday of conceptual analysis there was a prevalent view that philosophy could help non-philosophers avoid confusions in their own areas, so that its practice was taken to furnish them with a prophylactic against crooked thinking. They would then be able to do for themselves what philosophers who thought of themselves as 'underlabourers' might do for them. But, as we saw, this makes it hard to find anything distinctively philosophical in what confers such clarificatory value.

Philosophy as therapy

Whatever its merits, this preventative conception of the subject should not be confused with the later ideas of Wittgenstein. Wittgenstein has, for the most part, a very different and more precise notion of the problems faced by individuals who can be helped by the practice of philosophy, and with it a much more restricted view of the nature of its benefits and of the scope of its potential beneficiaries. For Wittgenstein, the practice of philosophy is essentially a cure, not a prophylactic against intellectual ills. To be cured one must already be suffering from a disease, and the victims of the disease, Wittgenstein implies, are principally those who are already, in some sense, philosophers. 'The philosopher', he writes, 'is someone who has to cure in himself many diseases of the understanding'.[45] These diseases arise from 'an urge to misunderstand' 'the workings of our language' as a result of being in the grip of misleading pictures – the picture of the mind as inner, for example. Wittgenstein's aim, 'to show the fly the way out of the fly-bottle', is to provide a therapy for the sufferer. The image illustrates the typical symptoms of the disease, which is, like the fly, to be 'tormented'. Thus the 'real discovery' is 'one that gives philosophy peace, so that it is no longer tormented by questions which bring *itself* in question' – bring itself in question, that is, as a technique for answering them. Thus, 'The philosopher's treatment of a question is like the treatment of an illness',[46] which, once a cure is achieved, removes the symptoms.

There has been considerable controversy over the extent to which Wittgenstein's aims are purely therapeutic, in which case his justification

---

[45] Wittgenstein 1998: 50.
[46] Wittgenstein 1958: §§ 109, 309, 133, 255.

of the subject is, in our terms, of its practice, or whether he also advances positive claims of supposedly additional value. Certainly he writes that, 'We may not advance *any kind of theory* … and description alone must take its place.' But it is open to debate whether such a description of the way our language works is in itself a valuable product of philosophy or simply, as he puts it, a collection of 'reminders for a particular purpose'[47] that form part of the therapy. Some have taken Wittgensteinian therapy to be directed, rather like psychoanalysis, at 'individuals' *troubled states of mind*',[48] which would restrict its clientele even more, since few philosophers are as tormented as Wittgenstein. But this seems to confuse the symptoms, as we termed them, with the disease, from which philosophers may suffer without exhibiting symptoms. This allows the therapy's client base to include all those who espouse theories in philosophy's traditional problem areas. Whether the therapy will work depends on whether Wittgenstein is right in his diagnosis of these philosophical problems or whether those like David Papineau are right in such claims as that 'nearly all important philosophical problems are occasioned by real tensions in our overall theories of the world, and that their resolution therefore calls for substantial theoretical advances, rather than mere conceptual tidying'.[49]

One does not need, however, to be tied to a Wittgensteinian diagnosis of philosophical problems or to his therapeutic method to find the subject's value principally, at least, in its practice. We can see both Socrates and Wittgenstein, for example, as similarly uncovering assumptions, exposing them to criticism and raising fresh questions for investigation. And one can find in this process the value of philosophy as constantly laying its own findings open to revision in the drive to get things right, as arguably no other subject does. That such a subject exists in a society may be held to foster a culture of critique and change rather than of acceptance and stasis. Indeed, one might see philosophy as providing a model for politics and social thought in this respect, even when these introduce empirical premises which, arguably, are not philosophy's concern. For we can see its practice as paradigmatic of how such intellectual inquiries should be conducted, without reliance upon authority or 'the tyranny of custom', as Russell calls it.

---

[47] Ibid.: §§ 109, 128.   [48] Baker 2003: 212.   [49] Papineau 2002: 4.

To the response that this makes philosophy's value culture relative we should reply robustly. As we understand the terms, to be critical is a virtue and to be uncritical is a vice; we cannot conceive what it would be for it to be otherwise. Similarly, to refuse to change in the light of criticism can only be, other things being equal, rigid and unreasonable, and this too can only be a vice. It is because nothing is sacred in philosophy that it is the guardian of these often awkward virtues of criticality and reasonableness, and its practice is a constant exercise and paradigm of them. A society in which these intellectual virtues are exercised will, in this regard, be better than one that is not. But this scarcely implies that it is better than those societies in which other virtues like deference to authority and respect for tradition take precedence. For such societies are different from the former sort in ways that may, perhaps, outweigh their relative paucity of the intellectual virtues philosophy cultivates. Whether and how this might be so is, of course, yet another philosophical question.

It is important to stress here that any claim to the effect that the value of philosophical practice lies at least partly in its fostering of certain intellectual virtues is not to be confused with either of two other possible claims. One, which we have already discussed, is that its value lies in imparting various thinking skills, for, as we saw in Chapter 7, skills and virtues are usually taken to be distinct. The other possible claim is that philosophy inculcates moral virtues. We have touched on this thesis obliquely in considering, somewhat sceptically, whether a normative ethics might produce moral improvement. But the idea that it is specifically the practice of philosophy which might do so is a distinct and narrower claim. It would stand up, on the assumption that this practice does nurture intellectual virtues, only if these virtues were ipso facto moral virtues. This is to say more than that they contribute in some way to moral virtue which we can, perhaps, accept. For, to take two especially relevant examples, openness to criticism may make for the moral virtue of tolerance, or the desire to get things right for conscientiousness. If true, this would imply that the practice of philosophy might be morally improving, but only indirectly so, since these moral virtues are not what the practice inculcates. The view that the intellectual virtues in question are themselves moral virtues is, however, the subject of philosophical debate. An answer depends inter alia on one's conception of the scope of the moral. But a positive answer would need to find a reply to John Henry Newman's challenge that 'a cultivated intellect ... a candid, equitable, dispassionate mind ... may attach ... to the profligate, to the heartless, – pleasant, alas, and attractive as he shows when decked in them'.[50] Is it that such a philosopher just lacks some of the moral virtues, or may he or she simply not be virtuous at all?

Conclusion

In this chapter we have suggested various ways in which Russell's question about the value of philosophy might be answered. Distinguishing the products of philosophy from its practice, we also contrasted the possible value of philosophy to individuals and to society at large. Among the products of philosophy have been, on the one hand, piecemeal analyses of concepts and, on the other, more systematic studies which present comprehensive world views or which are intended to contribute to them. We distinguished again between the possible value such products might have in subtracting erroneous notions from our store of ideas from their value in adding something worthwhile to it. Many world views involve evaluative elements, and we asked whether it was reasonable to hope for some moral improvement from such productions. Applied ethics sometimes seeks more directly to influence moral judgements, and the merits of this aspiration were discussed. Turning to the practice of philosophy, we considered several conceptions of its value, and ended optimistically by canvassing the idea that it might foster various intellectual virtues.

[50] Newman 1947: 107.

References

Ambrose, A. 1992. 'Linguistic Approaches to Philosophical Problems', in R. Rorty (ed.) 1992a, pp. 147–55.

Apel, K.-O. 2001. 'What Is Philosophy?', in Ragland and Heidt (eds.), pp. 153–82.

Aristotle. 1976. *The Nicomachean Ethics*, trans. J. A. K. Thomson and H. Tredennick. Harmondsworth: Penguin.

1984. 'Metaphysics', trans. W. D. Ross. In J. Barnes (ed.), *The Complete Works of Aristotle*, Vol. II. Princeton: Princeton University Press.

Arrington, R. L. and Glock, H.-J. (eds.). 1996. *Wittgenstein and Quine*. London: Routledge.

Augustine. 1961. *Confessions*, trans. R. S. Pine-Coffin. Harmondsworth: Penguin.

Austin, J. L. 1962. *Sense and Sensibilia*, ed. G. J. Warnock. Oxford: Oxford University Press.

1979. *Philosophical Papers*, ed. J. O. Urmson and G. J. Warnock. Oxford: Oxford University Press.

Ayer, A. J. 1949. 'Science and Philosophy', in *Ideas and Beliefs of the Victorians*. London: Sylvan Press, pp. 205–14.

1969. *Metaphysics and Common Sense*. London: Macmillan.

1984. *Philosophy in the Twentieth Century*. London: Unwin Paperbacks.

Babich, B. 2003. 'On the Analytic-Continental Divide in Philosophy: Nietzsche's Lying Truth, Heidegger's Speaking Language, and Philosophy', in Prado (ed.) 2003a, pp. 63–103.

Baker, G. 2003. *Wittgenstein's Method*. Oxford: Blackwell.

Baker, L. R. 2007. 'Naturalism and the First-person Perspective', in G. Gasser (ed.), *How Successful is Naturalism?* Heusenstamm: Ontos Verlag, pp. 203–26.

Barnard, F. M. (ed.) 1969. *J. G. Herder on Social and Political Culture*. Cambridge: Cambridge University Press.

Bealer, G. 1998. 'Intuition and the Autonomy of Philosophy', in DePaul and Ramsey (eds.), pp. 201–39.

Beaney, M. (ed.) 2007. *The Analytic Turn: Analysis in Early Analytic Philosophy and Phenomenology*. New York: Routledge.

Beaney, M. 2009. 'Analysis', in E. N. Zalta (ed.), *The Stanford Encyclopedia of Philosophy*. Available at: http://plato.stanford.edu/entries/analysis/.

Bennett, M. R. and Hacker, P. M. S. 2003. *Philosophical Foundations of Neuroscience*. Oxford: Blackwell.

Biletzki, A. 2001. 'Introduction: Bridging the Analytic-Continental Divide', *International Journal of Philosophical Studies* 9: 291–4.

Bix, B. 2003. 'Raz on Necessity', *Law and Philosophy* 22: 537–59.

Blackburn, S. 2004. 'Foreword', in H. Carel and D. Gamez (eds.), *What Philosophy Is*. London: Continuum, pp. xiii–xviii.

Boer, T. de 1986. 'An Ethical Transcendental Philosophy', in R. A. Cohen (ed.), *Face to Face with Levinas*. Albany, NY: SUNY Press, pp. 83–115.

Bontempo, C. J. and Odell, S. J. (eds.) 1975. *The Owl of Minerva: Philosophers on Philosophy*. New York: McGraw-Hill.

Botton, A. de 2000. *The Consolations of Philosophy*. London: Hamish Hamilton.

Boulter, S. 2007. *The Rediscovery of Common Sense Philosophy*. Houndmills: Palgrave Macmillan.

Bouveresse, J. 2000. 'Reading Rorty: Pragmatism and Its Consequences', in Brandom (ed.) 2000a, pp. 129–45.

Bowie, A. 2003. *Introduction to German Philosophy*. Oxford: Polity Press.

Brandom, R. B. (ed.) 2000a. *Rorty and His Critics*. Oxford: Blackwell.

Brandom, R. B. 2000b. 'Vocabularies of Pragmatism: Synthesizing Naturalism and Historicism', in Brandom (ed.) 2000a, *Rorty and His Critics*, pp. 156–82.

2002. *Tales of the Mighty Dead: Historical Essays in the Metaphysics of Intentionality*. Cambridge, MA: Harvard University Press.

Braver, L. 2011. 'Analyzing Heidegger: A History of Analytic Reactions to Heidegger', in D. O. Dahlstrom (ed.), *Interpreting Heidegger: Critical Essays*. Cambridge: Cambridge University Press, pp. 235–55.

Brennan, J. 2008. 'Beyond the Bottom Line', *Oxford Journal of Legal Studies* 28: 277–96.

Broad, C. D. 1927. *Scientific Thought*. London: Kegan Paul, Trench, Trubner & Co.

Carnap, R. 1959. 'The Elimination of Metaphysics through Logical Analysis of Language', trans. A. Pap, in A. J. Ayer (ed.), *Logical Positivism*. London: George Allen and Unwin, pp. 60–81.

1967. *The Logical Structure of the World*, trans. R. A. George. London: Routledge and Kegan Paul.

1992. 'On the Character of Philosophic Problems', in R. Rorty (ed.) 1992a, pp. 54–62.

Carr, D. 1999. *The Paradox of Subjectivity: The Self in the Transcendental Tradition*. New York: Oxford University Press.

Cassin, B. 2000. 'Who's afraid of the Sophists?', *Hypatia* 15: 102–20.

Cavell, S. 1979. *The Claim of Reason*. New York: Oxford University Press.

1988. *In Quest of the Ordinary*. Chicago: Chicago University Press.

2002. *Must We Mean What We Say? A Book of Essays*, updated edn. Cambridge: Cambridge University Press.

Cerbone, D. R. 2003. 'Phenomenology: Straight and Hetero', in Prado (ed.) 2003a, pp. 105–38.

Chase, J. and Reynolds, J. 2011. *Analytic versus Continental: Arguments on the Methods and Value of Philosophy*. Durham: Acumen.

Churchland, P. M. 2008. 'Eliminative Materialism and the Propositional Attitudes', in W. G. Lycan and J. J. Prinz (eds.), *Mind and Cognition: An Anthology*, 3rd edn. Oxford: Blackwell, pp. 231–44.

Cobb-Stevens, R. 1990. *Husserl and Analytic Philosophy*. Dordrecht: Kluwer Academic Publishers.

Cockburn, D. 2001. *An Introduction to the Philosophy of Mind*. Houndmills: Palgrave Macmillan.

Code, L. 1987. *Epistemic Responsibility*. Hanover, NH: University Press of New England.

Cooper, D. E. 1994. 'Analytic and Continental Philosophy', *Proceedings of the Aristotelian Society* 94: 1–18.

2009. 'Visions of Philosophy', *Royal Institute of Philosophy Supplement* 65: 1–13.

Crane, T. 2006. 'Is There a Perceptual Relation?', in T. S. Gendler and J. Hawthorne (eds.), *Perceptual Experience*. Oxford: Oxford University Press, pp. 126–46.

Crary, A. and Read, R. (eds.) 2000. *The New Wittgenstein*. London: Routledge.

Critchley, S. 2001. *Continental Philosophy: A Very Short Introduction*. Oxford: Oxford University Press.

Cummins, R. 1998. 'Reflection on Reflective Equilibrium', in DePaul and Ramsey (eds.), pp. 113–27.

Dancy, J. 2004. *Ethics Without Principles*. Oxford: Clarendon Press.

Deleuze, G. and Guattari, F. 1994. *What Is Philosophy?*, trans. H. Tomlinson and G. Burchill. London: Verso.

Dennett, D. C. 1991. *Consciousness Explained*. Boston: Little, Brown and Company.

2003. 'Who's On First? Heterophenomenology Explained', *Journal of Consciousness Studies* 10 (9–10): 19–30.

2006. 'Higher Order Truths about Chmess', *Topoi* 25: 39–41.

DePaul, M. R. 1998. 'Why Bother with Reflective Equilibrium?', in DePaul and Ramsey (eds.), pp. 293–309.

DePaul, M. R. and Ramsey, W. (eds.) 1998. *Rethinking Intuition: The Psychology of Intuition and Its Role in Philosophical Inquiry*. Lanham, MD: Rowman and Littlefield.

Derrida, J. 1982. 'White Mythology', in his *Margins of Philosophy*. Chicago: Chicago University Press, pp. 207–71.

Derrida, J., Moore, A. W. et al. 2000. 'Discussion', *Ratio* 13: 373–86.

Descartes, R. 1985. *The Philosophical writings of Descartes, Volume 1*, trans. J. Cottingham et al. Cambridge: Cambridge University Press.

Diamond, C. 1996. 'Wittgenstein, Mathematics and Ethics', in H. Sluga and D. G. Stern (eds.), *The Cambridge Companion to Wittgenstein*. Cambridge: Cambridge University Press, pp. 226–60.

Dietrich, E. 2011. 'There Is No Progress in Philosophy', *Essays in Philosophy* 12: 329–44. Available at: http://commons.pacificu.edu/eip.

Dilthey, W. 1976. *Selected Writings*, trans. H. Rickman. Cambridge: Cambridge University Press.

Dummett, M. 1978. 'Can Analytic Philosophy be Systematic and Ought it to Be?', in his *Truth and Other Enigmas*. London: Duckworth, pp. 437–58.

  1993. *Origins of Analytical Philosophy*. Cambridge, MA: Harvard University Press.

  2010. *The Nature and Future of Philosophy*. New York: Columbia University Press.

Eddington, A. S. 1928. *The Nature of the Physical World*. Cambridge: Cambridge University Press.

Feynman, R. 1986. 'Appendix F: Personal Observations on the Reliability of the Shuttle', *Report of the Presidential Commission on the Space Shuttle Challenger Accident*, Volume II. Washington DC: Presidential Commission. Available at: http://history.nasa.gov/rogersrep/v2appf.htm.

Foley, R. 1998. 'Rationality and Intellectual Self-Trust', in DePaul and Ramsey (eds.), pp. 241–56.

Føllesdal, D. 1996. 'Analytic Philosophy: What Is It, and Why Should One Engage in It?', *Ratio* 9: 193–208.

Friedman, M. 2000. *A Parting of the Ways: Carnap, Cassirer, and Heidegger*. Chicago: Open Court.

Gadamer, H.-G. 1976. *Philosophical Hermeneutics*, trans. and ed. David E. Linge. Berkeley: University of California Press.

  1989. *Truth and Method*, 2nd rev. edn, trans. J. Weinsheimer and D. G. Marshall. London: Sheed and Ward.

Gallagher, S. and Zahavi, D. 2008. *The Phenomenological Mind*. London: Routledge.

Garver, N. 1973. 'Preface', in J. Derrida, *Speech and Phenomena and Other Essays on Husserl's Theory of Signs*, trans. D. B. Allison. Evanston, IL: Northwestern University Press, pp. ix–xxix.

Gettier, E. L. 1963. 'Is Justified True Belief Knowledge?', *Analysis* 23: 121–3.

Gilbert, P. and Lennon, K. 2005. *The World, the Flesh and the Subject: Continental Themes in the Philosophy of Mind and Body*. Edinburgh: Edinburgh University Press.

Glendinning, S. 2006. *The Idea of Continental Philosophy*, Edinburgh: Edinburgh University Press.

Glock, H.-J. 2004. 'Was Wittgenstein an Analytic Philosopher?', *Metaphilosophy* 35: 419–44.

2008. *What is Analytic Philosophy?* Cambridge: Cambridge University Press.

Goldman, A. and Pust, J. 1998. 'Philosophical Theory and Intuitional Evidence', in DePaul and Ramsey (eds.), pp. 179–97.

Grayling, A. C. and Greenfield, S. 2010. 'Is Hawking Right to Attack Philosophy?' *Today*, BBC Radio 4, 8 September 2010.

Grice, H. P. 1989. *Studies in the Way of Words*. Cambridge, MA: Harvard University Press.

Griswold, C. L. 2002. 'Plato's Metaphilosophy: Why Plato Wrote Dialogues', in C. L. Griswold (ed.), *Platonic Writings / Platonic Readings*. University Park, PA: Pennsylvania State University Press, pp. 143–67.

Gutting, G. 1998. '"Rethinking Intuition": A Historical and Metaphilosophical Introduction', in DePaul and Ramsey (eds.), pp. 3–13.

2009. *What Philosophers Know: Case Studies in Recent Analytic Philosophy*. Cambridge: Cambridge University Press.

Habermas, J. 1986. 'Philosophy as Stand-in and interpreter', in K. Baynes, J. Bohman and T. McCarthy (eds.), *After Philosophy: End or Transformation*. Cambridge, MA: MIT Press, pp. 296–316.

1990. *The Philosophical Discourse of Modernity*, trans. F. Lawrence. Oxford: Polity Press.

2006. 'Levelling the Genre Distinction between Philosophy and Criticism', in L. Thomassen (ed.), *The Derrida-Habermas Reader*. Edinburgh: Edinburgh University Press, pp. 13–34.

Hacker, P. M. S. 1996. *Wittgenstein's Place in Twentieth-Century Analytic Philosophy*. Oxford: Blackwell.

1998. 'Analytic Philosophy: What, Whence, and Whither?', in A. Biletzki and A. Matar (eds.), *The Story of Analytic Philosophy: Plot and Heroes*. London: Routledge, pp. 3–34.

2009. 'Philosophy: A Contribution, not to Human Knowledge, but to Human Understanding', *Royal Institute of Philosophy Supplement* 65: 129–53.

Hagberg, G. 2007. 'Wittgenstein's Aesthetics', in E. N. Zalta (ed.), *The Stanford Encyclopedia of Philosophy*. Available at: http://plato.stanford.edu/entries/wittgenstein-aesthetics/.

Hampshire, S. 1975. 'A Statement about Philosophy', in Bontempo and Odell (eds.), pp. 89–101.

Hawking, S. and Mlodinow, L. 2010. *The Grand Design*. London: Bantam Press.

Heidegger, M. 1962. *Being and Time*, trans. J. Macquarrie and E. Robinson. Oxford: Blackwell.

1971. *Poetry, Language and Thought*, trans. A. Hofstadter. New York: Harper and Row.

1988. *Basic Problems of Phenomenology*, trans. A. Hofstadter. Bloomington: Indiana University Press.

1993. 'What Is Metaphysics?', trans. D. F. Krell, in M. Heidegger, *Basic Writings*, ed. D. F. Krell. New York: HarperCollins, pp. 93–110.

1995. *Phänomenologie des religiösen Lebens*, ed. M. Jung, T. Regehly and C. Strube. Frankfurt a. M.: Vittorio Klostermann.

1996. *Einleitung in die Philosophie*, ed. O. Saame and I. Same- Speidel. Frankfurt a. M.: Vittorio Klostermann.

Himma, K. E. 2002. 'Substance and Method in Conceptual Jurisprudence and Legal Theory', *Virginia Law Review* 88: 1119–228.

Hobson, R. P. 2004. *The Cradle of Thought: Exploring the Origins of Thinking*. London: Pan Macmillan.

Holmes, R. 2008. *The Age of Wonder: How the Romantic Generation Discovered the Beauty and Terror of Science*. London: Harper Press.

Hume, D. 1975. *Enquiries concerning Human Understanding and concerning the Principles of Morals*, ed. L. A. Selby-Bigge and P. H. Nidditch. Oxford: Clarendon Press.

1978. *A Treatise of Human Nature*, ed. L. A. Selby-Bigge and P. H. Nidditch. Oxford: Clarendon Press.

Hursthouse, R. 1999. *On Virtue Ethics*. New York: Oxford University Press.

Husserl, E. 1959. *Erste Philosophie (1923/24), Zweiter Teil*, ed. R. Boehm. The Hague: Martinus Nijhoff.

1965. 'Philosophy as Rigorous Science', in *Phenomenology and the Crisis of Philosophy*, trans. and ed. Q. Lauer. New York: Harper & Row, pp. 71–147.

1970. *The Crisis of European Sciences and Transcendental Phenomenology*, trans. D. Carr. Evanston, IL: Northwestern University Press.

1973. *Experience and Judgment: Investigations in a Genealogy of Logic*, trans. J. S. Churchill and K. Ameriks. London: Routledge and Kegan Paul.

1982. *Ideas Pertaining to a Pure Phenomenology and to a Phenomenological Philosophy, First Book: General Introduction to a Pure Phenomenology*, trans. F. Kersten. Dordrecht: Kluwer Academic Publishers.

1995. *Cartesian Meditations: An Introduction to Phenomenology*, trans. D. Cairns. Dordrecht: Kluwer Academic Publishers.

Jackson, F. 1998. *From Metaphysics to Ethics: A Defence of Conceptual Analysis*. Oxford: Clarendon Press.

Johnstone, H. W. 1978. *Validity and Rhetoric in Philosophical Argument*. University Park, PA: Dialogue Press.

Joll, N. 2010. 'Contemporary Metaphilosophy', *Internet Encyclopedia of Philosophy*. Available at: http://www.iep.utm.edu/con-meta/.

Kant, I. 1929. *Critique of Pure Reason*, trans. N. Kemp Smith. London: Macmillan.

Kauppinen, A. 2007. 'The Rise and Fall of Experimental Philosophy', *Philosophical Explorations* 10: 95–118.

Kekes, J. 1980. *The Nature of Philosophy*. Oxford: Blackwell.

Kelly, S. D. 2008. Review of D. W. Smith's *Husserl*, *Times Literary Supplement*, 25 April 2008.

Knobe, J. 2007. 'Experimental Philosophy', *Philosophy Compass* 2 (1): 81–92.

Knobe, J. and Nichols, S. (eds.) 2008a. *Experimental Philosophy*. New York: Oxford University Press.

Knobe, J. and Nichols, S. 2008b. 'An Experimental Philosophy Manifesto', in Knobe and Nichols (eds.) 2008a, pp. 3–14.

Kornblith, H. 2006. 'Appeals to Intuition and the Ambitions of Epistemology', in S. Hetherington (ed.), *Epistemology Futures*. Oxford: Clarendon Press, pp. 10–25.

Kriegel, U. 2007. 'The Phenomenologically Manifest', in Noë (ed.), pp. 115–36.

Kuhn, T. 1962. *The Structure of Scientific Revolutions*. Chicago: University of Chicago Press.

LaFollette, H. 2003. 'Introduction', in H. LaFollette (ed.), *The Oxford Handbook of Practical Ethics*. Oxford: Oxford University Press, pp. 1–11.

Lang, B. 1990. *The Anatomy of Philosophical Style*. Oxford: Blackwell.

Lazerowitz, M. 1970. 'A Note on "Metaphilosophy"', *Metaphilosophy* 1: 91.

Levinas, E. 1998. *Collected Philosophical Papers*, trans. A. Lingis. Pittsburgh: Duquesne University Press.

Levy, N. 2003. 'Analytic and Continental Philosophy: Explaining the Differences', *Metaphilosophy* 34: 284–304.

Lewis, D. 1983. *Philosophical Papers, Volume 1*. New York: Oxford University Press.

Locke, J. 1997. *An Essay Concerning Human Understanding*, ed. R. Woolhouse. Harmondsworth: Penguin.

Lycan, W. G. 1996. 'Bealer on the Possibility of Philosophical Knowledge', *Philosophical Studies* 81: 143–50.

MacIntyre, A. 1990. *Three Rival Versions of Moral Enquiry*. London: Duckworth.

Magee, B. 1982. *Talking Philosophy: Dialogues with Fifteen Leading Philosophers.* Oxford: Oxford University Press.

Marx, K. 1969. 'Theses on Feuerbach', in L. Feuer (ed.), *Marx and Engels: Basic Writings on Politics and Philosophy.* London: Collins, pp. 283–6.

McCulloch, G. 1995. *The Mind and Its World.* London: Routledge.

McDowell, J. 1996. *Mind and World*, 2nd edn. Cambridge, MA: Harvard University Press.

1998. *Mind, Value and Reality.* Cambridge, MA: Harvard University Press.

McGinn, C. 1993. *Problems in Philosophy: The Limits of Inquiry.* Oxford: Blackwell.

2002. *The Making of a Philosopher.* New York: HarperCollins.

Meisels, T. 2008. *The Trouble with Terror.* Cambridge: Cambridge University Press.

Merleau-Ponty, M. 1964a. *The Visible and the Invisible*, trans. A. Lingis. Evanston, IL: Northwestern University Press.

1964b. *The Primacy of Perception*, ed. J. M. Edie, various trans. Evanston, IL: Northwestern University Press.

2002. *Phenomenology of Perception*, trans. C. Smith. London: Routledge.

Misak, C. 2000. *Truth, Politics, Morality.* London: Routledge.

Moore, G. E. 1953. *Some Main Problems of Philosophy.* London: George Allen and Unwin.

1959. *Philosophical Papers.* London: George Allen and Unwin.

1991. *Principia Ethica.* Cambridge: Cambridge University Press.

Morrow, D. R. and Sula, C. A. 2011. 'Naturalized Metaphilosophy', *Synthese* 182: 297–313.

Mulligan, K. 1991. 'Introduction: On the History of Continental Philosophy', *Topoi* 10: 115–20.

Mulligan, K., Simons, P. and Smith, B. 2006. 'What's Wrong with Contemporary Philosophy?', *Topoi* 25: 63–7.

Nadelhoffer, T. and Nahmias, E. 2007. 'The Past and Future of Experimental Philosophy', *Philosophical Explorations* 10: 123–49.

Nagel, E. 1955. 'Naturalism Reconsidered', *Proceedings and Addresses of the American Philosophical Association* 28: 5–17.

Nagel, T. 1979. *Mortal Questions.* Cambridge: Cambridge University Press.

1986. *The View from Nowhere.* New York: Oxford University Press.

Newman, J. H. 1947. *The Idea of a University.* New York: Longman.

Nietzsche, F. 1990. *Beyond Good and Evil: Prelude to a Philosophy of the Future*, trans. R. J. Hollingdale. London: Penguin Books.

Noë, A. (ed.) 2007. 'Special Issue on Dennett and Heterophenomenology'. *Phenomenology and the Cognitive Sciences* 6 (1–2): 1–270.

Norris, C. 1985. *The Contest of Faculties*. London: Methuen.

2011. 'Hawking Contra Philosophy', *Philosophy Now* 82: 21-4. Available at: http://www.philosophynow.org/issue82/Hawking_contra_Philosophy.

Nozick, R. 1989. *The Examined Life*. New York: Simon and Schuster.

Nussbaum, M. 1990. *Love's Knowledge*. Oxford: Oxford University Press.

1997. *Cultivating Humanity*. Cambridge, MA: Harvard University Press.

2010. *Not for Profit*. Princeton: Princeton University Press.

O'Neill, O. 2009. 'Applied Ethics: Naturalism, Normativity and Public Policy', *Journal of Applied Philosophy* 26: 219-30.

Overgaard, S. 2010. 'Royaumont Revisited', *British Journal for the History of Philosophy* 18: 899-924.

Padilla Gálvez, J. (ed.) 2010. *Philosophical Anthropology: Wittgenstein's Perspective*. Heusenstamm: Ontos Verlag.

Papineau, D. 2002. *Thinking about Consciousness*. Oxford: Oxford University Press.

2009. 'The Poverty of Analysis', *Proceedings of the Aristotelian Society Supplementary Volume* 83: 1-30.

Passmore, J. 1961. *Philosophical Reasoning*. London: Gerald Duckworth.

Peacocke, C. 1991. 'The Metaphysics of Concepts', *Mind* 100: 525-46.

Perloff, M. 2011. 'Writing Philosophy as Poetry: Literary Form in Wittgenstein', in O. Kuusela and M. McGinn (eds.), *The Oxford Handbook of Wittgenstein*. Oxford: Oxford University Press, pp. 714-28.

Philipse, H. 2009. 'Can Philosophy Be a Rigorous Science?', *Royal Institute of Philosophy Supplement* 65: 155-76.

Plant, B. 2012. 'This Strange Institution Called "Philosophy": Derrida and the Primacy of Metaphilosophy', *Philosophy and Social Criticism*. doi: 10.1177/0191453711430930.

Plato. 1892. *The Dialogues of Plato*, trans B. Jowett, 3rd edn. Oxford: Oxford University Press. Available at: http://oll.libertyfund.org/?option=com_staticxt&staticfile=show.php%3Ftitle=166.

1989. *The Collected Dialogues*, ed. E. Hamilton and H. Cairns, various trans. Princeton: Princeton University Press.

Popper, K. R. 1968. *Conjectures and Refutations: The Growth of Scientific Knowledge*. New York: Harper & Row.

1975. 'How I see Philosophy', in Bontempo and Odell (eds.), pp. 41-55.

Posner, R. A. 1996. *Law and Legal Theory in England and America*. Oxford: Clarendon Press.

Poulakos, J. 1983. 'Towards a Sophistic Definition of Rhetoric', *Philosophy and Rhetoric* 16: 35-48.

Prado, C. G. (ed.) 2003a. *A House Divided: Comparing Analytic and Continental Philosophy*. Amherst, NY: Humanity Books.

Prado, C. G. 2003b. 'Introduction', in Prado (ed.) 2003a, pp. 9–16.

Price, H. 2004. 'Naturalism without Representationalism', in M. De Caro and D. Macarthur (eds.), *Naturalism in Question*. Cambridge, MA: Harvard University Press, pp. 71–88.

Priest, G. 2006. 'What Is Philosophy?', *Philosophy* 81: 189–207.

Prinz, J. J. 2008. 'Empirical Philosophy and Experimental Philosophy', in Knobe and Nichols (eds.) 2008a, pp. 189–208.

Pust, J. 2001. 'Against Explanationist Skepticism Regarding Philosophical Intuitions', *Philosophical Studies* 106: 227–58.

Putnam, H. 1975. 'The Meaning of "Meaning"', in his *Mind, Language, and Reality: Philosophical Papers, Volume 2*. Cambridge: Cambridge University Press, pp. 215–71.

  1992. *Renewing Philosophy*. Cambridge, MA: Harvard University Press.

  1997. *Realism with a Human Face*. Cambridge, MA: Harvard University Press.

  2004. 'The Content and Appeal of "Naturalism"', in M. De Caro and D. Macarthur (eds.), *Naturalism in Question*. Cambridge, MA: Harvard University Press, pp. 59–70.

Quine, W. V. O. 1953. *From a Logical Point of View*. Cambridge, MA: Harvard University Press.

  1960. *Word and Object*. Cambridge, MA: MIT Press.

  1969. 'Epistemology Naturalized', in his *Ontological Relativity and Other Essays*. New York: Columbia University Press, pp. 69–90.

  1975. 'A Letter to Mr. Ostermann'. In Bontempo and Odell (eds.), pp. 227–30.

  1981. *Theories and Things*. Cambridge, MA: Harvard University Press.

  1995. *From Stimulus to Science*. Cambridge, MA: Harvard University Press.

Quinton, A. 2005. 'Continental Philosophy', in T. Honderich (ed.), *The Oxford Companion to Philosophy*. Oxford: Oxford University Press. Oxford Reference Online.

Ragland, C. P. and Heidt, S. (eds.) 2001. *What Is Philosophy?* New Haven: Yale University Press.

Ratcliffe, M. 2007. *Rethinking Commonsense Psychology: A Critique of Folk Psychology, Theory of Mind and Simulation*. Basingstoke: Palgrave Macmillan.

Reid, T. 1969. *Essays on the Intellectual Powers of Man*. Cambridge, MA: MIT Press.

Rescher, N. 2001. *Philosophical Reasoning: A Study in the Methodology of Philosophizing*. Oxford: Blackwell.

Robinson, H. 1994. *Perception*. London: Routledge.

Rorty, R. 1979. *Philosophy and the Mirror of Nature*. Princeton: Princeton University Press.

1982. *The Consequences of Pragmatism*. Minneapolis: Minnesota University Press.

1989. *Contingency, Irony and Solidarity*. Cambridge: Cambridge University Press.

1991a. *Objectivity, Relativism and Truth*. Cambridge: Cambridge University Press.

1991b. *Essays on Heidegger and Others*. Cambridge: Cambridge University Press.

Rorty, R. (ed.) 1992a. *The Linguistic Turn: Essays in Philosophical Method*. Chicago: Chicago University Press.

Rorty, R. 1992b. 'Introduction: Metaphilosophical Difficulties of Linguistic Philosophy', in Rorty (ed.) 1992a, *The Linguistic Turn: Essays in Philosophical Method*, pp. 1–39.

1992c. 'Twenty-five Years After', in Rorty (ed.) 1992a, *The Linguistic Turn: Essays in Philosophical Method*, pp. 371–4.

1995. 'Response to Hartshorne', in H. J. Saatkamp (ed.), *Rorty and Pragmatism*. Nashville: Vanderbilt University Press, pp. 29–36.

1996. 'Something to Steer by', *London Review of Books* 18 (12): 7–8.

1997. 'What Do You Do When They Call You a Relativist?', *Philosophy and Phenomenological Research* 57: 173–7.

1998. 'Pragmatism as Romantic Polytheism', in M. Dickstein (ed.) *The Revival of Pragmatism*. Durham, NC: Duke University Press.

1999. *Philosophy and Social Hope*. London: Penguin.

2000a. 'The Decline of Redemptive Truth and the Rise of a Literary Culture'. Available at: http://olincenter.uchicago.edu/pdf/rorty.pdf.

2000b. 'Response to Bouveresse', in Brandom (ed.) 2000a, pp. 146–55.

2003. 'Analytic and Conversational Philosophy', in Prado (ed.) 2003a, pp. 17–31.

2004. 'Philosophy as a Transitional Genre', in S. Benhabib and N. Fraser (eds.), *Pragmatism, Critique, Judgement*. Cambridge, MA: MIT Press, pp. 3–28.

2006. 'Habermas, Derrida and the Functions of Philosophy', in L. Thomassen (ed.), *The Derrida-Habermas Reader*. Edinburgh: Edinburgh University Press, pp. 46–70.

2007. *Philosophy as Cultural Politics*. Cambridge: Cambridge University Press.

Russell, B. 1956. *Portraits from Memory and Other Essays*. London: George Allen and Unwin.

1959. *My Philosophical Development*. London: George Allen and Unwin.

1998. *The Problems of Philosophy*. Oxford: Oxford University Press.

Ryle, G. 1949. *The Concept of Mind*. London: Hutchinson.

1956. 'Introduction', in A. J. Ayer et al., *The Revolution in Philosophy*. London: Macmillan, pp. 1–11.

1971. 'Autobiographical', in O. P. Wood and G. Pitcher (eds.), *Ryle*. London: Macmillan, pp. 1–15.

2009a. *Collected Papers, Volume 1: Critical Essays*. London: Routledge.

2009b. *Collected Papers, Volume 2: Collected Essays 1929–1968*. London: Routledge.

Sacks, O. 1986. *The Man Who Mistook His Wife for a Hat*. London: Picador.

Sandel, M. J. 2005. *Public Philosophy: Essays on Morality and Politics*. Cambridge, MA: Harvard University Press.

Sandford, S. 2000. 'Johnny Foreigner', *Radical philosophy* 102 (July/August): 42–5.

Santas, G. 2001. *Goodness and Justice*. Oxford: Blackwell.

Sartre, J-P. 1966. *Existentialism and Humanism*, trans. P. Mairet. London: Methuen.

Schlick, M. 1992. 'The Future of Philosophy', in Rorty (ed.) 1992a, pp. 43–53.

Searle, J. 1983. *Intentionality: An Essay in the Philosophy of Mind*. Cambridge: Cambridge University Press.

    1999. 'The Future of Philosophy', *Philosophical Transactions of the Royal Society of London* B 354: 2069–80.

Sellars, W. 1991. *Science, Perception and Reality*. Atascadero: Ridgeview.

Sesonske, A. 1968. 'To Make the Weaker Argument Defeat the Stronger', *Journal of the History of Philosophy* 6: 217–32.

Siewert, C. 2011. 'Philosophy of Mind', in S. Luft and S. Overgaard (eds.), *The Routledge Companion to Phenomenology*. London: Routledge, pp. 394–405.

Simons, P. 2001. 'Whose Fault? The Origins and Evitability of the Analytic-Continental Rift', *International Journal of Philosophical Studies* 9: 295–311.

Singer, P. 1972. 'Moral Experts', *Analysis* 32: 115–17.

Skidelsky, E. 2000. Review of Allain de Botton's *The Consolations of Philosophy*, *The New Statesman*, 27 March 2000.

Skilleås, O. M. 2001. *Philosophy and Literature*. Edinburgh: Edinburgh University Press.

Smart, J. J. C. 1975. 'My Semantic Ascents and Descents', in Bontempo and Odell (eds.), pp. 57–72.

    1993. 'Why Philosophers Disagree', in J. Couture and K. Nielsen (eds.), *Méta-Philosophie: Reconstructing Philosophy? Canadian Journal of Philosophy, Supplementary Volume* 19. Calgary: University of Calgary Press, pp. 67–82.

Smith, A. D. 2002. *The Problem of Perception*. Cambridge, MA: Harvard University Press.

    2003. *Routledge Philosophy Guidebook to Husserl and the Cartesian Meditations*. London: Routledge.

Smith, B. *et al.* 1992. Letter in *The Times* (London), 9 May 1992. Available at: http://ontology.buffalo.edu/smith/varia/Derrida_Letter.htm.

Smith, D. W. and Thomasson, A. L. (eds.) 2005. *Phenomenology and Philosophy of Mind*. Oxford: Clarendon Press.

Soames, S. 2003. *Philosophical Analysis in the Twentieth Century, Volume 1*. Princeton: Princeton University Press.

Sosa, E. 1980. 'The Raft and the Pyramid', *Midwest Studies in Philosophy* 5: 2–25.

1998. 'Minimal Intuition', in DePaul and Ramsey (eds.), pp. 257–69.

Stich, S. 1998. 'Reflective Equilibrium, Analytic Epistemology and the Problem of Cognitive Diversity', in DePaul and Ramsey (eds.), pp. 95–112.

Strawson, P. F. 1956. 'Construction and Analysis', in A. J. Ayer et al., *The Revolution in Philosophy*. London: Macmillan, pp. 97–110.

1959. *Individuals: An Essay in Descriptive Metaphysics*. London: Methuen.

1985. *Skepticism and Naturalism: Some Varieties*. London: Methuen.

1992. *Analysis and Metaphysics: An Introduction to Philosophy*. Oxford: Oxford University Press.

2011. *Philosophical Writings*, ed. G. Strawson and M. Montague. Oxford: Oxford University Press.

Stroud, B. 'What Is Philosophy?', in Ragland and Heidt (eds.), pp. 25–46.

Taylor, C. 1995. *Philosophical Arguments*. Cambridge, MA: Harvard University Press.

2007. *A Secular Age*. Cambridge, MA: Harvard University Press.

Turner, G. W. 1973. *Stylistics*. London: Penguin.

Uniacke, S. and Carter, A. 2008. 'Editorial', *Journal of Applied Philosophy* 25: 1.

Villa, D. 2001. *Socratic Citizenship*. Princeton: Princeton University Press.

Waismann, F. 1959. 'How I See Philosophy', in A. J. Ayer (ed.), *Logical Positivism*. London: George Allen and Unwin, pp. 345–80.

Wang, H. 1985. *Beyond Analytic Philosophy: Doing Justice to What We Know*. Cambridge, MA: MIT Press.

Weber, Z. 2011. 'Issue Introduction', *Essays in Philosophy* 12 (2): 195–9. Available at: http://commons.pacificu.edu/eip.

Weinberg, J. M., Nichols, S. and Stich, S. 2008. 'Normativity and Epistemic Intuitions', in Knobe and Nichols (eds.) 2008a, pp. 17–45.

White, A. R. 1975. 'Conceptual Analysis', in Bontempo and Odell (eds.), pp. 103–17.

Whitehead, A. N. 1933. *Adventures of Ideas*. Cambridge: Cambridge University Press.

Wild, J. 1958. 'Is There a World of Ordinary Language?', *The Philosophical Review* 67: 460–76.

Williams, B. 1985. *Ethics and the Limits of Philosophy*. London: Fontana Press.

2003. 'Contemporary Philosophy: A Second Look', in N. Bunnin and E. P. Tsui-James (eds.), *The Blackwell Companion to Philosophy*. Oxford: Blackwell, pp. 23–34.

2006. *Philosophy as a Humanistic Discipline*, ed. A. W. Moore. Princeton: Princeton University Press.

Williamson, T. 2007. *The Philosophy of Philosophy*. Oxford: Blackwell.

Winch, P. 1958. *The Idea of a Social Science*. London: Routledge.

Wisdom, J. 1953. *Philosophy and Psychoanalysis*. Oxford: Blackwell.

Wittgenstein, L. 1958. *Philosophical Investigations*, trans. G. E. M. Anscombe. Oxford: Blackwell.

   1961. *Tractatus Logico-philosophicus*, trans. D. F. Pears and B. F. McGuiness. London: Routledge and Kegan Paul.

   1967. *Zettel*, ed. G. E. M. Anscombe and G. H. von Wright, trans. G. E. M. Anscombe. Berkeley: University of California Press.

   1968. *On Certainty*, ed. G. E. M. Anscombe and G. H. von Wright, trans. D. Paul and G. E. M. Anscombe. Oxford: Blackwell.

   1979. *Wittgenstein's Lectures 1932–35*, ed. A. Ambrose. Oxford: Blackwell.

   1998. *Culture and Value*, revised 2nd edn, ed. G. H. von Wright and H. Nyman, trans. P. Winch. Oxford: Blackwell.

Wood, A. 2001. 'Philosophy: Enlightenment Apology, Enlightenment Critique', in Ragland and Heidt (eds.), pp. 96–120.

Yeo, R. 1993. *Defining Science: William Whewell, Natural Knowledge and Public Debate in Early Victorian Britain*. Cambridge: Cambridge University Press.

Zabala, S. 2007. 'Introduction: Gianni Vattimo and Weak Philosophy', in S. Zabala (ed.), *Weakening Philosophy: Essays in Honour of Gianni Vattimo*. Montreal: McGill-Queens University Press, pp. 1–34.

Zahavi, D. 2007. 'Subjectivity and Immanence in Michel Henry', in A. Grøn, I. Damgaard and S. Overgaard (eds.), *Subjectivity and Transcendence*. Tübingen: Mohr Siebeck, pp. 133–47.

Index

For EU product safety concerns, contact us at Calle de José Abascal, 56–1°,
28003 Madrid, Spain or eugpsr@cambridge.org.

www.ingramcontent.com/pod-product-compliance
Ingram Content Group UK Ltd.
Pitfield, Milton Keynes, MK11 3LW, UK
UKHW030901150625
459647UK00021B/2699